Most African countries have a population composed of a multitude of language groups, and most African citizens have a varied language repertoire allowing them to rely on different languages for use in the home, at school, in the market, at work, and in communicating with political authorities. *Language Repertoires and State Construction in Africa* analyzes the complex language scene in Africa today and asks whether this distinctive web of language use is symptomatic of the early stage of state construction. If so, one would expect that as each of these states develops there will be a rationalization of language use and agreement on a common language within the country's borders. Alternately, Africa's language scene may be the result of a particular historical context of state construction, with the implication that political development will not lead to the one-state, one-language outcome typical of the idealized nation-state. Relying on comparative analysis and the techniques of game theory, Laitin delineates Africa's most common pattern of state building, leading up to what he calls a "3 ± 1 language outcome." Game theory not only allows him to speculate on Africa's future, but it allows him as well to make recommendations to language planners on how that future might be arrived at more peacefully and efficiently.

Language repertoires and state construction in Africa

CAMBRIDGE STUDIES IN COMPARATIVE POLITICS

General editor
PETER LANGE   Duke University

Associate editors
ELLEN COMISSO   University of California, San Diego
PETER HALL   Harvard University
JOEL MIGDAL   University of Washington
HELEN MILNER   Columbia University
SIDNEY TARROW   Cornell University

This series publishes comparative research that seeks to explain important, cross-national domestic political phenomena. Based on a broad conception of comparative politics, it hopes to promote critical dialogue among different approaches. While encouraging contributions from diverse theoretical perspectives, the series will particularly emphasize work on domestic institutions and work that examines the relative roles of historical structures and constraints, of individual or organizational choice, and of strategic interaction in explaining political actions and outcomes. This focus includes an interest in the mechanisms through which historical factors impinge on contemporary political choices and outcomes.

Works on all parts of the world are welcomed, and priority will be given to studies that cross traditional area boundaries and that treat the United States in comparative perspective. Many of the books in the series are expected to be comparative, drawing on material from more than one national case, but studies devoted to single countries will also be considered, especially those that pose their problem and analysis in such a way that they make a direct contribution to comparative analysis and theory.

OTHER BOOKS IN THE SERIES

Kornberg and Clarke   *Citizens and Community: Political Support in a Representative Democracy*

Language repertoires and state construction in Africa

DAVID D. LAITIN
University of Chicago

CAMBRIDGE UNIVERSITY PRESS
Cambridge, New York, Melbourne, Madrid, Cape Town, Singapore, São Paulo

Cambridge University Press
The Edinburgh Building, Cambridge CB2 2RU, UK

Published in the United States of America by Cambridge University Press, New York

www.cambridge.org
Information on this title: www.cambridge.org/9780521413435

First published 1992
This digitally printed first paperback version 2006

A catalogue record for this publication is available from the British Library

Library of Congress Cataloguing in Publication data
Laitin, David D.
Language repertoires and state construction in Africa / David D. Laitin.
p.   cm. – (Cambridge studies in comparative politics)
Includes bibliographical references (p.   ) and index.
ISBN 0-521-41343-5
1. Language planning – Africa.   2. Language policy – Africa.
I. Title.   II. Series.
P40.5.L352A3565   1992
306.4′49′096–dc20   91-34685
                                                              CIP

ISBN-13 978-0-521-41343-5 hardback
ISBN-10 0-521-41343-5 hardback

ISBN-13 978-0-521-03327-5 paperback
ISBN-10 0-521-03327-6 paperback

I lovingly dedicate *Language Repertoires and State Construction in Africa* to Frances and Daniel Laitin. Their assiduous concern that my Brooklyn accent might hold back my professional advancement and their occasional bribes to induce me to speak "correctly" alerted me to the market value of standard English. These parental lessons inspired the language games developed in this book.

Contents

Preface

Language Repertoires and State Construction in Africa, relying on data about language interests, use, and change, draws the national outlines of Africa's future states. The analysis demonstrates that "language rationalization" (the emergence of a single, dominant language in each state, which becomes the official one for education, administration, and cultural life) will not be the typical pattern of African national development. Instead, for most of Africa the multilingual state will be the norm. The multilingual pattern there will not resemble that of Switzerland, Belgium, or Canada; it will have distinct parameters, caused by the particular constraints of building a postcolonial state in the twentieth century. Because African states will have a distinct pattern of national development in the course of state construction, political scientists need to ask what this pattern implies for economic growth, political stability, democratic structures, and political ideology. This book concentrates on the analysis of language change and provides only a preliminary assessment of the social, economic, and political implications of Africa's model of state construction. It attempts to make sense of the cacophony of voices demanding more rational language policies in Africa and offers modest suggestions about how some of the fervently expressed goals might be achieved without courting political chaos and further economic decline.

However great my commitment to speak to current issues in African affairs, this book was written primarily as a contribution to political science, through its use of game theory to analyze cultural politics and through its incorporation of historical variables to reveal distinct patterns of state construction.

GAME THEORY

My analysis of trends in language use relies upon basic principles of game theory. Game theory (with some modifications) gives me the tools to analyze the myriad forces seeking to influence language outcomes in Africa today. It allows me to go beyond the predictions of primordial and cybernetic theories in understanding the construction of nations. Primordialism, which conceives of ethnic identity as rooted in blood, has no grasp on cultural change at all. And cybernetic theory, which portrays individuals as nodes in communication networks, cannot appreciate the manipulation of social networks by political forces. Going beyond these theories, the game analysis, as applied here, points to a future "equilibrium" for many African states that I call a "3 ± 1 language outcome." The identification of a stable language outcome, one that gives an important role to indigenous languages, will be of interest to Africanists. And political scientists should appreciate the identification of distinct patterns of national development, based on the microanalysis of players, preferences, and strategies.

Some justification for the use of game theory is surely in order. Game theory originated in the mid-1940s, and although it began to be applied in political science (or at least international relations) by the mid-1950s, its influence in the field of comparative politics in general, and on theories of culture in particular, has been minimal. In such cultural domains as language, religion, and kinship, notions of "players," "strategies," and "rules" have been considered inappropriate at best, grotesque at worst. In my own previous work on religion in Yorubaland (Laitin, 1986, chap. 7), I argued that the rational-choice assumption is insufficient to explain patterns of group mobilization. The rational-choice foundations of game theory, especially the deduction of actor preferences from actor choices – justified by the elegantly proved theory of "revealed preferences" – seem to eliminate from political research the reciprocal impact of structural constraints, individual purposes and strategies.

In my use of game theory in this book, I have therefore sought to gather independent data on language preferences and choices in Africa. By so doing, I lose much of the mathematical and formal elegance of game theory as demonstrated in current economic models. But my approach has its advantages. I can gain an appreciation of certain actor choices in the real world that do not fully reflect rational calculations. With independent data on actor preferences, I can determine whether the present language outcome is in equilibrium or unstable, in disequilibrium. Furthermore, revealed-preference theory binds the analyst to the assumption that the status quo represents an equilibrium. My interest in politics leads me to a rather different assumption, namely that society is often in disequilibrium and that the play of politics is usually about people, unhappy with the status quo, seeking to undermine apparent equilibria. The attainment of new equilibria through political action, a theme which does not consume the attention of most game theorists, gets extended treatment. In this book, then, I have carved out an arena for politics within the world of game theory.

HISTORICAL VARIABLES AND STATE CONSTRUCTION

In this book I also have taken advantage of some new thinking about the role of history in state-building processes. To claim that the state-building process today is identical with state building in the fifteenth century would obviously be naïve. But merely noting that the historical context today is different is insufficient. What must be demonstrated is that specific historical factors have a discernible effect on the type of state building that takes place. Making a theoretical connection between historical context and state-building outcomes, and then using historical evidence to enrich and develop theory, is the goal of contemporary historical sociology.

The standard example given to illustrate this point is the historical connection of war making to the development of the western European state. War making was a significant ingredient in the development of the administrative capacity to ensure the monopoly of violence in a large territorial area, the distinguishing feature of a modern state. In the world of the Cold War, heavy constraints against war making by weak states were imposed by the great powers. This may have made the world more peaceful, but it may also have made state building in the postcolonial era a more difficult process.

Consider this parallel example related to themes developed in this book. It is said that in Spain, during the Inquisition, gypsies who were found guilty of speaking their own language had their tongues cut out. With policies of this sort, it is not difficult to understand why it was possible, a few centuries later, to legislate Castilian as the sole official language of the monarchy. But when Emperor Haile Selassie of Ethiopia pressed for policies promoting Amharic, infinitely more benign than those of the Inquisition, speakers of Tigrey, Oromo, and Somali claimed that their groups were being oppressed, and the international community was outraged. Nation-building policies available to monarchs in the early modern period are not available to leaders of new states today.

These historical differences need to be specified and elaborated, so that we can develop a more scientific and historically sensitive understanding of the development of the state. In this book, one aspect of nation building will be highlighted: the attempt by states to influence the language repertoires of their citizens. Through this analysis I shall illuminate not only the dynamics of language politics in Africa but the larger dynamics of state construction as well.

ACKNOWLEDGMENTS

In writing a book that spans a continent as diverse as Africa, I have undoubtedly missed many subtle undercurrents of language use in particular settings. But my errors are surely fewer than they might have been, due to the help of a number of readers of an earlier version of this book. Carol Myers Scotton, Carol Eastman, Edgar Polomé, Tom Lodge, Johannes Fabian, Brian Weinstein, Bernd Heine, Anthony Appiah, Ronald Kassimir, Jean Laponce, Peter Lange, Jonathan Pool, and William Foltz all saved me from embarrassment and gave me ideas that helped my revisions. David Cohen of Northwestern University and Jennifer Widner of Harvard both invited me to present this material to faculty seminars at their universities, from which I profited.

The Social Science Research Council provided me with research funding, for which I am grateful. The council's Committee on Africa, which reviewed the project, however, was less than enthusiastic about my methods. Council reviewers of an earlier manuscript feared that the epistemological positivism revealed in what I call my "strategic theory" obscured rather than revealed the complex language scene in Africa. My response is that Africa need not be orientalized; its politics can be revealed by the same scientific techniques used to study politics anywhere. This does not imply that politics in Africa and in Europe are the same. Positivism, if it finds similarity where there is difference, is hardly science. My goal has been to use scientific methods to find the underlying mechanisms behind difference, so that we can sustain a compelling research program on the development of the African state.

PART I

Language repertoires and the state

1

Language repertoires as political outcomes

Cabdrivers are universally renowned as a source of political gossip. In October 1969, as a Peace Corps volunteer in Somalia, I was anxious to hear the latest gossip on my weekly shopping trip to Muqdisho, for a military coup had just occurred. Rumors about the assassination of the civilian president, the political chaos that ensued in naming his successor, and the foreign intrigue that had encouraged the military officers to stage a coup were rife.

I hailed a cab to drive me from the vegetable market to the fish market and anticipated a lively conversation. Thanks to my Peace Corps language training, I was able to talk politics with the driver in the Somali language. Having been in the country a mere five months, I was rather proud of my language achievement. As we reached the fish market, I asked him how much the fare was, and he responded "Cinquanta." Not knowing Italian, the colonial language in southern Somalia, I told him that I did not understand. He responded, in Somali, that I must be an idiot if I can't learn foreign languages.

Anecdotes like mine about the cabdriver show only the tip of the iceberg when it comes to explaining the kaleidoscopic language scene in Africa. It is not uncommon to meet people in all walks of life who speak many languages. My cabdriver claimed facility in Somali, Arabic, and Italian, each of which belongs to a distinct language family. Multilingualism is so common in Somalia that the driver could hardly believe I could not count to fifty in Italian. Not only are most individuals multilingual in Africa, but most countries are multilingual as well. Nigeria, with more than four hundred distinct speech communities, tops the list; language heterogeneity is the norm, rather than the exception, for most African countries.

But perhaps, as many believe, the process of modernization will bring Africa more in line with the rest of the world. The evidence of a careful scholar who has quantified the world's languages would support this view. His study shows that the number of living languages in the world is precipitously declining (Laponce, 1987, 188). Yet the evidence from Africa does not point to a significant reduction in the number of indigenous languages playing important communicative roles. Rather, African languages appear to be reproducing themselves over the generations. Meanwhile, new languages are emerging in the diverse environments of African cities, as pidgins, lingua francas, and other argots become used in an increasing number of social settings. While the world trend may be that of a reduction in the number of living languages, Africa is apparently bucking that trend.

The language scene in Africa is dynamic. Studies of the role of Sango in Bangui, of Amharic in the markets of Dire Dawa, of pidgin English in West African literature, of Afrikaans in the mines of South Africa, of Hausa among the butchers in Ibadan, and of Lingala in the Zairian army, are individually fascinating. They give the reader a keen sense of diversity and change. Yet one may ask, Are there any patterns within this complexity? Will Africa's language future look like Europe's, like India's, or have its own particular features? Can Africa's distinctive past – political, economic, and cultural – explain its configuration of language use? What will Africa's patterns of language change mean for democracy, for equality, for economic growth, and for cultural autonomy?

These questions are often posed in terms of a core concern as to whether indigenous languages can have an official voice in Africa's future. This concern has been articulated by African politicians, civil servants, and intellectuals, some of whose voices are recorded in this book. At times they speak as champions of their own mother tongue, arguing that each of the languages of Africa reveals and preserves Africa's rich cultural heritage. Yet at other times these same intellectuals, or their ideological kin, passionately advocate a politics in which each country chooses a single, indigenous language as the official language of state. How can both goals be reconciled in a multilingual society? And if they are not, will the pragmatists, who support the status quo of continued reliance on the language of the former colonial state, ultimately win out, making Africa's states deaf to indigenous-language discourse?

THE LANGUAGE REPERTOIRE

A state's language policy seeks to influence, yet is a product of, the language repertoires of its citizens. It is therefore imperative to discern these repertoires and to analyze the forces leading to their change. A "repertoire," according to the *Oxford English Dictionary*, is "a stock of dramatic or musical pieces which a company or player is accustomed or prepared to perform; one's stock of parts, tunes, songs, etc." A "language repertoire" is the set of languages that a citizen must know in order to take advantage of a wide range of mobility opportunities in his or her own country. The language repertoire of an entire citizenry consists in the set of languages that the model citizen must know in order to play an active role in family, society, economy, and polity.

The notion of repertoire has a distinct advantage as a core concept of this study. Examining language repertoires, rather than mother tongues, enables us to see the overlapping use of different languages, by the same people, in different social contexts. It comprehends multilingualism as the norm, rather than as the exceptional case where a person goes beyond the mother tongue. And it suggests that languages allow one to play roles, not merely to convey information.

The concept of the language repertoire is a core concern in a sociolinguistic research program that has flourished for over a quarter-century. In 1964, in a seminal paper, John Gumperz defined the "verbal repertoire" as the "totality of linguistic forms regularly employed in the course of socially significant interaction" ([1964] 1971a, 152). Because Gumperz's data included all varieties of "linguistic forms," he was able to analyze dialect and language shifts in any "speech event." Therefore the dynamics of langue choice in a monolingual society (where, for example, the statement "It looks as if it isn't going to rain today" and the statement "It looks like it ain't gonna rain today" are analyzed as distinct linguistic forms) turn out to have the same structural characteristics as language choice in a multilingual setting (where the choice might be between Swahili and English, for example) (151–7).[1]

Although Gumperz insists that linguistic forms in any speech community must be "finite," and therefore rule bound, sociolinguists have been reluctant to quantify the speech forms in a community's repertoire. (For a heroic attempt to do so, see Ferguson, 1966.) The reason for their reluctance is that their research program is basically descriptive: It seeks to elucidate the entire range of language choice available to members of any speech community. Sociolinguists have been less concerned with the positivist goal of relating types of speech communities to social, economic, or political outcomes. They ask questions such as "Why is it difficult for an American who has studied Hindi for many years to get someone in New Delhi to speak Hindi to him or her?" rather than such questions as "Will New Delhi remain a political center without a single dominant language for elite communication, or will it become like Paris, London, or Peking, where a single language has become predominant?" For the questions sociolinguists ask, a clear specification of types of repertoires is not useful and, in fact, detracts from their emphasis on the complex variety of possible speech forms available in each speech community.

A theory that relates language to state construction cannot ignore such advances in the field of sociolinguistics, but it must adjust them to fit its own needs. I have therefore appropriated Gumperz's concept of language repertoire, but I put it to a somewhat different use. My definition of repertoire differs from Gumperz's in two regards. First, my unit of analysis for language repertoire is the individual, rather than the speech community. An individual's language repertoire may include a language that is not used in the community in which he or she lives. An Ndebele youth who travels to South Africa to work in the mines may learn Afrikaans, which may be of great value to him in South Africa but of no use in his speech community when he returns home. I am interested in language investments like this, which may have long-term implications for change in the community language repertoire or for employment opportunity for an individual in the future. In this sense, my unit of analysis is more "micro" than Gumperz's.

Second, my focus on the languages in the repertoire, rather than on the entire set of "speech forms," reflects a concern with the issue of administrative control over society, which is what state construction is all about. Governments administer taxes, schools, and judicial systems. They want to have some say in which language is used as the medium of instruction, or for keeping financial records for tax purposes, or for presenting appeals to overturn lower court decisions. Meanwhile, citizens have their own agendas, wanting to learn certain languages for occupational mobility or wanting to have services provided to them in a language they can understand. Sometimes, in the process of interaction between government and citizen, congeries of speech forms get named as languages. In reality these "languages" (Hindi, English, French, Chinese) are complex sets of speech forms, but in the process of state construction they become reified as bounded social facts. By counting only bounded languages as parts of a repertoire, my analysis is more "macro" than Gumperz's.

A consideration of language issues in India will illustrate my focus on bounded languages. Sociolinguists point out that a person could travel in India from north to south, or from east to west, and find that there is no place where one language zone begins and another ends. Instead, there are "dialect chains," such that one language merges into the next over a long series of small dialect shifts. From a sociolinguistic perspective, the speech forms in India, if not infinite, are quite numerous. Political scientists, on the other hand, recognize that in the process of India's political emancipation during the twentieth century, languages such as Hindi, Bengali, Tamil, and Kannada have become named as potential national languages; dictionaries and grammars have been published, attempting to give these languages a standard form; government panels and citizens have taken sides on whether these languages should play an important role in administrative, educational, and social life. (This has not been a peaceful or merely academic exercise. Whether Bhojpuri or Maithili are separate languages or dialects of Hindi; whether standard Hindi is closer to Sanskrit or Persian – are political questions of some consequence.) Politics in India has in an important way given boundaries to sets of speech forms which are in the process of becoming standardized modern languages.

State leadership going back at least as far as the Roman Empire has sought to classify peoples and languages through the creation of boundaries where one language ends and another begins. Meanwhile, ambitious politicians have alternately sought to reify those boundaries and to undermine them for purposes of gaining power and wealth. In the course of these political conflicts, languages inevitably get named and counted. My examination of state construction therefore compels me to name languages and count how many are used in citizen repertoires. How, I can then ask, does the process of state construction alter the language repertoires of its citizens or subjects? To address this question, I must develop a typology of language outcomes, which involves counting the languages in any individual's repertoire. Sociolinguists are justifiably nervous when a language repertoire is quantified, because this takes the focus away from the fluidity of speech forms. I shall quantify individual repertoires not because I reject the notion that speech forms are fluid but rather because the logic of state construction can best be appreciated when languages are specified as bounded social facts.[2]

To be sure, counting the elements in a repertoire is no mechanical task. Ambiguities abound. Does the ability to converse in Oyo Yoruba and Ijebu Yoruba, which are dialects of a common language, count as two languages or as one language in someone's repertoire? Suppose the normal speech of a dry-goods merchant is a mixture of Akan with English. Does this count as a single mixed language, as two languages, as Akan peppered with English, or as English salted with Akan? If a Luo market woman can lure a customer with a few words of Kikuyu but must move to Swahili to work out the details of the sale, how do we count

Kikuyu when we reckon her repertoire? What about religious languages, used only for prayers and incantations? Do they count as necessary to know in order for individuals to play active roles in their society?

The answers to these questions depend on what one wants to learn about language, the state, and Africa. My focus will be on the set of languages that might be important for local status in the community, job mobility in the wider society, and successful communication with political administration at all levels that impact upon the individual in his or her daily life. Since low-status speech forms in earlier historical eras, such as English and Italian, eventually became high-status national languages, the urban argots, mixed languages, and pidgins that are all held today in low esteem throughout Africa cannot be ignored in a diachronic study of state construction. They must be considered as emergent contenders for status as official languages. Religious languages, too, can be considered, if they help define a social group with a political constituency. I will therefore enter into my equations a wide variety of speech forms that are part of everyday life throughout Africa, but I shall also be sensitive to the interest and power of state builders who seek, for purposes of command and control, to limit the growth of diverse speech forms.

LANGUAGE, NATION, AND THE STATE

The conventional approach to the analysis of language pluralism in the new states of Africa has been to label Africa's nations "tribes" and to identify the project of cultural homogenization of the tribes who live within the boundaries of the internationally accepted state boundaries as one of "nation building." In this postindependence commentary, the recognition of a Luo or an Igbo nation was seen as retrograde, but embedding the Luo tribe into a "Kenyan nation" or the Igbo peoples into the "Nigerian nation" was seen as progressive. Ideology, education, and the political wizardry of charismatic founding fathers would provide the nurturing for thè integrated growth of these new nation-states.

Language issues never sat well in these abstract discussions of nation building. To be sure, Julius Nyerere, the most eloquent proponent of the nation-building project, could champion Swahili as Tanzania's national language. Many historical factors made this project feasible. Islamic trade routes brought Swahili as a lingua franca to all reaches of the country; Swahili is structurally close to the Bantu languages of Tanzania; German and British colonialists relied upon Swahili for colonial administration; no language group made up more than 10 percent of the country's population; and the people whose mother tongue is Swahili were never considered as a political threat to any other group. Charisma was still crucial. Nyerere's translation of Shakespeare's *Julius Caesar* into Swahili demonstrated not only the literary skills of the country's first president but his commitment to the ideal of weaving the Sukuma, Nyamwesi, Haya, Zigula, Yao, Nyakyusa, and other groups into a single nation. But for most newly independent African countries, the only language that could apparently serve as a lingua franca was the language of colonial domination. Nation building for Nigeria, Senegal, Ivory Coast, Ghana, and Zaire meant defining the nation – at least in its language component – in foreign terms. How could the cultivation of English in Nigeria, or of French in Senegal, be called "nation" building?

What most analyses of nation building ignored – as I shall elaborate in Chapter 2 – is that rulers may have a greater need to construct states (that is, to establish effective social control over a bounded territory) than to build nations. They may therefore have interests at odds with societal groups. These rulers may use the symbols of a nation, but their interests are oriented more toward the construction of organizations capable of maintaining order in society and extracting resources from society. Their battles with societal groups are not necessarily a matter of modern nationalists confronting anachronistic tribalists. These battles have much to do with the terms of the state's domination over society. The concern of this book is to see how one component of the nation – language – gets pulled into the battle for the institutionalized domination over society by a ruling cadre, otherwise known as state building.

STATE RATIONALIZATION

Language rationalization

The terrain that this book explores, then, is where language repertoires intersect with the consolidation of a modern state. My supposition is that rulers have an interest in "language rationalization," defined here as the territorial specification of a common language for purposes of efficient administration and rule. The sociological implication of this definition is that a citizen needs to have facility in a single language in order to take advantage of a wide range of mobility opportunities in the territory. Language rationalization has been just one part of a wider process of state rationalization which needs to be historically situated.

The nineteenth-century German sociologist Max Weber used the term "rationalization" to refer to the process by which a state establishes efficient and orderly rule.[3] The development of a professional civil service, with a well-specified division of labor, was for Weber the essence of rationalization in the modern state. The establishment of clear territorial boundaries, the standardization of the calendar, and of weights and measures, and the issuance of a common currency are important examples of state rationalization.

Weber did not systematically explore language rationalization.[4] Yet the use of state power, through administrative regulation and public education, to standardize language within the boundaries of the state is certainly one of the things covered by his concept of rationalization. Legal uniformity is easier to ensure when court decisions are delivered and recorded in a common language. Taxes can be collected more efficiently and monitored more effectively if merchants all keep their books in the same language. State regulations can be disseminated more efficiently if translations are not necessary. And territorial boundaries are easier to patrol if the population at the boundary speaks the language of the country's political center, one that is distinct from the language of the population on the other side of the boundary. Given these considerations, it is not surprising that rulers of states have sought to transform their multilingual societies into nation-states through policies that can be called "language rationalization."

Language-rationalization policies usually entail the specification of a domain of language use (e.g., appeals-court cases or church sermons) and a requirement that the language chosen by the ruler be employed within that domain. When rulers have established power over several territorially distinct speech communities, they are easily able to induce some members of these communities to become bilingual, so as to translate documents from the language of the speech community to the language of the ruler. To the extent that political rule is stable, more and more members of the newly incorporated speech community will find it useful to learn the language of the ruling elite. Language rationalization is successful when there is a sufficient number of bilinguals among linguistically distinct communities so that the business of rule can be transacted in a single language.

In many cases of successful state building, language change is greater than rationalization would demand. On the individual level, rationalization requires only what Blom and Gumperz (1971, 294–96) describe as the ability to employ "situational code switching." Code switching has been defined (Haugen, 1978, 21) as "the alternate use of two languages, including everything from the introduction of a single, unassimilated word up to a complete sentence or more into the context of another language." In situational code switching, speakers, when functioning in certain social domains (for example, when encountering a representative of the central authority) will find it useful to use aspects of the center's language. However, situational code switching is often complemented by "metaphorical code switching" as well. In this case, members of a peripheral region may begin to use the center's language among themselves, or in nonofficial domains with central authorities, in order to signal a possible change in socio-cultural identity. Metaphorical code switching could be the first step in a long process of relying on the language of the center for communications in virtually all social contexts. This would be the beginning of the process of "assimilation." When this occurs, as Benedict Anderson has elegantly illustrated (1983), a "nation" that is commensurate with state boundaries can most easily be imagined.

In the world of real states, there are no examples of the complete elimination of societal multilingualism. In fact, given the need for international communication, in few countries of the world in the twenty-first century will a monolingual repertoire be sufficient for most elites. More countries with rationalized language outcomes will follow the path of Sweden and the Netherlands. Although rationalization in Swedish and Dutch has been fully successful, most educated citizens speak at least English and German, besides the official languages of state business. Furthermore, within countries that are rationalized, multilingualism persists. Certain minority groups retain their languages despite changes in the rest of the society; immigrant groups characteristically retain the language of their home area for some generations; and dialects diverge within a single language, yielding de facto multilingualism even when members of each speech community claim to speak the same language (e.g., black American English). Of even greater political importance, groups that had assimilated into the language of the political center may find themselves parties to a "language-revival movement" that challenges basic assumptions as to whether the country involved really is a national state. This sort of question persists in politics because no clear distinctions can be drawn between societies as being "monolingual" or "multilingual," or between states as "multinational" or "nation-states." Ambiguity feeds political struggle.

Despite the ubiquity of minority speech communities, many states have successfully pursued language-rationalization policies. The cases of France, Spain, and Japan are especially noteworthy, because political analysts often portray these countries as "natural" nations, in invidious comparison with the "concocted" countries of Africa. Even Julius

Nyerere accepted this formulation when he is said to have claimed (ironically) that Africa's boundaries are so absurd that "we must consider them sacrosanct." The short vignettes of the so-called "model" nations that follow will show that language rationalization was achieved there not naturally but through political struggle. Despite the excessive reliance on cases such as France, Spain, and Japan to make it seem as though we live in a world of "united nations," not all modern states have rationalized as one-country, one-language states. The example most often cited is that of multilingualism in Switzerland. Its case is instructive for Africanists, because, although there is no single state language in Switzerland, language has been rationalized there in a more coherent way than in the typical nation-states. The purpose of the following vignettes is not to provide a nuanced analysis of language change in these countries, a task beyond my capabilities. Rather, I wish simply to stress (1) the importance of the state in the rationalization of society, and (2) the significant role of language as part of that rationalization process.

Language rationalization in France

In 1539, King Francis I issued the Edict of Villers-Cotterêts, which established Francien, the dialect of Ile-de-France, as the only official language of the realm. At that time many related dialects, such as Norman and Picard, had more literary prestige, but the Francien dialect was spoken at the capital around Ile-de-France, so it was politically more attractive. There were in the king's realm a number of German, Flemish, Catalan, and Basque speech communities as well. The many languages of the southern region, collectively called *la langue d'oc,* had long literary histories and were not mutually intelligible with Francien. But the purpose of King Francis's edict was not to change the language repertoires of his ordinary subjects from different speech communities; rather it was to give support to a national vernacular as opposed to Latin, which was the prestige language of education and law (Certeau et al., 1975). The language of the court immediately changed to Francien. It was not until 1762, however, when the Jesuits were expelled from France, that Francien could replace Latin in higher education. Language rationalization, then, was a long but successful process.

French did not become the widespread national language it is today until the final third of the nineteenth century. As late as 1863, by official estimates, about a quarter of France's population spoke no French (E. Weber, 1976, 67). The rigid centralization of administration organized by Napoleon, the rise of public education, which supplanted the

Catholic church in providing basic literacy, and the introduction of military conscription all worked to create in France a state in which virtually all citizens, in large part through sharing French as the "mother tongue," could imagine themselves as members of a common nation. To be sure, multilingualism remains a sociolinguistic fact in France today. In Brittany, Alsace, Provence and elsewhere, regional speech forms have survived in the face of French domination. Furthermore, post–World War II immigrants from Algeria, Turkey, Indochina, and eastern Europe retain the languages of their former homelands. And English has increasingly become a necessary language in elite repertoires. Yet there remains little doubt for people who live and work anywhere in France that the French language is the sole necessary component of their language repertoire, because the business of rule is conducted almost entirely in French. This language conformity that helped structure the nation was not "natural," however; it was created through policies of rationalization.

Language rationalization in Spain

Spain was multilingual when the Catholic monarchs, Ferdinand and Isabella, presided over the final reconquest of the peninsula from Muslim rule. Castilian, Catalan, Basque, and Galician were the major languages of Spain. The Habsburg kings, following the policy expressed in treaties of Ferdinand and Isabella, respected regional differences in language and in law. Spain's wealth from overseas conquest, however, attracted artists and writers from all over Europe, and Castilian became a language of prestige throughout the peninsula. The literary florescence of the Golden Century (mid-sixteenth through mid-seventeenth century) induced well-to-do families throughout the kingdom to educate their children in Castilian.

It was not until 1716 and the Decree of the Nueva Planta, under Spain's first Bourbon king, Philip V, that Castilian became Spain's language for official business. A series of decrees issued between 1768 and 1771 required all primary and secondary education to be in Castilian, and in 1772 all commercial establishments were required to keep their accounts in Castilian. Despite these laws, as we shall see in the section on language revivals, regional languages continued to be used in local government and in business life. Especially in Catalonia, the business of rule has never been conducted in Castilian alone. Spain's status as a nation-state, despite an active policy of state rationalization, was therefore never fully realized.[5]

Language rationalization in Japan

Japan,[6] because of its geography and long-term insulation from foreign influence, is often described as the quintessential nation-state. Yet even in Japan, regional dialects (*hogen*), at least until the age of mass media, were quite distinct. The four major *hogen* groups were those of eastern Japan (known as *Kanto*), western Japan, Kyushu, and Ryukyu, each with subdialects. The Japanese Alps, dividing Japan east to west, helped to form the most politically significant dialect divisions. There is a considerable folklore in the west about the deficiencies and lack of intelligibility of the eastern dialect, and vice versa.

Over the course of Japanese history, there were many forces which sustained language differences. The seventh-century borrowing of Chinese orthography created a division between written and spoken language which lasted over a millennium. In the Tokugawa period (1600–1868), the establishment of the provinces, or *han,* each with its own lord who blocked open communication with rival *han,* helped to sustain regional differences. On the other hand, the samurai, who served as military officers for the lords, were educated partly through manuals that emphasized the dialect of the capital city.

It was not until the Meiji period (1868–1912) that the notion of a standard Japanese language (*hyojungo*) emerged. The Meiji rulers, through national education programs, promoted this standard, based mainly on the Japanese spoken by one of Tokyo's middle-class speech communities (*Yamanote*), which had been heavily influenced by the eastern dialect. This composite is known as *kyotsugo.* Even after a century of standardization and its extensive use on radio and television, Japanese linguists report that people who speak some *hogen*, while they can understand *kyotsugo,* cannot themselves speak it. Their dialect, in turn, is hardly comprehensible to *Yamanote* speakers.

The political organization of the Japanese state created conditions that encouraged young students from the regions to use *kyotsugo* and to rely less on their *hogen.* Japan's nation-state was therefore, at least in part, created politically; the idea that Japan enjoyed a natural condition of linguistic homogeneity is historically suspect.

Switzerland as a multilingual state

Language rationalization did not occur in Switzerland, which remains a multilingual state.[7] Four languages – German, French, Italian, and

Romansh – all have official status in the Swiss confederation. The key to understanding Swiss language politics is that rationalization occurred not at the political center but at the cantonal level.

Swiss national identity developed over centuries, and did so without need of a common language. From the origins of the Swiss confederation, in the late thirteenth century, through the end of the eighteenth century, German was Switzerland's sole official language. In the sixteenth century, the confederation expanded into French- and Italian-speaking areas. The collapse of the confederation during the French Revolution and the installation by the French of the Helvetic Republic led to the formal recognition of French and Italian. With the fall of Napoleon, however, German again became Switzerland's sole official language. But civil war erupted in the early 1820s, only to yield to peace in 1848, after which German, French, and Italian were all accepted as national languages. In 1938, Romansh became a fourth national language but did not have the same full rights as the other three. Despite societal multilingualism and a history of some language conflict, the imagined community of Switzerland developed without homogenization of mother tongues.

Yet the notion of a common "Swiss" culture is built upon clear notions of cantonal autonomy. Each canton is permitted to set its own language policy, and the cantons have been strong language rationalizers. In 1970, 96 percent of the German Swiss lived in the German region; 92 percent of the French in the French region; and 79 percent of the Italian Swiss in the Italian region. It is quite difficult for Swiss citizens living outside their language region to get an accredited education (public or private) through the medium of their mother tongue. Therefore migration of people across language zones has been minimal for the past century.

The rationalization of language at the cantonal level is so important to Swiss national consciousness that language is one of the few areas in which the central government supports welfare redistribution. Because the Italian and Romansh areas do not have enough resources to invest in higher education and television in their languages, annual subsidies are sent to these cantons to help authorities defend their languages.

The case of Switzerland demonstrates that rationalization of language is not a necessary condition for the creation of a nation-state, but it also demonstrates how important language rationalization is to rulers, even in a country where political elites have come to terms with the inevitability of language diversity.

LANGUAGE HEGEMONY

As the state rationalizes administration in the courts, in the schools, in the army, and in the tax system, an increasing number of people living in the peripheral regions of the state find it useful to learn the official language, for greater job opportunities and in order to understand elite discourse. As the scope of state power expands, through the construction of roads and the destruction of internal tariff walls, the spread of the center's language is further enhanced. At first these citizens rely on the center's language in a limited number of situations, for instrumental purposes. But over generations the descendants of these "situational code switchers" may begin to see their regional language as "backward" and as improper for serious business. They may begin to view administration in the center's language as a natural and proper institution, even if some people of their region still do not speak it. The unassimilated masses may continue speaking the regional language for centuries, but a greater and greater number of them establishes command over the center's language, which is used normally in higher-status language domains.

Sociolinguists call the resultant social situation "diglossia" (Ferguson, 1959; Fishman, 1967; Haugen, 1978, 68–9), pointing to the asymmetric bilingual condition where matters of importance are the reserve of a "high language," while matters of affection or private affairs are discussed in a "low language." Since the descendants of those who relied on the regional language as their primary language themselves consider "their" language to be "low," they no longer rely on the center's language merely for instrumental purposes. They have begun to rely increasingly upon the center's language for normal interchange, and this is foundation for what Dorian (1981) describes as "language death." Normal reliance on the center's language, with vestiges of the regional language used occasionally to establish local solidarity (Fernandez, 1986), becomes the language repertoire of the model citizen. When this phenomenon becomes generalized, we can say that "language hegemony" has been achieved, as has been the case in France, China (at least the written language), and Great Britain.

Hegemony does not imply that there is a societal consensus or harmony. The symbols and structures of meaning of the regional languages remain but are carried, as I once wrote, by "half-forgotten poets and lonely philologists" (Laitin, 1988; 293). When conditions change, these embedded symbols can be brought to the fore and can serve the interests of a regional revival movement.[8]

LANGUAGE REVIVALS

Rationalization from the political center, even after long periods of hegemony, is sometimes countered by revival movements from the periphery. These movements are easy to get going, in large part because language is such an emotional issue. Yet they are difficult to sustain, because while people may vote for the revival of a language in desuetude, they may not like the idea of having their own children educated in it. It is a safer investment, most of the time, to educate children in the language of opportunity rather than in a language of folklore, however great its past.

In modern European states, strong revival movements have occurred in those regions where there was more economic growth in the region than in the political center (Gourevitch, 1979). Under these conditions, an alliance could form between cultural elites who always wanted to preserve the language and the regional bourgeoisie that was more interested in international business contacts than in national ones.

Regional languages that have enjoyed successful revival movements in contemporary states include Catalan in Spain, Flemish in Belgium, German in the southern Tyrol, Kannada in India, Estonian in the Soviet Union, and French in Canada. Languages that have enjoyed successful revival movements in countries that overcame colonial rule to become independent include Hebrew in Israel and Finnish in Finland. Languages with a history of unsuccessful revival movements include the Celtic languages in United Kingdom, Alsatian and the *oc* languages in France, and Maithili in India (Brass, 1974). A particularly long and involved revival movement supporting Landsmaal in Norway had mixed results (Haugen, 1966).

The successful revival movements teach us that apparently stable nation-states need not remain officially monolingual. Like Switzerland, countries can develop bases other than language to imagine themselves a community. Yet these revival movements also show us that when rationalization weakens at the center, the pressure for uniformity becomes even stronger within the region. Language legislation in Quebec, Catalonia, and Karnataka (where Kannada is official) have been far harsher in demanding within-region uniformity than their political centers were in demanding statewide uniformity.

COMPETING TYPOLOGIES

The notion of the language repertoire allows us to evaluate the extent to which state rationalization of language has occurred in a given country.

It also allows us to code countries along a single dimension – that is, in terms of how many languages a citizen needs to use in order to take advantage of a wide range of mobility opportunities in the country. African countries, on this dimension, fall into three categories, which I shall call *language rationalization,* the *2-language outcome,* and the *3±1 language outcome.*

Some African states are on the road toward language rationalization, though for reasons different from those that brought rationalization to European states. In the future these African states will have a single national / official language, with one language playing the role of lingua franca and official language of state business and education. Citizens will learn other languages, to be sure, but no particular language will be necessary for occupational mobility. The African states that are moving in this direction include Somalia, Tanzania, Botswana, Swaziland, Lesotho, Rwanda, Burundi, and Malagasy. In Chapter 7, I argue that forces converging toward rationalization (in French) have been set in motion in the Ivory Coast and (in Arabic) in Algeria.

A principal claim of this book is that rationalization will not be the African norm. In its stead, the 3 ± 1 language outcome will be both prevalent and stable in many African states.[9] This is an outcome in which citizens seeking occupational mobility and middle-class urban opportunities will need to have facility in 3 ± 1 languages. This repertoire includes their vernacular (their primary language), which will also be the language in which they receive their elementary education. The repertoire also includes an African lingua franca, usually promoted by a class of nationalist politicians. This language is useful for extralocal communication and is often taught as a compulsory subject in public school. Third, the language of colonial contact, serving not only as a means of international communication but as a key to business and technical communication within the country, is also an essential part of the citizen's repertoire. If the citizen's vernacular is the same as the lingua franca, he or she need learn only two (i.e., 3 − 1) languages; if the citizen's vernacular is distinct from the vernacular taught in the region of residence, he or she must then learn four (i.e., 3 + 1) languages.

Since the language scene in Africa is in flux, no country there has institutionalized the 3 ± 1 formula. The Indian situation, where the 3 ± 1 outcome has been clearly defined, will serve as a real-world illustration of the formula's political logic in Chapter 2. Nonetheless, some African countries – Nigeria, Zaire, Kenya, and Ethiopia – have gone a long way toward a 3 ± 1 outcome. This outcome is a strong possibility in many other African states (Ghana, Senegal, Congo, Sierra Leone, Liberia,

Mali, Malawi, Gabon, Benin, Chad, Niger, Burkina Faso, and Zambia). The emergent cases in Africa are illustrated in Chapter 7.

The third pattern in Africa is that of the 2-language outcome, in which citizens maintain their own vernaculars but communicate with citizens who speak other vernaculars through a common international language. No indigenous language is promoted by this state to serve as a lingua franca. For some of these states, the international language as used in the African country will become, or is in the process of becoming, a local variant or dialect of the international language. African states that are moving toward this outcome include Angola, Mozambique, South Africa, Namibia, Togo, Morocco, Tunisia, and Zimbabwe.

My typology of language outcomes – rationalization, the 2-language formula, and the 3 ± 1 outcome – seeks to balance parsimony (which permits theory) and subtlety (which encourages sensitivity to social and language realities). The real test of this typology is whether it highlights patterns of state building and cultural change that were previously obscure. But a preliminary test is whether it organizes data about language in Africa in a more plausible manner than earlier typologies. It is to the initial-plausibility criterion that we now turn.

Typologies of African "language situations" abound.[10] Early typologies, reflected in language atlases, focused on the language family most widely spoken in a particular region. To construct such a map, it is necessary to name and classify the relevant languages. This is no easy task, in large part because of the sheer number of languages involved. One compilation of African languages and dialects listed over five thousand names (Welmers, 1971). Also, we do not have enough reliable field data to support the elaborate construction projects of classifiers such as Guthrie (1970). Nonetheless, intrepid scholars have used systematic comparisons based upon criteria of sound and meaning. They have applied statistical formulas on rates of linguistic change to distinguish between large language "families" in Africa: Congo-Kordofanian, Nilo-Saharan, Afro-Asiatic, and Khoi-San. Each family is subdivided into "branches," then "groups," then "languages," and finally, "dialects." The goal is to collect sufficient data to justify the placement of each language in Africa in the correct category.[11]

For the purposes of this book, the architectonic clarity of the classification systems presents some problems. First, the classifications tell us little about mutual intelligibility. Mutual intelligibility is explained more by a need to communicate than by the percentage of shared words or sounds. Consequently, language policies that have attempted to standardize a set of dialects from the same language group into a common language have usually fallen on deaf ears. Second, these classifications tell us little about the typical language repertoire of real people in Africa. Consider a Maasai hops farmer (Maasai is of the Nilo-Saharan family, East Nilotic group), who, through his business contacts, may speak Swahili (of the Niger-Congo family, Bantu branch). He may therefore understand Kamba (a Bantu branch, within the Kikuyu group) better than, say, Luo (a Nilo-Saharan language but from the West Nilotic group). To predict his language skills on the basis of an abstract classification of his mother tongue would be to err significantly. Third, the standard classifications omit many languages, such as those from Europe, pidgins, creoles, and lingua francas – all of which play a central role in intra-African communication. The genetic classification system is helpful in giving names and boundaries to African vernaculars but is not adequate by itself for a typology of language situations.

A concern for language outcomes must focus instead on the communicative range permitted by facility in a particular language, and the set of languages people have at their disposal. We are therefore concerned in this book not with the classification of the "pure" language that is spoken by adepts in any particular region but rather with the communicative facility developed by Africans in different social and cultural milieus to permit them to attain particular social, economic, and political goals.

We can now turn our attention to the sociological classification of language situations within African states.[12] Joshua Fishman, who helped to found contemporary sociology of language as an academic discipline, has distinguished "developing nations" in terms of three cultural situations, which he calls types A, B, and C. In type A, "there is [a "consensus" that the country has] neither an over-arching sociocultural past . . . nor a usable political past that can *currently* serve integrative functions at the *nationwide* level. It is felt by *élites* in decision-making capacities that there is as yet no indigenous Great Tradition." In countries of type B, there is a consensus that "a single Great Tradition is available to provide the indigenized and symbolically elaborated laws, beliefs, customs, literature, heroes, mission, and identity appropriate for nationwide identification." In type C countries, there is a *"conflicting or competing multiplicity* of such Great Traditions" (Fishman, 1971, 30, 39, 45, emphasis in original).

Language decisions, Fishman believes, follow from this typology. Type A decisions generally involve accommodating to a foreign language that permits wider communication for technical ("nationist") development. Type B decisions require the replacement of a colonial language with a ("nationalistic") lingua franca. This often requires choosing between a high literary standard of the lingua franca (perhaps its vernacular form) and the popular dialect (the lingua franca's pidginized form). Type C decisions often require central coordination of strong regional pressures for the development of regional vernaculars. This typology has considerable merit and has been relied upon by many sociologists of language in their fieldwork. It captures well the reason why, in the age of nationalism and authenticity, so many African countries (of type A) give support to foreign languages as official media. It also captures the problems of the transition from the colonial language to using an indigenous language as the official standard.

But Fishman's typology, from a political scientist's viewpoint, is unnecessarily static and, therefore, apolitical. The notion of a Great Tradition poses as an objective situation, but it is in reality a claim by a set of elites or scholars about the historical centrality of a particular tradition. In some formulations, languages need to have a literary tradition in order to be the foundation for a Great Tradition. But research on oral traditions (e.g., Akinnaso, 1983, 174ff., 199ff.) shows that they can well have the philosophical and transcendental qualities that are usually associated with written traditions. The establishment of claims to be a Great Tradition and the challenges to them constitute a significant aspect of state (de)construction. Fishman's reference to "consensus" recognizes the subjective element in the recognition of a Great Tradition, but he does not take the next step to see that the establishment of a consensus is part of the political process. Furthermore, his indigenous / foreign dichotomy fails to recognize that what is foreign to one generation may be local to the next. Consider the case of France. Centuries of war, protection, and bargaining helped forge a consensus that the French language is a Great Tradition; language planning was part of the forging of a consensus. Whether French is foreign or indigenous to the people of Provence, Alsace, or, for that matter, Ile-de-France is a contextual question rather than a transhistorical one. Fishman's typology would lead us to think that it was the elite consensus that made type B decisions possible.[13] His typology overlooks the dynamics that result in a language becoming a vehicle for a Great Tradition or remaining an indigenous language.

Other linguists have sought to differentiate the language situations of different countries by making a complete inventory of the relative importance of languages within a country, the degree to which they are standardized, and the communicative functions they perform. Charles Ferguson has summarized these typologies and put their variables in "quasi-algebraic" form (Ferguson, 1966).[14] The advantage of these classification schemas is the amount of information they can accommodate. The disadvantage is, of course, the other side of that coin: They are thoroughly atheoretical, in the sense that they make no judgments about what is important. Some of the typologies have so many variables that numerous cells in their classificatory schema remain empty or house only one country. From a positivist viewpoint, the problem is that there are far more variables than possible observations, making any attempt to explain outcomes or to hypothesize effects of language situations subject to the methodological problem of overdetermination. This problem is not insurmountable: By focusing on the dependent variable, a scholar can pick for a particular research question only those variables that plausibly relate to differences on the dependent variable. But this leaves us with the question of what research programs are worth pursuing and what variables to emphasize.

The focus on language repertoires has some advantages over these classifications. We need not assess how "great" any tradition is or the relative importance of "literary" versus "oral" traditions. In the process of state formation, claims are often made about the greatness of particular traditions for political reasons, and these claims are part of the historical dynamic. Second, since the model to be developed in this book is dynamic, predicting both the emergence of new languages and the disappearance of old ones, the outcomes do not have to be revised in light of reduced or enhanced heterogeneity caused by the language politics itself. Third, we will have more observations than categories, a scientific situation that makes systematic comparison less unwieldy. Finally, the three language outcomes to be specified provide a plausible way to differentiate state-construction strategies in contemporary Africa.

PLAN OF THE BOOK

The core questions of this book can be posed anew: Will language rationalization occur in African states, as it has in many of the states of Western Europe and East Asia? Will certain languages achieve hegemony in African states at the expense of others? Will language-revival movements, stimulated by the desire for ethnic autonomy, be a recurrent aspect of African politics? Do language outcomes matter for economic development, democracy, social equality, or other vital concerns? And finally: Are African countries on their own historical trajectory, which will lead to language outcomes distinct from the experiences of Western Europe and East Asia?

Answers to these questions – some of them tentative and calling for further research – are embedded throughout this book. The plan of the book is as follows. Part I, for which this chapter serves as introduction, provides the conceptual tools in the sociology of language and the theory of the state. In Chapter 2, basic theoretical issues are addressed, and the "strategic theory" of language that is presented demonstrates that African states indeed are on a distinct language trajectory from the states of Western Europe and East Asia. In Chapter 3, the question of whether language outcomes matter is addressed. The answers here are only tentative, but show clearly that some of the radical claims about the importance of rationalization for development and democracy are ill founded.

In Part II, the book moves from the theoretical to the descriptive. Chapter 4 analyzes the sociology of language research conducted at the micro level in Africa. It focuses on what sort of languages are actually used in multilingual settings. Here the boundaries between languages break down, as Africans make eclectic use of a wide variety of speech styles to negotiate their daily lives. These mixed speech styles have an impact on government policies, and they are therefore presented as a key piece to the puzzle of projecting Africa's language future. Chapter 5 is descriptive on the macro level. It looks at the larger social and political forces – the colonial state, missionaries, international organizations, and the postcolonial state – to see how policies about language use have affected Africa's language scene.

The theoretical and descriptive are combined in the two chapters of Part III. In Chapter 6, a formal analysis is provided of the three patterns of language development in different African states. In Chapter 7, political vignettes are drawn from countries that reflect each of the three patterns. Finally, Part IV, Chapter 8 provides policy recommendations for those language planners who hope to construct a reasonable language future for Africa. Special consideration is given to those "reform mongers" who want to ease the pain of working toward the 3 ± 1 outcome.

2

Three theories explaining language outcomes

State rationalization, we have seen, implies cultural change. As rulers seek to rationalize rule within their historically contingent boundaries, the people who live within those boundaries will begin to face an altered world. New roads will open up regular contact with people who were previously foreign to them; boundary walls may close off contact, or radically change its nature, with people who were previously considered to be neighbors (Sahlins, 1989). Newly installed religious authorities may demand novel sorts of rituals and prayers; former ritual authorities may be banned from practice. And new languages may be required for petitions, licenses, or simply for bargaining with the tax collector. In light of state-building processes, people may alter their sense of national identity, their religion, and their language. How can we theorize about these changes so that we can understand the conditions under which cultural change occurs?

THE PRIMORDIAL THEORY OF CULTURE

The preeminent cultural anthropologist in the United States, Clifford Geertz, has conceived of the issue of cultural change in new states as a move from "primordial" to "civil" ties, transcended by an "integrative revolution" (Geertz, 1973; chap. 10). By a "primordial attachment," characteristic of social and political bonds in the new states, Geertz means

one that stems from the "givens" – or, more precisely, as culture is inevitably involved in such matters, the assumed "givens" – of social existence: immediate contiguity and kin connection mainly, but beyond them the givenness that stems from being born into a particular religious community, speaking a particular language, or even a dialect of a language, and following particular social practices. These congruities of blood, speech, custom, and so on, are seen to have an ineffable, and at times overpowering, coerciveness in and of themselves. . . .

The general strength of such primordial bonds, and the types of them that are important, differ from person to person, from society to society, and from time to time. But for virtually every person, in every society, at almost all times, some attachments seem to flow more from a sense of natural – some would say spiritual – affinity than from social interaction. (259–60)

"Civil" ties, on the other hand, the basis for unity in a modern state, are maintained "not by calls to blood and land but by a vague, intermittent, and routine allegiance to a civil state, supplemented to a greater or lesser extent by governmental use of police powers and ideological exhortation" (260). The "integrative revolution" is "the containment of diverse primordial communities under a single sovereignty" (277).

The fundamental contribution of this seminal essay (first published in 1963 and called "The Integrative Revolution: Primordial Sentiments and Civil Politics in the New States") was to elucidate the enormous difficulties that the postcolonial states were facing in the search for a political formula that could justify their existence to their own citizens. Urbanization, political movements seeking independence, and greater communication – those processes which we lump together as "modernization" – all led, not to the establishment of wider ties commensurate with the boundaries of the new states (Indonesian; Nigerian; Lebanese), but rather to the radical expression of identities (Javanese; Igbo; Shi'ite) that often created ethnic, racial, linguistic, or religious tensions within the new states. Modernization was not leading inexorably to the creation of civil ties; rather, it was ripping the patchwork-quilt fabric of the new states (Geertz, 1963).

The problems with this conceptualization, however, are many. First, the radical dichotomy between modern "civil" states and traditional "primordial" states was too sharply drawn, as Geertz himself acknowledges in the 1973 reprint of the article (260–1). It would be absurd to claim that those Italian immigrants to the United States who organized as Italians to preserve their language were acting "primordially," whereas their grandchildren, who rely on the use of English to preserve American integrity by keeping out Salvadorians, are acting "civilly." This family has not overcome primordialism; rather, the cultural basis for their political action has changed. Second, Geertz's use of the language of disease ("abnormally susceptible," "pathological," 259–60) to portray political claims based on primordial ties seems to ignore the many constructive, self-help political activities that are based on the same symbolic repertoire. Catalan literary societies, organized to promote the language of northeastern Spain, pressed for the democratization of Franco's authoritarian rule. The tie of the Catalan language served emancipatory – I should say, "civil" – goals.

The fundamental problem with the primordial theory for the purpose of understanding changing language repertoires in the process of state rationalization is that the dynamics of change are insufficiently specified. To be sure, Geertz refers to a range of policies – primordial compromise, balkanization, *Herrenvolk* fanaticism, and forcible suppression of ethnic assertion – that have been attempted, in a variety of mixtures, in new states for the purpose of bringing about change. But absent from Geertz's discussion is any analysis of the conditions – social, economic, demographic, or political – under which an "integrative revolution" is likely to occur. And absent as well is any systematic attention to the mechanisms by which people become "civil." Geertz points out that if this is to happen, people must cease being primarily Tamils and become Indians, cease being primarily Igbos and become primarily Nigerians. A theory about cultural "givens," however, has a conceptual handicap in examining cultural "takens." If under certain conditions people can adopt a new cultural identity (and they have been doing this in Europe for centuries), how can we say that our ties to language, religion, dress, or ethnic group are primordial in the sense of being deep and unchanging? More likely, even in traditional societies, people have been taking on new identities, dropping some gods and extolling others, imitating dialects of newly powerful groups, in every generation. Geertz's approach can explain why problems of ethnic tension appear inexorable; it is much less adequate to explain change.

An excellent example of the problems of primordial theory in regard to language change comes from the novel *The River Between*. Here, James Ngugi (who now writes under the name Ngugi wa Thiong'o), one of Kenya's leading literary figures, presents an image of modern schools popping up throughout Kikuyuland like "mushrooms. Often a school was nothing more than a shed hurriedly thatched with grass. And there they stood, symbols of people's thirst for the white man's secret magic and power. . . . The schools were soon overflowing with children, hungry for this thing." Clearly, the English language was a key ingredient of "the white man's secret magic" (Ngugi, 1965, 79). Meanwhile, Kikuyus, Kambas, and Kalenjins, migrating to the new urban environments in Nairobi, Nakuru, and Mombasa, learned to speak Swahili so that they could negotiate business in their new environment. This sort of scene was being reproduced nearly everywhere in Africa from the beginning of this century. Why was there such intense desire to add to one's language repertoire? Under what conditions did change in language repertoire lead to a new social or political identity? And why, in Africa, have the addition of languages to repertoires not led to the dropping of languages, at least over a generation or two, as has been the experience with other migrations? These are fundamental questions of social change that a focus on the primordialness of culture cannot address systematically.

THE CYBERNETIC THEORY OF NATION BUILDING

Karl Deutsch's views about nation building derive from his cybernetic theory of politics.[1] Cybernetics is the study of communications networks and the issues of regulation, command, and control. Social scientists who use cybernetics theory see states as one of the large set of organisms and organizations that are "held together by communication." From the point of view of cybernetics, modern states – like living cells and business firms – can survive only through the successful transmission and processing of information and through the adjustment of their own behavior in light of new information (Deutsch, 1966, chap. 5).

In contrast to the primordial notion of tribal givens, Deutsch emphasizes the cybernetic social processes of social mobilization and assimilation. By "social mobilization" Deutsch means the process of entering a wider, more intensive communications grid. Those people who do at least some of the following are, for Deutsch, socially mobilized: leave the village for the town; read a newspaper; pay taxes directly to the central government; have children who receive formal schooling; rely on a postal service to send and receive mail; register to vote; listen to the radio or go to the movies. Exposure to a wider society is the key to social mobilization (Deutsch, 1953, 126).

By "assimilation" Deutsch means the process of cultural unification in the wider society in which people are becoming socially mobilized. Assimilation takes place, in the quantitative cybernetic framework, when all groups within a society receive statistically more information that is common to all of them than they receive communications that are peculiar to particular groups (1953, 117–18). In differentiating his approach from that of primordial theory, Deutsch argues that the process of social mobilization and assimilation are "likely to be more powerful in uniting or destroying an emerging people or a newly-established state than are the mere static facts of the multiplicity of tribes or languages within its territory" (1966, 6).

Social mobilization and assimilation have different thrusts. The former creates society; the latter, community. A society is a group of individuals made interdependent by the division of labor, who have become a group through the process of working together. Society thus represents economic interdependence. A community is created by shared values. The shared values of a culture develop from a particular configuration of internal and external stimuli that lead to a common filtering of information. Given a common reaction to the same stimuli, communication among people who share a culture becomes routine and easy. "In so far as a common culture facilitates communication," Deutsch reasons, "it forms a community." To illustrate the two concepts, Deutsch points out that "individuals of different cultures often live in one society, such as Czechs and Germans in Bohemia, or Moslems and Hindus in Bengal. For many years they may exchange goods and services but relatively little information" (1953, chap. 4).

A "people" or a "nationality" forms when all the members of a society have a complementary communications network. "Membership in a people essentially consists in . . . the ability to communicate more effectively, and over a wider range of subjects, with members of one large group than with outsiders." (Four languages are officially recognized in Switzerland, and yet, according to Deutsch, Swiss citizens are able to communicate with one another quite effectively, so language is a useful but not a necessary tool for complementarity of communication [1953, 97]). The future for nation building in the new states, from this model's perspective, lies in the creation of a communications network within the boundaries of a society that is more intensive than the communications network that spans state boundaries. When this occurs, the possibility for a complementary communications network, and thus the sense of a nation comprising all the people who live within the state, is enhanced.

Deutsch's cybernetic model, applied in 1966 to the new states (perhaps too optimistically, from the present point of view of nation builders), envisioned the process of assimilation as eventually victorious. In contemporary Africa, he wrote, the rates of cultural change are likely to be faster than they were in medieval Europe, because the move to the cities is making "natives . . . free from the (tribal) customary way of life." And so, "It seems likely from the experience of ethnic minorities in other parts of the world that the process of partial modernization will draw many of the most gifted and energetic individuals into the cities or the growing sectors of the economy away from their former minority or tribal groups, leaving these traditional groups weaker, more stagnant, and easier to govern" (1966, 5). The social fact of "retribalization" (Cohen, 1969) within Africa's cities, where primordial attachments seemed stronger in the modern than in the traditional sector, was not considered by Deutsch.

How long will the process of assimilation take in the new states,

Deutsch inquires? He does not claim to know but presents the European case as a point of reference (1942; 1966, 8–9). The Saxons were forcibly incorporated into the Frankish empire and forcibly converted to Christianity during a period of violence that lasted from 772 to 804. It took another century, until 919, before a Saxon prince, wearing Frankish clothes, ascended the imperial throne as Henry I, symbolizing the integration of the Saxons into the Frankish empire. Even though their languages were mutually intelligible, language assimilation had not occurred five centuries later, when Bible translations into High German (Frankish) and Low German (Saxon) reflected still-distinct tongues. Smaller minorities required from one hundred to four hundred years to assimilate linguistically: the Langobards in Italy (588–750); the Scandinavian-speaking Normans in Normandy (955–1050); the French-speaking Normans in England (1066–1400). The implication is that the process of the development of nations within the new states of Africa and Asia will take generations.

The cybernetic approach to language, culture, and the state is far more adequate than the primordial approach, if only because it embeds a theory of change without giving up an explanation for the pervasiveness and power of ethnic loyalties. Cultural communities are primordially linked because they have for longer periods shared a common communications filter. But they are not eternally so, because social change exposes people to new filters, and new communications networks create common experiences. The systematic study of social mobilization (which both differentiates peoples and opens them to new networks) and assimilation (which brings them together) will permit us to model cultural shifts and language assimilation.

The fundamental flaw in this powerful model is that it treats human beings as nodes in a communication network, who merely send and receive messages.[2] Deutsch encouraged political scientists to count the flow of first-class mail within state boundaries as a percentage of all first-class mail that was sent and received. Over time, his model predicts, if the percentage grows, so will the sense of people within those boundaries that they are one people. But, as Stanley Hoffmann has pointed out (1960, 45), it matters a great deal who sent those messages and what they said. A nasty letter from President DeGaulle to Prime Minister Adenauer could set back the course of European nation building, even though it would count, in Deutsch's model, as a bit of trans-European information that would work toward the creation of a new community.

Rulers, civil servants, and peasants – to take just three social strata – have different levels of resources and different interests. But people from these strata will use available resources to influence the direction and scope of the communications grid around them. If a ruler effectively blocks commerce across a boundary, Deutsch's model predicts that communication would decline across that boundary, relative to communication within each boundary. If that ruler (with the acquiescence of his neighbor) sponsored a regional market in a boundary town, communication would increase across the border, and Deutsch's model would predict the development of a border community. But the source of change was not in the communications grid; the source of change was in the decision of a ruler. Similarly, civil servants could go out of their way to maintain a language used for official paperwork that is foreign to virtually all other members of the society. The resultant failure of the urban migrants from culturally diverse peripheries to assimilate into elite culture would be the direct result of a blocked communications grid. But the cause of the blocked communication could be found only in the interests and strategies of a professional group of civil servants. Finally, peasants may go out of their way to learn the language spoken by their lords, even though the probability of their getting a random message in that language is very low. If the strategy of the few becomes the habit of the many, the communications grid would be altered. But again: The cause of the change would be found in the actions of peasants, built upon their purposes and interests.

This criticism of the cybernetic model has been ably made by William Foltz, a student of Deutsch's who later collaborated with him. In the restatement of cybernetic theory that he presented as an article in a Festschrift honoring Deutsch, Foltz observes,

> *The Nerves of Government* concludes with invoking a powerfully simple goal for our labors as political scientists, "that men should be more able to act in politics with their eyes open." If we are to join with Karl Deutsch in working toward that end, we should not start out by building models in which men can only react to change with their eyes shut. (1981, 41)

Cybernetic theory applied to language shift is therefore deficient in explaining purposeful behavior in regard to altering communications grids or entering them.

Cybernetic theory can be challenged not only theoretically but empirically as well. Sociology of language research provides numerous examples to delimit the force of the cybernetic model. There has been an accumulation of evidence suggesting that change sometimes occurs with low levels of contact and that resistance to change sometimes occurs with high levels of contact (Weinreich, 1953, 106–9).

In revisionist research on the development of pidgins, William Samarin (1982) seeks to dispute the myth that in the upper Congo and the Ubangi River basins, contact between whites and Africans yielded a common language, facilitating previously restricted communication. After disputing the common theory that whites simplified African structures in order better to command, Samarin writes,

The Whites provided the [colonial] context, but it was the foreign Blacks who achieved communication by creating pidgins. These were the speakers of Fula, Serer, Temne, Wolof, Bambara, Soninke, Susu, Kru, Basa, Vai, Malinke-Sose, and Dhasonke – just to mention the languages represented by only fifty-three "Senegalese" soldiers recruited on the west coast of Africa in 1892 for the Casimir Maistre expedition to the French Upper Congo . . . who found it to their advantage to learn varieties of languages belonging to the Sango–Yakoma–Ngbandi–Dendi dialect cluster. It was they – not Van Gèle, Le Marinel, Ponel, Bobichon, de Poumayrac, or any of the other Whites at that time – who talked to the local inhabitants directly. The Whites were not even (or hardly even) spectators to what was going on because it was not going on under their very noses. [Present theory] does not . . . consider the possibility that Sango became a contact language precisely because the foreign Blacks established solidary and sanguine relations with indigenous Blacks. Out of the effort to achieve mutually satisfactory aims, they produced a pidgin. (417)

Contact between whites and blacks did not produce new linguistic forms, because, according to Samarin, there were no common aims. Contact between black soldiers and black indigenes did produce pidgins, because there were common aims. Common aims, rather than contact, is the operative variable.

Fabian's work (1986) on the development of Shaba Swahili in Katanga builds upon Samarin's insights. Fabian challenges the "evolutionary" view of language change, which shares assumptions with cybernetic theory. He demonstrates that the proposed evolutionary stages did not develop as expected in Shaba Swahili, for a creole seemed to develop without a pidgin preceding it. Furthermore, he shows that Shaba Swahili's role as a principal lingua franca after World War I was not the result of evolutionary growth but rather a sudden spurt after a long period when multilingual repertoires among the regional languages did not require people to rely heavily on Swahili for interethnic communication. Fabian consequently proposes a model that stresses a dialectic between interests using language for control amid a field of speakers seeking to use language for communication. Emphasis here is on strategic behavior in light of asymmetrical power relations rather than on the probability of language contact.[3]

The omnipresence of Swahili as a lingua franca in Kampala, recorded by Scotton (1972), poses yet another challenge to the cybernetic approach to language change. To be sure, in a multiethnic city there is a high degree of contact, and cybernetic theory predicts the development of some lingua franca. But why Swahili, when the level of contact with the Swahili trading system that carried Swahili throughout Tanzania was quite minimal? Why Swahili, when Ugandan elites have long refused to speak it, and when a highly educated woman could claim – without reproach – that Swahili was a "language of prostitutes only?" Mass surveys show similar disrespect for the language. Scotton's answer is based on what economists call "expected-utility theory." People make individual assessments of the benefits of speaking a language (multiplied by the probability of actually receiving them) and then subtract the cost of learning it. Scotton finds that because Swahili does not reveal ethnic origin or socioeconomic status, it is a useful code for everyday communication where individuals do not want to embroil themselves in status competitions. She concludes her sociolinguistic survey by attributing the considerable use of Swahili to its "good return" to Kampalans who learn and use it.[4]

Analysis of code switching – a topic on which I will have more to say in Chapter 4 – demonstrates quite graphically the strategic aspects of language shift (Scotton, 1983; Parkin, 1974). Language shifts are here seen not as methods of transmitting information but as strategies for repositioning oneself in the social order. Scotton argues that "speakers use code choices to negotiate their wants about relationships, with different choices symbolizing different wants" (116). Building upon Grice's notion of "conversational implicatures," Scotton theorizes about the strategy of using a "marked" code switch (one that is not normally expected) as an attempt to redraw social boundaries between the speakers.[5]

Language goals, as part of a broader political process, are not always fulfilled, in large part because language shift is costly and difficult and because other actors in the social system have different language interests. A decision to learn English when no schools are available to teach it, or to operate schools in the vernacular when most citizens refuse to matriculate, will have limited success. Language decisions, more so than most social-choice decisions, require coordination. Examples abound in Africa of language outcomes that are the result of strategic compromise rather than cybernetic processes. Take, for instance, Marcia Wright's politically astute analysis of German language policy in Tanganyika (Wright, 1965, 47). In the wake of the anti-German Bushiri Revolt of 1888–90, the German government took over the colony from private company rulers. The new governor wanted to administer the colony in

German but was able to procure crucial political support from the Muslim population only under the condition that the government rule through the Swahili medium, the language the Muslims used for trade. Meanwhile the Lutheran missionaries were running their schools through the medium of the separate vernaculars. Consequently, the government schools, because Swahili promised positions in the army and in local administration, were drawing students away from the missions. The Lutherans were in a strategic bind. Between the fear that teaching Swahili at the lower levels might cause detribalization and the fear that pressures from Africans to learn English at the upper levels would enhance England's political dominance in the region, the Lutherans gave grudging support to Swahili. This decision, Wright suggests, is part of the reason that modern Tanzania now has the basis for a standardized national language. Goals, opportunities, and conflicts of interest, rather than the forging of communication channels through routine interactions, explain the rise of Swahili as a national language.

Deutsch's analogy between the breakdown of tribal Europe and the process of nation building in 1960s Africa is therefore suspect, not because there is no lesson in European history for Africa's future but because Deutsch examines only what is panhistorically present (communications networks), not what is historically distinct. National development in Africa has brought to the stage a different set of relevant actors, with different interests and facing novel constraints. Only by examining the preferences and strategies of relevant actors, taking into account the constraints under which they act, can we develop a model of state consolidation that differentiates what is universal from what is historically specific. It is for this reason that I develop a strategic theory of state rationalization.

A STRATEGIC THEORY OF LANGUAGE AND THE STATE

Game theory

My theory of strategic analysis relies upon a simplified version of the theory of games developed by two mathematicians, John von Neumann and Oskar Morgenstern (1944).[6] Any reader who has successfully procured a visa into, or out of, an African country will have no trouble understanding strategic analysis and should be able to play even more complex games to challenge or elucidate the primitive models that I present in this book.[7] Most concepts necessary for understanding the models discussed here will be defined when introduced, but a few general comments may serve as introduction. Game theory assumes that individuals, groups, or organizations ("players") have a variety of goals that can be ordered in terms of their desirability. (Such an ordering is called a "preference function".) The attainment of their goals depends, however, on the choices made by other players. Players must therefore choose a course of action ("strategy") that takes into account the likely decisions of other players. When both players choose a strategy, the confluence of their choices is the "strategic outcome." We say that the outcome is in "equilibrium" when each player looks at the outcome and realizes that one could do no better by unilaterally changing one's strategy.[8]

Equilibrium outcomes need not be happy ones for either player. If both players could have chosen differently, with both doing better, we say that the outcome is a "deficient equilibrium." The classic example of a deficient equilibrium is the outcome of the "prisoners' dilemma" game, in which a district attorney separately interrogates two prisoners she thinks committed a felony together, forcing them into a "game" against each other. She tells each that (1) if he confesses alone, he will get a reduced sentence; (2) if neither confesses, both will be charged with a misdemeanor, but the punishment recommended will be somewhat harsher than the reduced sentence; (3) if he refuses to confess but the other player confesses, he will suffer the harshest sentence permitted by law; and (4) if both confess, both will get a standard felony sentence, worse than the sentence for a misdemeanor. Game theory can demonstrate that the equilibrium outcome is for each player to confess, even if each would do better if both refused to do so. From the players' point of view, the outcome is deficient.

Let us now move from the prisoners to rulers of states, who seek to change the language behavior of their key subordinates. Assume that a ruler controls a realm with a variety of culturally distinct regions, each having a lord who shares a language with the people of his region but is under the political control of the ruler. Suppose the ruler seeks to reduce the cost of the translations needed for collecting taxes, dispensing justice, and monitoring commerce by decreeing that all official transactions be recorded in the language of the central court. Why should the lord comply by learning and operating in the language of the ruler? (We assume the lord wants one day to be free of political bondage to the king and hopes to become the ruler of a realm in which his region would be the center.)

Let us postulate a "game" between that ruler and a single lord, in which the ruler has two choices (to administer in the language of the center or to administer in the language of each region), as does the lord

Matrix 2.1. Ruler's goals in state rationalization

	Ruler administers in	
Lord, in regard to ruler's language	Ruler's language	Lord's language
Learns	*A, C*	*B*
Doesn't learn	*A*	*C*

(to learn or not learn the language of the center). Given these sets of choices, there are four possible outcomes, as can be seen in Matrices 2.1–2.3. Let us assume that the ruler has three related goals (*A, B, C*) in regard to language, with $A > B > C$.

A. The short-term rationalization of language (i.e., use of the ruler's language as the sole medium of official communication). This would lower the transactions costs of rule, while at the same time compelling lords to pay the costs of learning a new language.
B. Rationalization made feasible over the long term.
C. Efficient short-term communication with the local lords.

Given these preferences, we can chart the goals fulfilled at the confluence of the ruler's and the lord's decisions, as shown in Matrix 2.1. Note, for example, that in the northwestern (NW) cell, the ruler has achieved rationalization (*A*) as well as short-term communication with the lords, who decide to learn the ruler's language (*C*). In the northeastern cell (NE), there is no rationalization, but because the lords are learning the ruler's language the chances of future rationalization are higher (*B*). Matrix 2.1 demonstrates that the northwestern cell is the most preferable outcome for the ruler, for he receives his first preference and one other. Given four cells and relying on ordinal preferences, we can assign the highest score (4) to this outcome. Following this logic, and recalling the ruler's preference function of $A > B > C$, the southwestern (SW) cell receives a 3, the northeastern a 2, and the southeastern a 1.

Now let us examine the preferences of the lord:

A. Maintain regional language as the official language of state business.
B. Be able to communicate with the central authority (for monopolies, for legal judgments).
C. Avoid having to learn a foreign language.

This set of goals leads us to Matrix 2.2. Following the same line of reasoning as in Matrix 2.1, we can assign in Matrix 2.2 a 4 to the SE cell;

Matrix 2.2. Lord's goals in state rationalization

	Ruler administers in	
Lord, in regard to ruler's language	Ruler's language	Lord's language
Learns	*B*	*A, B*
Doesn't learn	*C*	*A, B, C*

a 3 to the NE; a 2 to the NW; and a 1 to the SW. These two matrices are combined in Matrix 2.3. The first numeral in each cell is the score for column (in this case, the ruler); the second numeral is the score for row (in this case, the lord).

Students of game theory will see that the ruler has a dominant strategy: to administer in the language of the center, no matter what choice the lord makes.[9] The lord does not have a dominant strategy, but, if he is rational, he should assume that the ruler will pursue his own best course of action. With this assumption, the best the lord can do is learn the language of the ruler. The equilibrium outcome 2, 4 involves a successful rationalization of state language.

This formal and deductive finding resonates with the experiences of older states such as France, Spain, and Japan. Despite a fair degree of multilingualism in these realms, and considerable attachment to local mores, language rationalization occurred slowly, as Deutsch's work reminds us, but inexorably.

Two qualifications are in order. First, language rationalization did not always lead to the establishment of language hegemony, where citizens think it is natural and right and proper (i.e., part of *their* primordial identity) to speak in the language of the center. In Japan and France, hegemony was established; in Spain and China, although elites from all regions are capable of communicating officially in the language of the center, many of them consider their languages (or dialects) to be superior. They continue to rely on the language of the center because they accept the logic of state-rationalization strategy, rather than because they believe they are Castilians or Hans. Under conditions of rationalization without hegemony, the possibility of language-revival movements – especially when an outlying region becomes an engine of economic growth relative to the center – increases (Laitin, 1989b; Gourevitch, 1979). But even in China and Spain, where regions were powerful vis-à-vis the center, language rationalization did occur.

Matrix 2.3. The state-rationalization game

Lord, in regard to ruler's language	Ruler administers in	
	Ruler's language	Lord's language
Learns	2, 4*	3, 2
Doesn't learn	1, 3	4, 1

*For this and future matrices, an asterisk denotes an equilibrium outcome.

The second qualification to the deductive model concerns those states (Switzerland and the Soviet Union) that have not rationalized. These cases are anomalies for my strategic theory, and future research will necessarily put the strategic model to test. However, as the example of Switzerland suggests, where rationalization is not successful at the center, regional elites seek rationalization at the level of the region, with a greater desire for uniformity and less toleration for language minorities than the central rationalizers exhibited. The model would predict that language rationalization will be pursued more comprehensively within the autonomous republics of the Soviet Union, now that they have power to legislate in this domain, than it was for the Soviet Union as a whole under Stalin. The logic of state rationalization holds in these two cases, but at a different level.

With these qualifications aside, the question becomes: Is the same logic of rationalization at work in the new states that began independent state-building efforts in this century? Are they moving, slowly and painfully, to fit the mold of previously constructed states? Geertz and Deutsch would have us think so.

The 3 ± 1 language outcome in India

An examination of India reflects a substantially different dynamic. If the outcome of a game differs from what equilibrium theory predicts, the game theorist must ask if the set of choices has changed, if the preferences of players have altered, or if the players themselves are different. My research in India has pointed to substantial differences from earlier state-building experiences in preferences and players in the postcolonial state, leading to the 3 ± 1 outcome.[10]

Let us review the elements of the 3 ± 1 outcome in India. India is a federation of states, with a separation of powers between the state governments and the federal (called the All-Union) government. In regard to language policy, English and Hindi share the de facto status of "link languages," that is, languages used for All-Union business and between states and the All-Union government. The Indian constitution (1950) stipulated a fifteen-year period after which Hindi would replace English as India's sole link language. But this provision, as 1965 neared, brought great consternation to southern India, where Hindi is not widely spoken. Recognizing pressures from the southern states, Prime Minister Jawaharlal Nehru acknowledged the de facto reality that English and Hindi would continue to share official status at the All-Union level and that no Indian would be compelled to use Hindi. Today, while some states are relying on state languages for communication with All-Union authorities, nearly all business of rule at the All-Union level is carried out in either English or Hindi. Although some business matters are handled entirely in English (e.g., record keeping by the state-owned oil company) and others entirely in Hindi (e.g., recent army manuals), these two languages share space in virtually all areas. (For instance, although nearly all applicants to the civil service, The Indian Administrative Service, take their examinations in English, they could take them in Hindi.) Public school students must demonstrate facility in the two All-Union languages.

The third language that socially mobile Indians must learn is the language of the state in which they are living. In many states, the medium of instruction throughout primary school is the official language of the state. Many states provide essential services (health, transport) that virtually require facility in the state language. That is the third language; what about the ± 1? Those who live in Bihar, for instance, where the state language is Hindi, need learn only two languages. (Some in the north can get by, but not with bright job prospects, with Hindi only.) Those minorities whose primary language is neither the state language nor one of the All-Union languages must equip themselves with four languages if they want to get through the school system and have reasonable job prospects in the modern sector.[11]

Language in the twentieth-century state. Let us now examine India's state-building logic, since that has important implications for our analysis of Africa. Two historical factors have implications not only for the preference functions of actors but also for the specification of who the players are. The first factor has to do with the role of language in governing a twentieth-century state as opposed to an eighteenth-century state. The second factor has to do with the establishment and institutionalization of colonial bureaucracies in the period before political independence was achieved. Both factors alter the nature of the language-rationalization game.

In thinking about state rationalization, it is fundamental to recognize that the relationship between language and the state changed vastly in the late nineteenth century. In the era of modern nationalism, all states have engaged in a number of activities in which the language used has had a noticeable effect on the general population. Because states were in competition with one another, successful innovations in one state became a point of reference for others. Those states that provided compulsory education for the young, drafted "citizens" into a national army, and employed a large number of literates in a rationalized bureaucracy became powerful and were consequently attractive models for less prominent states. For the initial cases of state consolidation, the expansion in functions occurred after state rationalization of language had been successfully completed. In France, for example, there was sufficient (though not widespread) knowledge of French in the mid-nineteenth century so that a teaching corps and an officer corps could run a school system and an army in French (E. Weber, 1976).

With twentieth-century state building, rulers have felt it necessary for their states to perform all "natural" state functions. This phenomenon can be partly attributed to the competitive model of state functions and to the "modular" (i.e., easy to copy in outline) nature of nationalist ideology (Anderson, 1983). The ideology of necessary state functions came out clearly in the words of the Kher Commission, examining the question of a national language for India. "Modern Governments," the commission reasoned,

concern themselves so intimately and so extensively with all aspects of social and even individual existence that inevitably in a modern community the question of the linguistic medium becomes an important matter of concern to the country's governmental organization. In the conduct of legislative bodies, in the day-to-day dealings with citizens by administrative agencies, in the dispensation of justice, in the system of education, in industry, trade and commerce; practically in all fields in which it has to interest itself in modern times, the State encounters and has to tackle the problem of the linguistic medium (Kher, 1956, 11).

There was no question as to whether the Indian state should perform only those functions performed by European states in early periods of rationalization. In terms of the strategic model, this historical change has two implications: The preferences of the rulers, given the state's new functions, will be different; second, the rulers will be "playing" the language-rationalization game directly with the citizenry whose compliance they seek, rather than ignoring their subjects' preferences in the search for language coordination with lords.

Consider the implications of these changes for the state-rationalization logic in India. As in state rationalization, there are four possible outcomes, based on the confluence of state choices (to administer in Hindi only, or in a mixture of languages) with the aggregate of individual decisions (to learn or not learn Hindi). For the Indian Union (and let us assume that the position of the Kher Commission represented the state rationalizers), administration in Hindi, with the masses learning Hindi, is the best outcome. Administration in regional languages while the population learns Hindi is the second-best outcome, because this means that in the long term Hindi could play its role as the link language of the subcontinent. If the people in the regions refuse to learn Hindi, however, the commissioners are reluctant to impose it upon them. The state must communicate with (and serve) the people, rather than ignore them. Thus, the third choice is administration in the language of the region when the mass of the population does not know Hindi. The fourth choice is administration in Hindi when the masses do not know it.

For the "people of India in the non-Hindi zones," their preference, as represented by their party leaders, is to have administration in their regional languages without the necessity to learn Hindi. They seem quite willing to learn Hindi, however, as long as it is not a requirement of citizenship. (In Tamil Nadu, for example, where politicians have been adamant against Hindi imposition, the percentage of students who study Hindi voluntarily is quite high. One piece of evidence reveals that 79.9 percent of students in Madras secondary schools were studying Hindi voluntarily in 1954–5 (Kher, 1956, 82).) Thus, their second choice is administration in the regional language while they become fluent in Hindi. Finally, I assume that if the authorities in Delhi were able to impose Hindi as the all-India language, the people would prefer to know it rather than not.

The confluence of these preferences is presented in Matrix 2.4. Game theorists know this configuration as "chicken," or "brinkmanship." It has two equilibria (2, 4 and 4, 2), but neither equilibrium could be predicted based on assumptions of rational action. The 3, 3 outcome, sometimes called the "natural outcome," in which the state administers in the regional languages and the people learn Hindi, is subject to cheating and betrayal. I suggest that the language scene in India, in this regard, looks like "iterated chicken." Whenever Delhi comes out with a proposal for an "all-Hindi day" (a day when Hindi is to be used for all memoranda) in the civil service, it faces protest and ridicule; the authori-

Matrix 2.4. State rationalization in India

Indian people in non-Hindi zones	Union administers in	
	Hindi only	Hindi, English, and regional languages
Learn Hindi	2, 4*	3, 3
Don't learn Hindi	1, 1	4, 2*

ties quickly retreat and claim that they never will impose Hindi on an ungrateful population. Meanwhile Indians from all over the country pay rupees to see the latest Hindi-language films. They come out discussing the plot but during a census they tell census takers that they do not understand Hindi. The Union authorities promote Hindi but deny that they will impose it; the people from non-Hindi zones learn Hindi but deny that they can use it. Neither equilibrium – state direction or societal defection – is stable over iterated play.

Bureaucracy in the postcolonial state. The second historical factor that distinguishes the Indian case from the European ones concerns the effect of modern colonialism on political–bureaucratic relations. In the postcolonial state, there is a conflict of linguistic interest between national politicians and senior bureaucrats, one in which the latter group has a strategic advantage. State builders of early modern Europe had an administrative service loyal to them. Max Weber, in his classic study of bureaucracy, notes the modern (after the consolidation of states) development of officials in an administrative hierarchy who earn a salary that is paid irrespective of their loyalty to the ruler. The burden of contemporary state builders is that they were handed modern bureaucracies in order to accomplish tasks best performed by loyal knights and retainers.

Robert Price's portrayal of the dilemmas for leadership of a civil service that operates according to norms different from the goals of the political elite emphasizes the breakdown of Weberian bureaucratic norms (1975). But while Ghanaian bureaucrats quickly adopted corrupt practices that subverted the goals of a neutral civil service, they never abjured the perquisites of office (regular salary payments, health benefits) enjoyed by their European predecessors. An entrenched bureaucracy with high status and cost presented a challenge to political leadership.

This problem also applies to the issue of language rationalization. It becomes clear that the political elite who fought for independence had different interests from the administrative elite that remained on salary during the period of transition from colonialism to independence.[12] The contention here is that the bureaucrats had a vested interest in the perpetuation of the colonial language as the official language of state, while the politicians had a mixed interest in developing an indigenous language for official purposes but also in getting compliance and support from the bureaucracy.[13]

This conflict of interest fits into the game-theory perspective, and can be modeled using tools similar to those employed to model the state-rationalization game. Rather than using the normal form matrix, I rely here on the extensive form, or "tree," a technique that is more sensitive to the temporal dynamics of choice. Let us begin with the Congress party, India's nationalist party, whose leaders had demonstrated since the 1920s a preference for official support for India's indigenous languages. Congress elites (call them P, for their political role) had a choice at the 1948–9 constitutional convention. They chould have chosen English as a link language and given permission to the states to develop state languages as they wished; or they could have chosen Hindi / Hindustani as the link language with the hope of developing it into a truly national language.[14] The historical record tells us that as nationalists they preferred the second alternative to the first. Let us reckon, however, that their second goal was to operate in the same language as the Indian Administrative Service (B, for bureaucrats), since bureaucratic support was necessary for what was then called "development planning and administration." In other words, P and B both operating in Hindi was P's first choice; P and B both operating in English was second; P operating in Hindi while B is operating in English was third; and P operating in English with B operating in Hindi was fourth.[15]

The preferences for B are less equivocal. As salaried officials, they had great societal status. (Their worth on the marriage market, as indicated by the marital classified advertisements in the *Times of India*, suggests they were the most sought-after spouses in India, almost irrespective of caste; they have recently been supplanted by managers in multinational corporations who have a "green card" enabling them to work in the United States.) The most important skill distinguishing this class from others in India was their command of the English language. Their education in English was a capital investment paying great dividends; movement from English to Hindi as India's official language would be inconvenient for their careers; it would be perilous for their children, who had a considerable advantage over other Indian youth in that their families transmitted English more effectively than did Indian schools. From the point of view of *B,* administration in English as a link language was preferred, whether or not Hindi played a role in electoral politics or became the national language.

Let us now reckon the preferences of the politicians in states outside the Hindi zone (call them *V,* for their identification with regional vernaculars).[16] They had been in a political bind in regard to writing the Constitution. They did not want Hindi but could not be seen to oppose it openly. At best, they could delay its implementation through the strategy of using English as an interim language. Especially in the south, where English had spread very well through mission education, political leaders sought to lengthen the period of transition. They were therefore pleased at the bureaucratic resistance; in fact, a disproportionate number of senior bureaucrats was from the south, and regional interests must surely have been part of the reason for bureaucratic resistance to the use of Hindi.

Regional elites, as previously mentioned, supported the development of the state language as the normal language of school, business, literature, and everyday life. But they also recognized that, despite the electoral support such a policy might have, individual residents will often subvert the policy if they see a language of wider communications as commanding respect and being necessary for jobs. The choice of the regional elites, then, is as follows. They could promote the regional language for use in a wide variety of domains: in school, as the medium of instruction; in courts, as the medium of justice; and in government offices, as the medium of administration. Or they could promote the regional language as a cultural marker to be used in local ceremonies and in family domains. I call the choice to expand the domains of a language's use "promote," and the choice to give honor to the language in a restricted number of domains "symbol." I assume that the state elites prefer vernacular development ("Promote") if the market signals about a language of wider communication are unclear but prefer symbolic uses ("Symbol") if there is a clear signal.[17]

The Indian national-language game is portrayed on Tree 2.1. The Congress party (*P*) chose Hindi; the Indian Administrative Service (*B*) chose to "reject" that choice and to continue operating in English. The state-level elites (*V*), seeing ambiguous signals, chose to seriously promote the vernaculars. The outcome in India gave the Congress party a low score: There is neither rationalization nor an indigenous national language. The bureaucracy got a medium score: They continue to operate in English, but Hindi is encroaching into the civil service, making for an

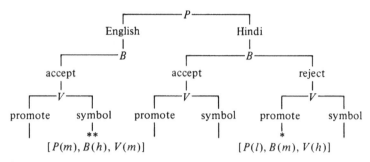

* = Actual outcome; ** = strategically rational outcome.

Tree 2.1. Nonrationalization of language in India. [*Key:* For scores, *h* = high; *m* = medium; *l* = low. *P(m)* = medium score for Congress politicians, etc.]

ambiguous future. For example, as Dua (1985, 204) points out, the All-Union government must respond to correspondence coming from Hindi states in Hindi. The state elites earned a high score: They can develop the vernaculars without facing an unambiguous challenger.[18]

To a considerable extent this outcome has been reflected in India's political formula, at least since 1956, when the government accepted in principle the reorganization of India into language-based states. Since then, new states have been created which reflect the language of the region. The best estimate for the 1980s is that only 2.7 percent of the Indian population has as its primary language a language different from the official language of their state (Schwartzberg, 1985). States have been strong and active rationalizers of language. Yet they are required by constitutional mandate to protect the linguistic rights of minorities, who have successfully used the courts to ensure themselves the right to use their own language for education. Meanwhile the All-Union government operates in both Hindi and English.

The tree formalization suggested to me, when I published my account of the Indian rationalization project (1989a), that the Congress party did not play the national-language game strategically.[19] If it had reckoned the preferences of the civil service and the state politicians (instead of decrying the former as neocolonialists – as Nehru and other Congress-party members were wont to do – and the latter as irrational traditionalists), it could have done better for itself by choosing English. To be sure, the political climate made the explicit choice of English an apparent impossibility. But a decision to postpone the issue of language until after independence – a stance that had some chance of success – would have been a de facto choice for English, in large part because independence represented a symbolically important moment for unifying nationalist policies. Choosing English would have been accepted by the bureaucrats and might have led the state elites to give symbolic support to the state languages. Congress would have reached a moderate score (it would have gotten rationalization without indigenization); the bureaucrats would have received a high score (they would be fully secure in their language investments); and the state elites would have received a moderate score (they would have their language in use, but only in the cultural and family realms, not in the business or technical realms).[20]

The outcome that did occur in India may not have reflected strategic rationality on the part of P, in that by choosing Hindi they received a lower score than if they had chosen English (assuming that B and V acted rationally). The outcome nonetheless appears to have become institutionalized. To support this claim, I cited the election in 1977 of the Janata government, which was brought to power in the wake of Prime Minister Indira Gandhi's ill-fated state of emergency in which civil liberties were suspended. In the postemergency government, 221 out of 299 elected representatives of Janata came from Hindi-speaking areas. This represented a government clearly committed to a Hindi vision of India. Once in power, however, the Janata party immediately stood behind Nehru's language concessions (K. L. Gandhi, 1984, chap. 3). English would remain the language of elite domains; the non-Hindi states would not face the imposition of Hindi. In light of this experience, the 3 ± 1 language policy in India appears now to be in a state of equilibrium, because the costs of change, for any party, outweigh the benefits of the status quo.[21]

Africa's twentieth-century state development has many parallels to India's. The colonial experience, with institutionalized bureaucratic forms that preceded self-government, is like India's. So also is the coincidence of state building with a period when states are intricately involved in the lives of their citizens. But Africa is in many ways distinct from India, and African states themselves are quite diverse. To the extent that I find a dynamic toward a 3 ± 1 language outcome in African states, I will be pushed to generalize the model presented in Tree 2.1. I will need to show that the strategically nonrational actions of the Indian politicians are likely to be replicated by African leaders. Or, alternatively, I will need to demonstrate that there are other paths to the 3 ± 1 formula. I shall build upon the strategic models presented in this chapter to give a fine-grained analysis of Africa's language outcomes. If this goal is accomplished, a piece of the puzzle of the dynamics of twentieth-century state construction can be placed into the larger picture of state theory.

CONCLUSION

This chapter has reviewed three theories that purport to explain the relationship of language to state construction. The primordial theory of cultural anthropology correctly posited that attachment to language and other symbolic forms would exacerbate the problems of establishing a national culture for the leaders of the new states. But in predicting that primordial ties would remain dominant, the theory was unable to explain previous cases where cultural groups became assimilated into new national cultures. The cybernetic alternative was able to explain both the stability of primordial ties and their shift. In this sense, it has been more powerful. But it does not take into sufficient account the preferences of actors nor the historical constraints under which states have formed.

The strategic theory does not deny that people are attached to their own language and culture, nor does it deny that people prefer to communicate with those who best understand them and that understanding is a function of regularity of interaction. In this sense, the theory presented here is less an alternative, and more a complement, to the work of Geertz, Deutsch, and their followers.

A methodological point: Although the language-rationalization game and its derivatives posit rational actors, they are distinctive from the game-theoretical models that pervade the literature of economics. Microeconomic models rely on "revealed-preference theory," which essentially means that the outcomes are used as data from which to ascertain actor preferences. This intellectual strategy has merit if you seek to develop a general theory of, say, how parents choose family size, based on the expected marginal payoff of each additional child. Here data on preferences ("I like large families, so . . .") may obscure some important general phenomena ("I want more children, but housing circumstances make it impossible"). The games presented here began with assumptions about preferences based on a reading of the historical record. And the historical record, especially when the model moved to later developers, was crucial in capturing changed preferences that led to new equilibria. The strategic models presented here are attuned to the social, economic, and political environments in which they are applied. Any recommendations that follow from these models will not have the ring of the International Monetary Fund's admonitions to today's African leaders – "Privatize!" – advice that has very little practical application. These models are meant to speak to Africa's real choice situations in regard to language.

3

Do language outcomes matter?

If the strategic theory proposed in Chapter 2 were accepted without qualification, we could model the payoffs for learning any particular language, the opportunity costs of maintaining a multilingual repertoire, and predict as an equilibrium outcome the eventual coordination of the most efficient means of societal communication. The model might share characteristics with what game theorists call a "coordination game," so called because both parties have an interest in coordination, even though they have a conflict of interest concerning the coordination point. Consider the game played among small computer firms that are deciding whether to promote computers that rely on DOS machine language or Apple machine language. Each firm knows that aggregate sales will be higher if there is an industry standard. Since all firms have a clear interest in a coordinated solution, game theory predicts that one of the two equilibria (all Apple, or all DOS) will eventually be reached, the outcome depending on the relative gains for early DOS switchers into Apple, compared to the gains for early Apple switchers into DOS. Once a "tip" into one language begins, the firms using the minority language will cascade into the camp of the majority. Computer-language rationalization would be the result.

Such models cannot be blindly applied to shifts in natural languages in real social, cultural, and political settings.[1] First, the basic insight of primordial theory, despite its inability to explain change and the strategic use of cultural markers, remains: People have an apparently intractable attachment to their language or dialect which is not subject to easy calculation. Their decisions to learn another language, to assimilate into another language group, or to speak a language they do not know well in order to consolidate a transaction all have complex implications. An individual's preference concerning language choice therefore involves numerous concerns, having to do with personal identity, social and economic opportunity, and political ideologies and structures. It will be impossible to discuss actor strategies without a clear sense of how language outcomes matter to people. This is not to say that I reject any form of "expected-utility" analysis; rather, it is to say that the "expected utility" of a language repertoire cannot be as neatly defined as the expected utility of "profits" is, in the computer-language case.[2] It is crucial to understand the bases for language utilities before we can reckon them. In this chapter, then, I try to get at some fundamental issues concerning the sources of language preferences, or utilities, taking into account people's assessments of the consequences of different language outcomes.

The question posed by the title of this chapter, then, asks whether something more than the advantages of societal coordination is at stake in the strategic choice of managing a language repertoire. For most sociologists of language, the question appears to have an obvious answer, but in fact it does not. On the one hand, politicians and poets, citizens and foreigners, and speakers of majority and minority languages have spoken eloquently about the cultural implications of language policy in Africa. The brilliant Kenyan novelist and dramatist, Ngugi wa Thiong'o, wrote a compelling polemic, *Decolonising the Mind: the Politics of Language in African Literature* (1986), in which he argued that African artists must stop using European languages if they are to lead their people to political emancipation. Echoing this presumption of importance is Ike Nodolo, who wrote, in the *Journal of Modern African Studies,* that a "common medium of communication" is one of Nigeria's "pressing needs" (1989, 679). The Ugandan poet Okot p'Bitek recites the lament of an Acholi woman who is lost in a world of colonial language dominance:

> My husband says
> Some of the answers
> Cannot be given in Acholi
> Which is a primitive language
> And is not rich enough
> To express deep wisdom.
> He says the Acholi language
> Has very few words
> It is not like the white man's language
> Which is rich and very beautiful
> A language fitted for discussing deep thoughts.
>   (Quoted in Chishimba, 1986, 164)

The pages of the literary and cultural journal *Présence Africaine* have been filled for the past generation with similar calls for cultural independence won through the elevation of African vernaculars to the commanding heights of national communication. A number of Ph.D. dissertations in linguistics, written by Africans, (which are cited in Chapter 8) echo these same themes. Many African intellectuals, although they might not agree on particular policies, would agree that language policies matter deeply.

On the other hand, because of the political, economic, and social problems that African countries have faced over the past quarter-century, the language issue has most often been on the back burner. In the Nigerian constitutional debates of 1979, far more attention went to the issue of which legal tradition to use in the court system (Islamic law or British common law) than to the question of a common language. Occasionally countries have had conferences for linguists, which have drawn up manifestos calling for more research and rational policies, but rarely have these calls been seriously considered by top government officials. Tanzania, Guinea (under Sékou Touré), and Somalia have been exceptions here, but in most African countries other pressing concerns have taken precedence. We can only assume that language reform has not mattered all that much, so that it could be profitably ignored.

A coherent answer to the question of this chapter must break the issue down and ask, How do language outcomes matter, and to whom? This question has a psychological, an economic, a cultural, and a political dimension. Let us unravel the question into its separate threads, which will allow us to give a nuanced answer to our question.

PSYCHOLOGICAL FACTORS

People care intensely about the language demands put upon them, at least in the modern era. The late and astute anthropologist Robert Armstrong, once director of the Institute for African Studies at the University of Ibadan (Nigeria), put this matter in psychological terms:

> In the great area between Yaoundé . . . and Dakar . . . from 500 to 1,000 different languages are spoken. . . . These languages are important to the people who speak them and who, speaking them, become complete human beings. So important, indeed, are their respective languages that people make them the very symbol and banner of the cultural and tribal differences that today rack Africa. . . . Thus it is obvious that when we discuss language problems of developing nations, we are not merely discussing cabinet and ministry decisions, the

recommendations of international conferences, the statistics of examination results, and the experience of pilot teaching projects. People still kill each other
over language questions. (Armstrong, 1968, 227)

This psychological element cannot easily be ignored. In 1984–5, I was
carrying out field research in Spain on the revival of the Catalan language. On my final day in Barcelona, I was sitting in a café, and an
American businessman recognized me and sat down. He asked me
about my work, and in response to my short description, he asked me
what I thought of the bilingual movement in the United States. Without
giving me a moment to answer, he excoriated the bilingual activists for
tearing at the fabric of American society, and as he did so his face turned
purple. I quietly answered that, as a political scientist, I could see that I
had chosen an important topic, because people get so aroused by its
politicization.

Even where language controversies have been broadly settled, as in
Belgium, the issue will flare up suddenly, like those trick birthday can-
dles that cannot conclusively be blown out. In a Flemish-speaking village
inside the French-speaking zone, a mayor was relieved of office for
refusing to speak French, a language he could speak with fluency. The
issue almost brought down the government in Brussels. The *New York
Times* reported the mayor's behavior as an atavistic return to his roots
(19 October 1986). Atavism hardly explains his motives. He refused to
speak French because the social meaning of using it for his constituents
was that of capitulation to cultural tyranny. For the Flemish speakers in
the French zone of Belgium, there is clearly a psychological burden in
living outside their own linguistic zone. Because symbols evoked by
hearing one's own (or a foreign) language have deep psychological reso-
nance among constituents, politicians cannot be merely technocratic
about its use. And because people feel that it matters, in an important
way it does matter.

African literary figures have expressed this burden in the strongest
terms, but they are merely expressing what many ordinary Africans feel
so clearly when they hear voices of authority admonishing them in a
language they can barely comprehend. Consider this fragment composed by a Haitian poet:

> Sentez-vous cette souffrance
> Et ce désespoir à nul autre égal
> D'apprivoiser, avec les mots de France
> Ce coeur que m'est venu du Sénégal?

[Do you feel this suffering
And this unequaled despair
Of taming, with the words from France
This heart which came to me from Senegal?]

Or these words from a Malagasy poet:

Truly our conference [the Second Congress of Negro Writers and Artists] is one of language thieves. This crime, at least, we have committed ourselves. We have stolen from our masters, this treasure of identity, the vehicle of their thought, the golden key to their soul, the magic *Sesame* which opens wide the door of their secrets, the forbidden cave where they have hidden the loot taken from our fathers and for which we must demand a reckoning. (Wauthier, 1967, 31)

These statements reflect a deep ambivalence about language in Africa. On the one hand, reliance on European languages is considered to be a sellout of one's own heritage. On the other hand, its use opens up a world of interlocutors who could not be reached through the medium of African vernaculars. In a series of provocative papers, Ali Mazrui (1966, 1968) has explored the often bitterly ironic situation through which colonial languages became necessary to further African nationalism. Mazrui embellishes the irony by pointing out that it was from the corpus of English literature that African nationalists got the idea that the African vernaculars ought to be extolled and promoted. Further, Mazrui points out, it was the European languages that facilitated communication among diverse Africans, and this communication was a necessary condition for the success of the nationalist movements. The practical need for European languages, combined with the deep psychic need to rely on indigenous languages, give the language question in Africa its drama and tell us why the outcomes so profoundly matter to individual Africans.

Still on the psychological level, other issues besides pride are involved. Suppose an individual lives in a society in which he or she can operate successfully in all social domains in a single language. Compare that with a situation in which most individuals who are successful in their societies need to use three languages. What are the costs and benefits for the individual of these different outcomes?

Some scholars (e.g., Laponce, 1984, 8–19) emphasize the costs of multilingualism for the individual, concentrating on memory and the time it takes to solve complex problems. Others (e.g., Peal and Lambert, 1962) point to a methodological flaw in the research that shows deficiencies among bilinguals: Socioeconomic status is rarely controlled for. They point out that in Canada bilingualism offers an intellectual advantage, improving the individual's ability to manipulate abstract concepts.

It is doubtful whether the issue of the respective effect of monolingualism and multilingualism on intellectual development will ever be resolved in the abstract. But research on concrete cases can tell us a good deal about the particular problems faced by individuals in light of Africa's multilingual outcomes. A. Colot describes the experience of a typical student just starting primary school in Dakar: "He will immediately have to learn and speak in a foreign language," leading to "a brutal rupture of his family life" (1965, 130–50) The apparently unbridgeable gaps between the family and the state, and between traditional and modern authority, are surely widened by the functional separation in Dakar between French as the language of school and authority and Wolof as the language of home and community.

The pressure to teach in the languages of science, of modernity, and of the available textbooks, was of course great in the early independence years. But evidence from a survey in Uganda (Ladefoged et al., 1971, 131 ff.) suggests that long-term individual academic achievement is not enhanced by early immersion in English. The crucial variable to explain achievement had to do with staff turnover, competence, and commitment. Elsewhere in Africa, educational authorities are moving away from immersion programs in European languages for primary school students. The psychic costs of immersion seem not to yield clear pedagogical benefits in the long term.

Admittedly impressionistic, the evidence points to a fascinating psychological quality about language. People are willing to learn languages other than their mother tongues as instruments for the fulfillment of economic or social goals. As the newly learned language(s) begin to replace the mother tongue in a widening circle of social domains, however, many people feel a sense of loss, of alienation from their roots, of betrayal. This sense of betrayal is passed on through the generations, even to children who have never heard the language of their ancestors. Revival movements of "dead" languages, led by intellectuals who have never spoken that language (for example, in the Basque country in Spain) use that sense of guilt and betrayal to political advantage. People can be mobilized to support terrorism, secession, or federalism in the name of language revival, in large part because of the psychological power of the sense of rootlessness that language loss imposes upon its speakers and their descendants.

SOCIOECONOMIC FACTORS

Language and economic growth

Do countries that have a single speech community whose language is the sole official language of the state perform better economically than countries with diverse speech communities that rely on a foreign language for important government business? An affirmative answer to this question is often assumed. During the twenty-five-year struggle in Somalia concerning what script was to be used to write Somali, Yaasiin Cismaan, the son of the inventor of an indigenously developed script, argued that "almost all the difficulties and obstacles which hinder the rapid course of progress in all fields derive exclusively from the negligence of this sacrosanct duty toward their mother tongue. It is logical that a nation ought to find itself in an embarrassing situation when it neglects such a fundamental duty." He concluded that Somali backwardness in the trades, in agriculture, in livestock breeding, in fishing, in weaving, in leather work, and in carpentry was caused by "ignorance" and the inability to write in one's own language (quoted in Laitin, 1977, 101).[3] Mahatma Gandhi, although he supported the cultivation of regional languages, sometimes implied a deeper desire for India to become linguistically homogeneous. In one of his essays in *Harijan,* he held up the model of Japan as meriting admiration, in large part because the country contained a single speech community. The Japanese, he wrote, "economise their energy. Those who need to learn [other languages] do so for enriching the Japanese thought with knowledge which the West alone can give. . . . The rapid progress was due to the restriction of the learning of the Western mode to a selected few and using that for transmission of the new knowledge among the Japanese through their own mother-tongue" (quoted in Kher, 1956, 26). The frequent calls for a single national language by African intellectuals reflect the belief that development is associated with the choice of an indigenous language as the sole official language for politics and economics.

Correlation analysis involving all countries of the world suggests that there is a positive statistical relationship between societies with diverse speech communities and low levels of economic development (Pool, 1972). Cross-sectional data compiled by Lieberson "indicate that the more [linguistically] diverse nations are less urbanized, poorer, have lower newspaper circulation, and greater illiteracy, consume less energy, have less domestic mail. . . . [T]hese . . . results are consistent with a model in which diversity and national development are inversely linked" (Lieberson, 1981, 20–1). Scholars who provide policy advice (e.g., Allan, 1978) accept these results and argue that economic development presupposes the settlement of the language question and therefore depends upon agreement on a single national language.

The data are not so clear. First, the multinational correlations are not strong, and language diversity rarely explains more than a quarter of the variance on any of the dependent variables. Second, many countries with impressive economic performance, such as Switzerland, Belgium, and Canada, are linguistically diverse. So language uniformity is clearly not a necessary condition for socioeconomic development. Third, and more important, the cross-sectional studies reporting these correlations do not demonstrate causal links. Lieberson, in noting the pitfalls of the correlational studies, organized a data set for twenty-three European countries from 1930 to 1960. Changes in the level of language diversity did not explain any variance in socioeconomic development. Thus any advice assuming that changes in language diversity would yield changes in economic development is scientifically suspect. Fourth, these studies ignore a standard intervening variable, the age of a country. As Lieberson explains his findings:

It is as if there are two clusters of nations, with one cluster consisting of pre–World War II nations that are generally more developed and less diverse than the second cluster of post–World War II nations. The correlations between diversity and development are created because these two separate clusters exist, but it is only a slight overstatement to say that within each cluster there is essentially no association between the developmental characteristics and mother-tongue diversity. (Lieberson, 1981, 37–8)

African data, based on socioeconomic indicators from forty African countries, cannot demonstrate a statistical relationship between language diversity and economic growth. Pearson product-moment correlations show no relationship between the growth of GNP per capita and the percentage of people who speak the dominant vernacular, or the existence of a lingua franca, or the level of standardization of the dominant vernacular, or the government promotion of a vernacular. There is a positive relationship between the primacy of the first language over the second language (dividing the percentage of speakers of the first vernacular by the percentage of speakers of the second vernacular) and GNP growth. This finding turns out to be spurious, however, because thirty-seven of the forty countries are coded in the bottom decile. Two of the three countries at the top (Lesotho and Botswana) have higher GNP growth, for reasons having little to do with language primacy (Morrison et al., 1989). We can say, then, that language diversity and economic growth in Africa are unrelated.

The call for the elimination of language diversity to foster socioeconomic development is therefore clearly based on faith, not science. Yet there is a mirror argument: the contention that African countries can catch up to Western science only if they train their students in the European languages. In a report issued in 1964 by the Kenya Education Commission, chaired by S. H. Ominde, a national immersion program in English was strongly advocated for the schools. The commission argued:

First the English medium makes possible a systematic development of language study and literacy which would be very difficult to achieve in the vernaculars. Secondly as a result of the systematic development possible in the English medium, quicker progress is possible in all subjects. Thirdly, the foundation laid in the first three years is more scientifically conceived, and therefore provides a more solid basis for all subsequent studies, than was ever possible in the old vernacular teaching. . . . In short, we have no doubt about the advantages of English medium to the whole educational process. (Quoted in Gorman, 1974a, 441)

This view, that expertise, systematic learning, and science can be fully developed through use of a nonindigenous language, is equally based on faith.

The package of European languages, technical efficiency, and socioeconomic progress is often too neatly tied. For Ominde, only the cost of abandoning English or French – losing access to the world's knowledge – was reckoned. But socioeconomic and developmental gains are associated with vernacular development as well. I have untied this package elsewhere (Laitin, 1983, 338):

What has become accepted as "technological rationality" throughout the world encompasses a mixed bag of both highly efficient methods of production and a whole set of cultural forms which accompanied technical advance as it developed in England, France, the United States, and elsewhere in the West. The dominant mode of development theory has conflated the technical and cultural forms, and its proponents have argued that technological progress requires extensive "westernization." But in Japan, where linguistic barriers have been particularly high, there was an incentive to separate the "technical" from the "Western," making more probable the development of distinct organizations and market strategies, and with it the potential to break the hegemony of the economic order dominated by the advanced industrial states of the West. By this argument, while policies of linguistic association might induce "catch up" [with the more economically developed countries], policies of linguistic dissociation [i.e., support for vernaculars] might induce "challenge" [to their economic domination].

I went on to argue that linguistic dissociation might have some positive implications for economic efficiency. First, leaders who seek to induce change in productive methods would have an easier time communicating with the people whose behavior is targeted. Promotion of the vernacular might create what I called an "institutionalized audience" in the rural areas – among both peasants and civil servants – capable of reacting to the subtleties of the ideological and technological information sent (usually through radio) by the center. Additionally, an administration that operates in the local languages will be better able to respond to the development needs of the people, as the people see those needs. More directly associated with development, vernacular promotion (for example, giving all technical education in indigenous languages) would help to plug the brain drain, since moderately well trained Africans would no longer have credentials easily enabling them to get comparable jobs in Europe and North America at higher wages (Godfrey, 1976).

It would be imprudent to deny the benefit that individual Africans derive from easy access to French or English, even if those Africans who have such access feel ambivalent about it. This ambivalence reflects considerable tensions, which can of course be exploited politically. The most telling example of the tensions in regard to popular attitudes comes from Soweto in South Africa, where black parents saw English as the language of their children's future and saw Afrikaans and their own vernaculars as education for oppression (Hirson, 1981). African intellectuals, especially writers, have felt this tension acutely, recognizing the irony of selling books in English and French while being able to reach most of their own people only in the vernaculars (Achebe, quoted in Mazrui, 1975; Ngugi, 1986).[4]

But the economic benefit that has been associated at the individual level with speaking a European language may have already begun to decline. The political economy of Africa since independence, while it certainly gives no support for the strategy of dissociation, hardly gives promise to those who have cast their lot with notions of "westernization" or the assimilation of European languages as the key to wealth. Given the unfulfilled promise of westernization that has included modern education provided through the medium of European languages, the expected utility of assimilation into African urban culture is not high. For any individual, given the economic and political difficulties that have faced most African countries, maintaining one's first language is an investment in returning to subsistence farming and herding if urban life becomes unbearable, as has been the case in Uganda in the 1970s and 1980s, and in Liberia, Rwanda, and Somalia in the early 1990s. Macro forces, then, hold little promise for high societal payoffs for rapid language shift; these forces translate into risk-averse strategies of individuals who learn the languages of power but make sure that their children have facility in at least one of the languages of subsistence society.

Multilingualism and social mobility

Language situations relate not only to economic development but also to issues of social and economic equality. As Pierre Alexandre points out,

Herein lies one of the most remarkable sociological aspects of contemporary Africa: that the kind of class structure which seems to be emerging is based on linguistic factors. . . . This minority [who have facility in a European language], although socially and ethnically as heterogeneous as the majority [who do not command facility in a European language], is separated from the latter by that monopoly which gives it its class specificity: the use of a means of universal communication, French or English, whose acquisition represents truly a form of capital accumulation. (1972, 86)

The classic empirical work on the relation between language (dialect) shift and social equality is that of Labov (1968). He found that the English of inner-city black Americans has tended to diverge over time from standard American English. The lack of contact between the two societies (inner-city blacks and the predominantly white middle-class) has reinforced language barriers between those two strata, and the language barriers themselves make egalitarian remedies difficult to implement.

In Africa, when the preferred language of the elite is distinct from the languages of the lower strata, the isolation of the elite has been described as "elite closure" (Scotton, 1990). When an elite relies on a language for intra-elite communication (French and English, in Africa) but relies on a different lingua franca for communication with the masses, there is "downwards accommodation," which itself sustains elite closure. (In the United States, the lower strata seek to use standard English when they talk to middle-class employers, and this condition of upwards accommodation tends to erase the closure effects.) Scotton observes that "downwards accommodation seems to be the rule in much of Africa. In West Africa and eastern Zaire, the elite learns enough Swahili to communicate with the masses; along the East African coast, a pidginized or creolized form of English is used to communicate across groups; and in other countries an indigenous lingua franca, such as Dyula in the Ivory Coast, is used for these purposes" (Scotton, 1990, 39). The point here is that reliance on European languages for official purposes and technical domains, while vernaculars and creoles are relied upon for communication between elites and the people, leads to a system of stratification that is inherently inegalitarian in that it puts up extra barriers to social mobility.

Dr. O. O. Oyelaran of the Department of African Languages and Literatures at Obafemi Awolowo University in Nigeria uses the term "exclusion" in a way similar to Scotton's "elite closure." He writes (1990, 24):

It is my considered opinion that the vast majority of Nigerians are excluded in the primary sense from participating in the productive life of the nation. The minority, just because they – the minority – can read or write the English language, see themselves as the anointed heirs to the imperial masters whose purpose they (the minority) served effectively in order to strip Nigerians of their . . . meanings, values and activity.

Closed or excluded from elite discourse, the great majority of African citizens face linguistic barriers to social mobility.

Statistical research gives limited support to these general observations linking indigenous language policies to social and economic equality. In 1979, I examined language outcomes in four African countries. In two of them, language policies did not give any group linguistic capital denied to others. In Tanzania, Swahili was the official language, was widely spoken, yet was the mother tongue of very few. Intra-elite communication and communication between the elite and the ordinary people were, by government policy, both to take place through Swahili. In Kenya, where knowledge of Swahili is far less widespread than in Tanzania, English became the de facto official language. Under Kenyan conditions of linguistic diversity, the use of a European language – known by only a small percentage of the people, but a percentage that includes members of all ethnic groups – was less discriminatory than choosing an indigenous language. In the other two countries, language policy reinforced social stratification. In Ethiopia, where Amharic, which is spoken by about half the population, is the official language, many language groups felt alienated from their polity. And in Senegal, where a high percentage of the population speaks Wolof, the choice of French as the official language helped sustain elite closure. The socioeconomic data from these four countries show that the linguistically inegalitarian states (Ethiopia and Senegal) tended to pursue policies that held back social mobilization, unlike the linguistically more egalitarian countries (Tanzania and Kenya). The linguistically inegalitarian states had lower school enrollment, lower communication rates (as measured by newspaper circulation and radio broadcasting), and lower literacy rates.

In a related study, Tanzania's language policies were seen to have egalitarian consequences (Polomé and Hill, 1980, chap. 14). The study reported that the ratio of primary school students to secondary school students is quite high, by African standards, and argued that this reflects a national commitment to raise the floor before raising the ceiling. Also, adult literacy campaigns are better administered in Tanzania than elsewhere in Africa. This again shows a greater interest in cultivating general skills for the masses than in cultivating special skills for the elites. Of course, this policy creates a new social divide, between those with and without a secondary education. Yet policies that effectively bring national vernacular literacy are, on the whole, more egalitarian in the African context than those that focus on training a small elite which operates in a language distinct from the ones spoken in the wider society.

Field research in Somalia demonstrated an association between language policies in which the lower strata's voices can be officially heard in their own language and a government that is attentive to the needs of those strata. To be sure, socialist policies in Mozambique and Angola, both countries where Portuguese was formerly the language of politics, show that the relationship is not one-to-one. But limited comparative data show that elite closure in Africa, in which social barriers between elites and masses are becoming rigid, is being helped along by language policies that exclude the voices of the masses.

Elite closure has until now mostly brought individual strategies of remedy: Individuals have sought to develop facility in the language of elite discourse. But the opportunity for political entrepreneurs in the regions to articulate general language demands, seeking official recognition of regional languages as "elite" languages, is ready to be exploited. There is no reason to assume that the cost of organizing general opposition to state language policies is prohibitively high or that there will be insufficient reward for political entrepreneurs to champion such efforts.

Consider the situation of most women in rural Africa. Tensions and ambivalences about language must be deeply felt by these women especially. The data are clear: African women are far more likely to be monolingual in the vernacular than African men. Women have less facility in the lingua francas and in the languages of the colonial state (Ladefoged et al., 1971, 25; Whiteley, 1974a, 48, 231; Barton, 1980, 194–5). We have evidence that lack of "linguistic capital" among women prevents participation, even on the local level (J. F. O'Barr, 1976, 80–1). These data do not tell us much about women's preferences in regard to language politics. In a similar situation in Bombay, a sociolinguist found that women sought literacy in the language of clinics, road signs, and pamphlets – things they wanted to be able to read – while eschewing

literacy programs in their vernaculars (Rajyashree, 1986). This suggests
that they accepted the language hierarchy and wished members of their
family to climb it. But in Africa, can women be mobilized to support
vernacular politics, which would provide them with higher relative linguistic capital, or are language investments in children their principal
means of achieving language mobility? Can they be mobilized on language issues at all? These are questions that require further research to
answer.

Issues involving language and social stratification are by no means
answered by these studies. Suppose education is provided in the language of the masses, but excellent jobs in the economy are withheld
from them, due to their lack of facility in the language of the market?
Immigrants, or children who learn the economically elite language at
home or in private school, will become the new economic elite. In
colonial Zaire, mission-educated children who spoke and were literate
only in their mother tongues watched as West Africans got remunerative
administrative and military jobs demanding French (Yates, 1978, 34–5).

On the other hand, bureaucratic jobs no longer hold great economic promise in Africa. Economic catastrophe brought "structural-
adjustment" programs to many African countries in the late 1980s and
early 1990s. These programs were designed to reduce the payrolls of
inflated bureaucracies in African states. This meant that the jobs of the
African managerial classes, especially in government, were no longer
secure. Literacy in English, French, or Portuguese was no longer a ticket
to a sinecure in the capital city. These programs translate, then, into a
lower expected utility for facility in a European language and to the
declining marginal utility of such facility as jobs in the public sector
(opened up by the disappearance of colonial civil servants) began to
decline.

Two issues concerning social mobility and language are therefore at
stake in Africa today. First, as elite closure becomes institutionalized,
social groups with less access to elite languages may mobilize politically
to seek general changes in societal language policies that would be more
egalitarian. Second, as "structural adjustment" takes its toll, the expected value of speaking European languages will continue to decrease.

CULTURAL FACTORS

There is a cultural dimension to the issue of language outcomes that was
partially touched upon in the discussion of individual pride. That issue is
generally understood as one of "language relativity," and it builds upon

Sapir's notion of "the tyrannical hold that linguistic form has upon our orientation in the world" (quoted in Slobin, 1971, 120). The thesis developed from this insight (now in the bolder formulation of Sapir's student, B. L. Whorf)

holds that all observers are not led by the same physical evidence to the same picture of the universe, unless their linguistic backgrounds are similar, or can in some way be calibrated [and] that users of markedly different grammars are pointed by their grammars toward different types of observation and different evaluations of externally similar acts of observation, and hence are not equivalent as observers, but must arrive at somewhat different views of the world. (1956, 214, 221)

Scholars in socio- and psycholinguistics have all but abandoned this heavily determinist formulation. Carefully controlled laboratory studies could not, on the whole, reject the null hypothesis that language does not affect our conceptual schema (Carroll, 1964:110, but see Bloom, 1981, and Lucy, 1987, for confirmatory data).

A less determinist formulation, however, although confirming evidence is still scarce, prospers in anthropological linguistics. Language relativity is a thesis that does not easily die. In a review of Whorf, the philosopher Max Black wrote some scathing criticisms but admitted, "I do not wish the negative conclusions reached to leave an impression that Whorf's writings are of little value. Often enough in the history of thought the unsoundest views have proved the most suggestive. Whorf's mistakes are more interesting than the carefully hedged commonplaces of more cautious writers" (1959).

In my Peace Corps experience, I developed an appreciation for Whorf's attractive ideas. I served on a faculty which was asked to teach English to secondary school graduates in Somalia (who had had Arabic or Italian as the medium of instruction), so that they would be able to teach in intermediate school, where English was the medium. Even though they and their prospective students were all Somali speakers, the ministry of education required that subject matter be taught in English. This policy helped to unify the formerly separate northern (English) and southern (Italian) educational curricula.

Each day the TEFL (Teaching English as a Foreign Language) faculty went over the day's English-immersion program, and we moved back and forth between Somali and English. I gradually recognized that the choice of language was not merely a matter of convenience but of strategy. The head of the program, for example, switched into English at various times, because he felt more comfortable exerting authority in English than in Somali. I asked myself whether legislation requiring the use of certain languages for specified functions would have the effect of giving different people strategic advantages. This was the question which led me to Whorf's formulations.

Two years later, doing field research for my dissertation, I was in Waajeer, the Somali-speaking region of northeastern Kenya, to test these notions out (Laitin, 1977, chaps. 6–8). The data, which I shall summarize here, lent some support to the language-relativity hypothesis. Secondary school students who were bilingual in English and Somali answered interview questions and participated in structured role-playing sessions in both languages. I had hypothesized, based on my impressions observing conversations in the society, how and why approaches to certain kinds of problems would be different depending on which language was used for the interview or role-playing session.

The most telling difference between the two sets of answers concerned the concept of authority, the idea I had picked up participating in the faculty meetings. In one role-playing situation, I structured a conflict between a headmaster who had written an exceedingly difficult final examination and the teacher of that subject, who wanted to protest the difficulty of the examination. In the English dialogues, the Somali respondents tended to justify their stand by virtue of their role, that is, in terms of who had the right to set the questions. Again and again in the English dialogues, the respondents would make claims like this: "Since I am the English master, you leave the English to me. You are the headmaster of the school, but you are not supposed to interfere with my subjects." A typical response by the headmaster was "In this school, I am the one who is supposed to know what is going on."

Although there is nothing inherent in the Somali language which would prevent someone from making those claims, such claims were rarely made in the Somali dialogues, perhaps because Somali social structure has few formalized roles. Constructions making role claims (e.g., "I am the headmaster") seem odd in the Somali language. In fact, a few respondents who made a role claim in the Somali dialogues reverted to English to express their thoughts. In the Somali-language dialogues, authority was generally determined not by role but by the substance of the issue. The teacher, the advocate of the easy test, would point out to the headmaster that "progress is through understanding bit by bit," while the headmaster would argue that "the children will be accustomed to easy tests and will not understand the hard one."

These data (in which the differences were statistically significant) indicated that in the Somali-language dialogues the "teachers" and "headmasters" saw each other as equals, with an equal claim to correctness on an educational issue. In the English dialogues, on the other hand, the teachers and headmasters saw each other as having certain rights and obligations which had a bearing on the educational claims being made. To an important degree, then, both the teachers and headmasters were seeing different people and making different claims, depending on which language they were speaking.

A second difference focused on the style of expressing political difference. In the Somali-language dialogues, political argument tended to have a more diplomatic tone, while in the English-language dialogues there was a more confrontational style. A third difference focused on political identity. In the English interviews, the Somali respondents were far more open to their Kenyan identity than they were in the Somali-language interviews. Finally, religious metaphors were far more prevalent in the Somali-language responses than in the English-language responses. I concluded from these experiments that the political culture of a society would reflect somewhat different concerns depending on which language was the prescribed language of political debate.

These issues are notoriously difficult to nail down in a convincing research design. My findings have been challenged by linguistic anthropologists such as Eastman (1979) and O'Barr (1978), both of whom remain unconvinced, owing to the limitations of the data. A political scientist has criticized my conclusions as claiming causality but demonstrating only correlation (Weinstein, 1983, 25–6). Yet the role-playing data are compelling: The substance of political debate, its emphases, and its core points of concern were different depending on whether respondents were required to rely on their primary language or the language of colonial conquest. The popular belief that the abandonment by the state of indigenous languages in official life will undermine national cultures is supported by the Somali data.

POLITICAL FACTORS

There is a state interest in language outcomes, just as there are psychological, economic, and cultural interests. In the words of Abdulaziz and Fox, "Of the many factors decisively affecting the capacity of the new governments to mount social, political, and economic structures that were essential to the building of self-governing nations, language was probably the most complex" (1978, 4). In a highly multilingual society, language policies that recognize all groups put heavy constraints on a young state, making more difficult the development of educational materials, the propagation of laws and administrative decrees, the production of national symbols, and the coordination of personnel throughout the country. It is little wonder that in the early years of independence, despite the commitment of many nationalist movements to promoting national languages, the new governments' language policies were built on inertia. As language planning came into better focus, however, the desire for the promotion of indigenous languages was countered by pressures from representatives of the state (in courts, in ministries) to have a standard language for official communication throughout the country. While an accounting of learning costs, as opposed to translation costs, might demonstrate certain configurations of multilingualism to be more efficient than the achievement of language uniformity, most political leaders in modern empires and states certainly have sought to promote a standardized language, just as they have sought to standardize the coinage and system of weights and measures (Friedman, 1977). States have an interest in standardization and perhaps also in passing off the cost of change onto their subjects.

If language diversity is a threat to the standardizing tendencies of state builders, is it an equal threat to committed democrats? Political-science approaches to democratic theory originally emphasized the importance of language uniformity for democratic stability (Dahl, 1971, 110–11). It was thought that democracy required public participation in open debate, which is difficult to sustain when citizens are unable to communicate effectively with each other. A public-choice analysis, showing how cultural diversity leads to democratic breakdown, confirmed this emphasis (Rabushka and Shepsle, 1972). More recent models of democracy, sometimes termed "consociational," suggest that a "decentralized" system, in which each language community has considerable autonomy, is a viable form of democracy. Belgium and Switzerland are used as models for the decentralized democracy (Lijphart, 1977). Since the 1970s, noting what has happened with the Catalan language in post-Franco Spain and with French in Quebec, we see that multilingual states may experience considerable tension in managing democracy but that multilingualism does not in itself preclude democratic stability. Specifying the precise conditions of language diversity and democratic stability remains on the political-science agenda.

CONCLUSION

For game theory, this chapter has a revealing message. The language game is a special form of the "coordination game." Like players in many standard coordination games, players whose languages become the standard receive short-term payoffs, and players whose languages are non-standard will have extraordinary transition costs, making all players reluctant to support coordination based on someone else's standard. As in some coordination games, players are uncertain as to whether there will be any welfare gains if a standard is agreed to at all. Given the political economy of 1990s Africa, it would be imprudent to allow one's children to ride the wave of monolingualism in a European language. While it is true that benefits can be achieved through learning a European language, the opportunity costs of maintaining one's first language are low. Furthermore, given the economic and political difficulties that face most African countries, maintaining one's first language is an investment in returning to one's home region if order cannot be preserved in the urban centers. And so, high uncertainty lowers the expected utility of a European language and lowers as well the opportunity costs of maintaining, through family interactions, one's first language.

Utility calculations, however, must also incorporate the psychological and cultural issues raised in this chapter. Perhaps unique to language coordination games, speakers of a particular language feel that their social values (or preferences) are themselves a function of the language they use to discuss their preferences. People often feel that they are in a world of reason when hearing arguments in their own language but in a world of bizarre preferences when hearing arguments in another language. The conservatism about language shift is not merely a calculation about economic gains and transition costs; it has something to do with a desire to live in a world in which common sense reigns. The political appeal for language preservation or revival by ethnic political entrepreneurs therefore has a stronger force than modelers who see language choice simply as a standard coordination game would predict.

PART II

Sociological and political forces described

4

The micro dynamics of language use in contemporary Africa

Varenasi, the holy city on the Ganges River in India, houses the political movement seeking to institute Hindi as India's sole official language. Well-known Hindi-language novelists, literary figures, and poets have worked in Varenasi, and they have become icons in the symbolic war that has been fought against English. The focus of political activity has been on the expanded use of the Hindi language for government regulations, public education, and political administration, at the expense of English, which is perceived as a foreign language of colonial domination. Hindi, mentioned in the constitution as India's future link language, was slated to supplant English by 1965. Political protest in southern India and bureaucratic intransigence in New Delhi, India's capital city, have delayed – some say forever – the full implementation of the constitutional design for a single, indigenous link language. In Varenasi, political forces have organized to fulfill the constitutional dream.

A casual walk through central Varenasi tells a different story. On nearly every street there are signs advertising yet another private school which has English as its medium of instruction. One can surmise that the citizens of Varenasi vote for Hindi education, yet send their own children to English-medium schools. The sum of numerous family decisions to vote for Hindi yet personally to subvert the goals behind that vote is the continued reliance upon English as India's de facto link language.

Any country's language outcome is built upon, and ultimately cannot defy, the innumerable language choices that ordinary people make, consciously or unconsciously, every day. If Mexican migrants in East Los Angeles turn their television sets to the major-network offerings, as opposed to that of Univisión, a Spanish-language channel, their children will more easily develop a native's facility in English. If, in Spain, the Catalan middle class routinely addresses bus drivers, sanitation workers, construction workers – most of whom are first- or second-generation migrants from Andalusia – in Catalan, these working-class men will more likely converse at home with their children in Catalan. If Kenyan store managers insist on speaking to their middle-class clientele in English, the likelihood of Swahili becoming the dominant language of Kenya, no matter what the laws say, will be severely reduced. People make these decisions often for personal reasons, but sociologists of language have discovered some broad patterns of language choice in linguistically diverse settings, suggesting that everyday decisions are responses to broader societal opportunities.

Although the purpose of this book is to determine the probable "macro," or societal, language outcomes for contemporary African states, it would be a grievous error to shut one's ears to the "micro" language choices that take place in everyday life. This chapter focuses on a set of language patterns that characterize African social life. Quantitative data cannot capture these patterns; instead we are looking for revealing examples of language use in Africa, so that we can put them into an interpretive frame. These patterns identify the micro mechanisms that help to drive the logic of the macro outcomes.

Consider this field report from a researcher working in Harare, Zimbabwe, where the Zezuru dialect of the Shona language and English are both widely spoken but have very different social meanings. The researcher would enter a shop in the West Harare market each day and say, "Mangwanani, changamire," to which he would get the English response, "Good morning, Sir." After he had suffered for many weeks the frustration of no one talking to him in Shona, he went into the store and said, "Good Morning, Sir," to which the shopkeeper responded, "Hausi imwe unonditaura kuChiZezuru here?" [Aren't you the one who always speaks to me in Zezuru?] Afterward Zezuru was their main language of conversation. Clearly, African language repertoires are complex, and they are in flux. Their rapid change, however, is not a sign of movement toward language rationalization or successful societal coordination relying on an agreed-upon standard language. Despite the continued high status of European languages and the significant expected utility of developing facility in them, few Africans have adopted these languages as their primary language, for use at home. In most African countries, there is, then, no emerging "focal point," or identifiable single-language equilibrium, that statesmen might support as a future national, or official, language. There is no micro basis for language rationalizaton in most African states – a point that has been broadly demonstrated in sociolinguistic research.

MULTILINGUALISM

The anecdote that I told in Chapter 1 about the Somali taxi driver illustrates the ubiquity of multilingualism in Africa, even in a linguistically homogeneous country like Somalia. Research from Ghana (Apronti, 1969) and Zambia (Kashoki, 1978, 35–45) demonstrates that multilingualism is the norm throughout Africa, with many Africans having facility in three or four languages. Kashoki's data show an average of two languages per person, going up to nearly three for those who have moved at least once in their lives and have lived in an urban area for at least six months.

Multilingualism as a social fact in Africa has had an important bearing on the organization of this book. While many other studies have focused on what "ought" to be the national or official language of a particular state in Africa, this study focuses on the set of languages in peoples' repertoires. The notion of the language repertoire makes the author of this volume – who has fluency in English alone – the exception, rather than assigning that role to the average African.

The social fact of African multilingualism has had an important impact on society as well. Languages are resources which can be sociologically exploited. Speaking three languages allows many Africans to travel widely, to seek diverse employment opportunities, and to settle in areas outside their home region without great difficulty. Also, as we shall see, multilingual repertoires allow an individual to show solidarity with or keep distance from an interlocutor; to show elite status or to hide it; to identify oneself with the locality, or with the region, or with the country, or to show oneself as a cosmopolitan.

CODE SWITCHING AND CODE MIXING

Code switching and code mixing are typical conversational devices used in multilingual settings.[1] Anthropologists have been sensitive to these conversations and refer to them as part of "situated talk," the study of which promises to deliver insight into deeper sociocultural realities (Gumperz and Cook-Gumperz, 1982, 1–2). "Code switching" refers here to the use of two different languages (or codes) in alternative utterances during a single conversation, or speech event. Early work by John Gumperz in Norway (Blom and Gumperz, 1971), India (Gumperz, 1964), and the American Southwest (Gumperz and Hernández-Chávez, 1972) has shown that each switch in code can be meaningfully inter-

Table 4.1. Code switching in Nairobi

Utterance	Language	Translation
K: Omera, nadi!	Luo	How are you, brother!
L: Maber.	Luo	Fine.
K: Ati,	Kikuyu	What?
nini?	Swahili	What?
L: Ya nini kusema lugha ambao huelewi mama?	Swahili	Why (try) to speak a language you don't know, Mum?
K: I know	English	I know
Kijaluo	Swahilized form	the Luo language
very well	English	very well
L: Wapi!	Swahili	Go on!
You don't know it at all	English	You don't know it at all.
Wacha haya, nipe mayai mbili	Swahili	Anyway, let's leave the matter, and give me a couple of eggs.
K: Unataka mayai.	Swahili	Do you want eggs?
Ariyo, omera?	Luo	Two, brother?
Haya ni	Swahili	OK, these are
tongalo	Luo	10-cent pieces (?)
Tatu	Swahili	Three.

preted. Code switching is so ubiquitous in multilingual areas that a particular switch often is so sociologically expected that to continue a conversation in the first language would be to signal an important change in the relationship of speakers in a conversation (Scotton, 1984).

In the multilingual urban environments of Africa, "code mixing" (the use of two or more codes within a single speech act) competes with code switching. Ethnolinguists report utterances such as this one, from Zaire, mixing French (in italics) with Lingala:

Est-ce que o-tun-aki ye soko akozonga *le lendemain?* [Did you ask him if he will return the day after tomorrow?] (Bokamba and Eastman, n.d., 5)

Scotton gives an example from Kenya, in English (italics) and Swahili:

Nikaona ina *taste lousy* sana. [And I thought it had a very lousy taste.] (1988, 74)

Excellent work on the use of code switching and mixing and interpretations of their use is now available (Parkin, 1974b, chap. 8). Consider the dialogue in Table 4.1, discussed by Parkin, which pits a Kikuyu market woman (*K*) against a Luo male customer (*L*). Parkin's core interpretation of this conversation is that it is the Swahili language that keeps the two conversants on neutral ground and allows them to transact their business effectively. But more than a sale was being transacted, and Parkin is sensitive to that. The Luo customer lets the Kikuyu stall keeper see that he knows she does not really speak his language ("he exposes her as having been using *his* language for her personal economic gain" [1974b, 195, emphasis in original]. The stall keeper was seeking to use the Luo language to establish solidarity with a new customer (whom she recognized, by dress or manner, as a Luo), but the customer exposes that strategy as merely instrumental, and he wins the first round. The stall keeper, hardly chastened, raises the stakes, showing her social status by switching to English. The customer then mixes his code, to show that he has equal status with the stall keeper but that he merely wants to make an economic transaction, without any one-upmanship. To do this he switches from English to Swahili, the neutral language. The stall keeper finally gets her victory, by making the sale, but presumably at the market clearing price. One may want to develop alternative interpretations of this rich snippet from the Kenyan language scene, but for present purposes it makes two points. It underlines the social fact of multilingualism in Africa, even for people in nonelite social roles. Second, it shows that languages are hardly kept distinct and that mixing and switching are part of everyday reality.

Akan–English code switching and mixing in Ghana (Forson, 1979) goes beyond strategic interaction. Seen as a standard verbal repertoire, social regularities in its use and structure can be identified. First, code switching occurs only between English and a Ghanaian vernacular, never between Ghanaian vernaculars. Second, code switching begins early in many children's lives. A typical case is that of a six-year-old child who tries to use all the English items he can name and incorporate them in his Akan sentences. Consider the following example from Joojo, who is nearly seven and has been at Achimota Primary School for four months (Forson's notation is not relevant to our concerns, but the reader should get a sense of the incorporation of English into this passage):

Wɔfa Kwakú, ɛ-yèa, ká kyèrɛ Mámà sɛ́ yɛ́n teacher sè obiá ' a ne parents m' bɛ́ visit nò, wó-à- ' e? [Uncle Kwaku, if you have the opportunity, tell Mama that our teacher says everybody's parents should come to visit him, O.K.?] (249)

Forson's third regularity notes that code switching rarely occurs in the written language or in ritual domains but nearly always in informal speech settings. He reports that of all the people he recorded, 77 percent felt that switching was somehow immoral or impure and that "we should stop switching." Yet switching and mixing continue, often by the same people who decry its use. Forson has an entire section of code-mixed responses to his question of whether Ghanaians should stop switching (209–10). One respondent said that the Fantes (those who speak the Fante dialect of the Akan language), especially, overdid the switching: "Mfantefóɔ. Òbiá ' a yɔ, but Mfantefóɔ déɛ wɔpɛ saá too much." [Fantes. Everybody does it, but as for Fantes, they like that too much.] When Forson alerted the respondent to his use of the mix, they both laughed, and the respondent excused himself in this way: "Sɛ́ ɛbɛdi a ' a nono! Wɔ́nom nà wɔdé baaeɛ́, na wɔde asane yɛn." [There we are! It was they who brought it, and they have infected us with it.] Not only is its use common, but code mixing has become institutionalized to such a degree that the resultant forms exhibit qualities similar to the development of a new language. In examples from Ghanaians of virtually all ages and educational levels, we can discount any notion that it represents an affectation of a particular class. It is a societywide phenomenon in a particular cultural milieu.

These examples of code switching and mixing should alert us to the methodological difficulties of specifying a person's language repertoire. Do we count each language as a member of the repertoire, or do we count – for example – the Akan–English mixed language as a single code itself? A government can demand that Swahili be the language of education or administration, but the people who use it may have already incorporated so much of another language into their use of Swahili that it is no longer the Swahili of the primers printed by the ministry of education. The boundaries of languages, from a micro view, are always shifting and affect the kind of choices or outcomes available on the macro level.

LINGUA FRANCAS

Lingua francas, described by Bernd Heine as languages of contact from areas in which the local peoples have different mother tongues, are essential elements of African language repertoires. In Africa, lingua francas serve many functions (1970, 20–1). Hausa and Dyula are used (when they act as lingua francas) as languages of trade. The word *dyula,* in parts of the western Sudan, has come to mean "traveling salesman." Languages such as Bambara, Lingala, Nyanja, and possibly Yaunde have become lingua francas of ethnically heterogeneous armies. The large rivers of Africa, including the Congo, Ubangi, and Niger, have created conditions favorable for the development of regional lingua francas, connecting diverse peoples whose economic lives center on river travel. Here Lingala, Sango, and Songhai can be mentioned. Certain African languages, such as Tswana-Tawana and Fanagalo, both in southern Africa, serve as lingua francas of the workplace. Whatever their original purpose, these lingua francas often develop wider sets of uses.

A diachronic analysis of lingua francas points to four routes that any lingua franca may take. First, it could serve as the primary language for the descendants of those people who had been using it as a second language. Second, it could lose its lingua franca role and serve only as the primary language of the group that originally spoke it, if it were no longer needed for intergroup communication. Third, it could remain as part of a permanent bilingual repertoire, reserved for specific functional domains. As Greenberg pointed out in his linguistic studies, "The Tuareg and the Arabs have been bilingual for centuries, employing Songhai and their own language without loss of ethnic identity or serious impairment of group membership" (1965, 56). Finally, a language may have been no one's vernacular until it develops as a lingua franca. Then a small but growing community, usually in an urban center, adopts that language and passes it on to their children as a mother tongue.

Heine's comprehensive survey of African lingua francas (1970) shows that they are ubiquitous throughout the continent, yet their boundaries rarely coincide with state boundaries. They therefore serve crucial communication functions but are not especially useful to state builders as a symbol of a national communications network. Also, these languages do not have the status of the vernaculars and are often considered of low value. Rarely is there a social group that seeks to promote their use in official domains. They represent, however, yet another type of language in the complex repertoires of contemporary Africans.

PIDGINS AND CREOLES

A "pidgin" has been defined as a lingua franca that is native to none of the speakers using it. A "creole" is a pidgin that has been passed on intergenerationally as a mother tongue (Bloomfield, 1933). Pidgins and creoles are vital means of communication all over Africa (Berry, 1971; Holm, 1989, vol. 2, Map 1). Pidgins were originally understood as the result of natives desperately trying to communicate with whites but failing to capture more than bits of the grammar. The term "pidgin," after all, apparently comes from a Chinese mispronunciation of the English word "business." Today historical linguists recognize that a pidgin is better understood as a language of contact among peoples of vastly different language repertoires. In Samarin's meticulous historical reconstruction of pidgin Sango (1982a), a more nuanced view is developed. He finds that pidgin Sango developed from a combination of an already pidginized Bangala, used by Africans of many different language groups, with French, the language of the new European traders. Later on, it was heavily influenced by standard Sango, and it then became known as pidgin Sango, even though its basis was in Bangala. In any event, the pidginization process involved the interaction of a number of parties seeking to communicate in a limited number of social domains – here, only trade. These pidgin languages, as they are used for an increasing number of domains, are fully able to develop into new natural languages. "Creolization" – when people pass a pidgin language on to their children as their mother tongue – is the beginning of the linguistic process of the development of a new natural language.

The importance of pidgins and creoles in Africa cannot be overstated. It would be impossible to capture much of what goes on in most of West African urban settings without an ear for a wide variety of local pidgins. These pidgins are therefore of key importance in understanding the micro dynamics of language use in contemporary Africa.

West African pidgin has many (often mutually unintelligible) dialects but is spoken widely throughout the coastal region and is popularly understood throughout much of the savannah to the north. It emerged in the slave factories and therefore has elements of Portuguese and Spanish, but mostly English, vocabulary, among European languages. Donor languages from Africa include Yoruba, Igbo, Ijo, Itshekiri, Kongo, Krio, Urhobo, Fante, Arabic, Hausa, and Twi. Among the African brigades in the British and French armies in World Wars I and II, the language spread as a lingua franca. Today it is playing an increasingly important role in popular culture, literature, the press, and everyday communication.

Nigerian pidgin English has evolved to such a degree that it is not mutually intelligible with English. Consider these examples from Anna Barbag-Stoll's phrase list (1983, 94–5):

Dat bin-tu tink sei him no pas os fo dis land. (The man who has just arrived from overseas said that he was more civilized.)

A no laik pipul wei dei tek konikoni wei. (I don't like people who are not straightforward.)

Clearly, this cannot be considered a "European" language, making the dichotomy between indigenous and nonindigenous, so common in the literature on the sociology of language, and even more common in popular debate about language in Africa, untenable.

Pidgin is no longer reserved for a set of restricted domains in Nigeria. Many Nigerians reported "thinking" in pidgin (Barbag-Stoll, 1983, 39). Yet it is still taboo for parents to address their children in pidgin. Status reasons, rather than semantic or syntactic impoverishment, explain why these pidgins have not played a preeminent role in discussions about the promotion of national languages (ibid., 37–9, 49, 117).

We should not, however, take an overly static view of social status. Status can change in the face of artistic innovation. Ken Saro-Wiwa is the author of a Wednesday-evening television series in Nigeria, a situation comedy called "Basi," which is watched by an estimated 30 million Nigerians each week. The language of the dialogue is pidgin, to the delight of the nationwide audience. Saro-Wiwa published *Sozaboy: A Novel in Rotten English,* which is written entirely in pidgin. Such sentences as "Person wey no get power make é no go war" capture the lilt of Nigerian pidgin. Because Saro-Wiwa graduated from the prestigious Umuahia College, studied at the University of Ibadan, and served in the national cabinet, everyone knows that standard English is part of his repertoire and that he is relying on pidgin out of a desire to communicate rather than because of any lack of standard-English skills.

Consider too this fragment from Wole Soyinka's childhood memoir, *Aké,* part of a scene that takes place early during the Second World War. Paa Adatan is deeply angered that he could not get into the British army. Standing in front of Soyinka's mother's shop, in the King's Market, he yells,

Ah, Mama Wole, this English people just wan the glory for den self. Den no wan' blackman to win dis war and finish off dat nonsense-yeye Hitler one time! Now look them. Hitler dey bombing us for Lagos already and they no fit defend we. (Soyinka, 1981, 110)

When a (future) Nobel Prize-winning author uses pidgin forms, first for effect, and then more to capture the voice of the people represented in his literary works, the signal is given that the pidgin speech form has a certain cachet. Taboos get broken when high-status people self-consciously ignore the rules. One can easily imagine the future growth in status of certain pidgins, to make their status commensurate with their use.

OTHER LANGUAGE INNOVATIONS

Innovation is the norm in Africa's multicultural settings. Interlanguage borrowing, for one, is quite common. Jan Knappert (1970) found in African languages from all over the continent trace words from Arabic, En-

glish, French, Portuguese, Afrikaans, and Hindi. He points out that from
these data it is possible to reconstruct external influence, as well as routes
of communication, in early times. For our purposes, we can see how
changes in language are no recent phenomenon. Mubanga Kashoki's
work on lexical borrowing in Zambia shows greater borrowing from English than from other African languages (which happened more fre-
quently in earlier periods). With so much intercontinental lexical borrowing, the distinction between indigenous and nonindigenous languages,
already threatened by the growth of pidgins, breaks down even more
(Kashoki, 1977b).[2]

Where borrowing is intense, specialized argots begin to appear.
Charles Adams has described the development of Sharamboko, a "camp
language," in Lesotho. It is akin to Sesotho, but speakers in a multiethnic urban setting borrow well-known words from contact languages and
give them highly specialized meanings (Adams, 1982). A related example comes from Kenya. Work by Zuengler (1982) demonstrates the
"nativization" process – not English becoming nativized; rather Kenya
developing an indigenous language of its own – in English-speaking environments. Standard vocabulary items from Swahili (e.g., *sufaria,* a pot)
or Kikuyu (e.g., *irio,* a food staple) take on semantic shifts and become
part of English. English also takes on a Kenyan ring, such as in the
expression "We hated each other like a woman and a snake" (Zuengler,
1982, 117). Innovations come from all sorts of mixtures. In the newspaper *Taifa Leo,* the word *ushambaboi,* meaning "the career of farm
work," comes from the Swahili *shamba* (farm) and the English "boy,"
here meaning "menial servant" (Laitin and Eastman, 1989, 58). These
sorts of innovations, with input from English, Kikuyu, Swahili, Luo,
Luhya, Kamba, and other languages, are a common component of Nairobi's language scene. Urban argots, sometimes considered "youth talk"
and at other times a new language, are the result. The name "Shang" has
been given to one of these speech forms, and only time will determine its
future.

STATUS OF COLONIAL LANGUAGES

As the phenomenon of "elite closure" (discussed in Chapter 3) and the
resourceful Kikuyu market woman's use of English as part of her code
switching reveal, the status of European languages in Africa and of
those who speak these languages well remains high. In Soyinka's *Aké,*
the young Wole imagines that the parsonage was often visited by God,
who would indeed attend the morning and afternoon services "but re-

served his most formal, exotic presence for the evening service which, in his honour, was always held in the English tongue" (1981, 1). These attitudes did not disappear with the colonial flags; knowledge of European languages is still a sign of erudition and success.

The status of the European languages has something to do with the economic payoffs for those who have skill in speaking and writing them, but the languages have an aura of formality that transcends their economic value. Consider this example from Kenya:

Kenya's 1969 constitution recognized English as the sole language of parliamentary debate, and literacy in English was a requirement for election to that assembly. However, when President Kenyatta delivered his first address to Parliament as Kenya's President, he added at the end of his address a short personal note in Swahili. In1974, Swahili became an official language of Parliament, side by side with English. An informal rule then developed about which language to use when. The "rule," as Eastman observed in November, 1985, is that code-switching . . . is *not* to occur. If a member of Parliament begins to speak in English, that member must continue to speak in English; if Swahili is the choice, Swahili must be continued. In fact if an MP addresses another MP in one language, the person addressed is supposed to respond in the language used by the addresser. This rule seems to work without exception when English is chosen but is sometimes breached with Swahili – due to the fact of many MPs not knowing Swahili well enough and disdaining it, even if they do know it. In a discussion of foreign currency accepted illegally for payment of a hotel bill in Mombasa, an MP from the coast [where Swahili is the vernacular] made a point in Swahili. This was met with mockery and derision in English with Swahili words thrown in, in response, only in sarcasm. It appears that people derive gain from not learning some Swahili in favor of learning some English. Thus, in a high-status arena such as Parliament, to *not* assimilate the national language pays off. (Laitin and Eastman, 1989, 56)

Kenyan president Daniel Arap Moi, in light of the status situation, often faces ridicule for his less than perfect command of English. In his principal public appearance on Kenyan Independence Day, 12 December 1989, he spoke in Swahili but spiced his speech with some English sentences. Probably fearing that his colloquial English was not quite up to snuff, he said in English (as reported by the Foreign Broadcast Information Service, 13 December 1989), "When you speak English, it does not mean that you change. English is used – even if I make mistakes, do you think I am ashamed? No. It is a commercial language, and it is one of communication." A high-status person in Africa must explain his weakness in command over the former colonial language; no such explanation is needed for parallel weaknesses in the vernaculars.

Yet, of the many sociolinguistic surveys done throughout Africa, there are few reports of Africans who have adopted English or French as their language of home life. There is evidence that in Abidjan, Ivory Coast (Djité, 1985, 51–2), some African families rely exclusively on French, and it could be considered a first language, or "mother tongue," to the children of those households. But through most of Africa, speaking English or French well is more like owning a Mercedes Benz – it gives you European cachet, but it cannot turn you into a European. European languages are a consumption item, or perhaps more an investment item, but Africans in most settings have not adopted the social and cultural identity of being native speakers of French or English.

The mirror image of this point is the social fact of the continued resiliency of African vernaculars. This point does not imply that there is no "language death" in Africa. Nancy C. Dorian's impressive work on language death (1981, 1989) models the slow but inexorable process by which community languages get reserved for ever-fewer social functions, until a "tipping point" is reached, after which these languages rapidly disappear and become mere primordial memories. This is an insufficiently studied but worldwide phenomenon. In Dorian's edited volume (1989), Dimmendaal analyzes the death of a variety of languages of hunter-gatherer societies in East Africa and shows how tipping occurs in the assimilation to the languages of pastoralists (Dimmendaal, 1989, 13–31). In another essay, Rouchdy (1989, 91–102) documents the increasing obsolescence of Nubian among Nubian peoples living in Egypt and feels the tipping point has already been reached. Many Nubians, even in rural areas, are now monolingual Arabic speakers. It is certainly true, then, that some African languages are dying.

The key social fact, however, is that these "tips" are not toward the cosmopolitan languages of Europe but toward indigenous languages more prestigious within the speakers' own societies. Furthermore, the languages facing death in East Africa all had minuscule numbers of speakers. In the case of Nubian, virtually the entire society had been displaced from its homeland by the construction of the Nile dams. The Nubians were more like immigrants into Egypt than indigenes. So the reports of language death reflect extremely limited and limiting cases. With enormous population growth in Africa, I can claim with some confidence that the absolute number of speakers of nearly all African languages has been increasing, rather than decreasing, in this century. A sociolinguist who has worked in Tanzania and Zaire reported to me that in 1970 he found many "detribalized youth" who relied extensively on Swahili slang, married outside their language zone, and yet were assiduously teaching their own children their mother tongue, so that they would be connected to grandparents and their wider family (Edgar

Polomé, personal communication). Although a number of languages will inevitably tip toward death in Africa during the coming century, the resilience of the major vernaculars and the adoption of multilingual strategies is of greater sociological significance.

CONCLUSION

On the basis of trends involving loanwords, code switching, pidgins, creoles, and lingua francas, language theorists often project a future for Africa not unlike the past in Europe. In medieval Europe, Brann (1981) points out, there was great multilingualism, a prestige language of external influence (Latin), and rising national languages that were once considered bastard languages of interethnic contact. These bastard languages developed prestige and support through their association with rising national states. Today these languages have achieved preeminence, and in some countries hegemony, in political, economic, and educational life. The future of Africa, as the borders of states make intrastate contact more probable than interstate contact, could well be the same.

Yet the sociodynamics of language use in contemporary Africa described in this chapter give no indication that such trends are in the making. And an examination of macro forces, in the chapter that follows, points to a similar conclusion: that multilingualism is not a transitional point on the route to state consolidation. The macro forces have sought to alter the patterns of everyday language use, and some of them have pushed toward rationalization. But the interaction of macro and micro forces, as we shall see, has made language rationalization and the massive language death predicted by Brann (1981) and Laponce (1987) highly unlikely.

5

Macro forces shaping the contemporary language situation in Africa

Previous approaches to the study of nation building have been apolitical. Primordial theory assumes that people inherit their identities and learn, quasi-genetically, to love their mother tongue, even if their mother has never spoken it. Cybernetic theory assumes that people are merely recipients of messages, slaves to the communications network in which they are inextricably enmeshed. Strategic theory introduces politics. It assumes that individuals, organizations, and states all have preferences about language and use available resources to fashion the communications network that surrounds them. Those who successfully fashion that network, strategic theorists further assume, seek to develop legitimating ideologies about the favored language; its new speakers recreate their own pasts, turning the merely instrumental into something primordial. This phenomenon, described as the "invention of tradition" (Hobsbawm and Ranger, 1983), demonstrates that the primordial is not always given; sometimes it is taken.

The description of Africa's current language scene at the micro level, in Chapter 4, downplayed the larger historical forces that create incentives, infuse status, and punish laggards. It is the purpose of this chapter to paint the macrohistorical picture. While history is necessarily the confluence of many interests and actors, with outcomes altered by fortune, this chapter treats the historical actors in Africa serially, one by one. By separating the historical forces, for analytical purposes, we can better appreciate the variety of mixes that have come to constitute Africa's present. By paying attention to preferences and strategies, we will be better able to see what occurred by design and what was the result of fortune's hand. Let us now consider these macrohistorical forces, with an eye to preferences and strategies.

PRECOLONIAL AFRICAN RULERS

In the historical reconstruction of precolonial states, there is evidence that the interest of rulers influenced the language repertoires of the ruled.[1] Atkinson (1985, 112–13) reports that in eighteenth-century western Acholi, due to the administrative and taxing power of nearby Luo states, "those who accepted the new socio-political order, whatever their linguistic origins, eventually spoke Luo as their primary language." Stanley Ambrose (1982, 109–11), relying on archaeological and linguistic evidence, reports that hunter-gatherer groups usually have adopted the language of their food-producing superiors and gives evidence from central Kenya and southeastern Africa. The more centralized the political institutions, one might infer from Ambrose's generalization, the greater the spread of the language among the progeny of nonspeakers. Charles Bird reports that the unusually broad spread and coherence of Mandekan in West Africa can be explained only by such factors as the creation of an "empire" that controlled and facilitated trade (1970, 146–59). What these speculative accounts share is a notion that African rulers had, in precolonial times, preferences not unlike those of their European counterparts. Trade itself does not explain these shifts; what explains them is the interest of those controlling or taxing the trade.

By this analysis, we can hypothesize that precolonial African states, to the extent that there was centralized administration, induced the population living within their boundaries to learn the language of the central court. The precolonial political logic in Africa is not, then, substantially different from that of language rationalization as analyzed in Western Europe and East Asia. The argument that the predominant element of African political culture is one that would chafe at rationalization or reject strategic calculation is, then, historically invalid.

COLONIAL STATES

As the once-revisionist Robinson and Gallagher thesis (1961) illustrated, the purposes and preferences of the colonial states in Africa were hardly clear. This is certainly true in regard to language policy. Yet it is crucial to sort out the different preferences of colonial states, at least to make sense out of the configuration of language interests in the early independence period.

France's language policy was unequivocal in its support for the sole development of French.[2] As its colonial empire was under construction, Third Republic France was undergoing its own rationalization campaign, seeking to cure the country of religious and regional attachment, which would only, according to republican logic, invite back feudal relations. Colonial administrators – ironically, many of them with roots in Brittany, Provence, and Corsica – sought the same sort of rationalization in Africa. These administrators believed that only French could counter the advance of Arabic, which was seen as a proxy for Islam, fanaticism, and rebellion. They also believed that French was necessary for easy administrative control. Consequently, by the early twentieth century these functionaries had made education in French for the children of chiefs compulsory. French was eventually taught to the masses as well, as part of the "moral conquest" that was on the verge of success in metropolitan France. By 1911, Governor General William Ponty prescribed that all administrative documents in French West Africa should be printed solely in French. Under colonial law, speaking French properly became a requirement for an African to "evolve" into a Frenchman. Under French administration, virtually no work was done to standardize African languages or to choose a small set of African languages for official promotion.

Britain had less lofty goals than did France. The primary goal of low administrative cost goes a long way to explain the British policy of offering inducements to missions to provide a sufficient number of English-speakers to staff the administrative apparatus, but relying in local administration indirectly on African languages. As Lord Lugard, the architect of indirect rule in Uganda and Nigeria, wrote to the Colonial Office from Nigeria in 1900:

I have also always felt that it was neither good policy nor fair upon charitable institutions that government should rely on Mission Societies and make little or no effort in tropical Africa to turn out a sufficiency of clerks, artisans and other trained natives to meet at least a part of its own demands – men with a sound secular education whether as clerks or artisans. (Quoted in Graham, 1966, 8–9)

In Southern Nigeria, Lugard relied almost exclusively on the missionaries, most of whom provided vernacular education at the early level. He offered small subsidies to the missionary schools to assure himself that some students would have sufficient skill in English to serve as petty clerks for the colonial administration. In the Muslim north, Lugard feared a potential rebellion, similar to what had plagued the British in the Sudan. He therefore proscribed Christian missionaries from operating in northern Nigeria, thereby holding back formal education in English. Eventually a Church Missionary Society (CMS) project to set up a boarding school for the sons of Muslim chiefs was accepted, but the CMS was not permitted to implement it. Instead the British government brought in Hanns Vischer to run the school as a secular institution. Vischer, like the CMS missionaries in the south, emphasized the local vernacular (Hausa) as the medium of instruction in the early years and gradually introduced English at higher levels. Vischer's consuming idea,

Graham asserts, was that a "liberal education must come first and . . . vocational training second. Thus by postponing the teaching of English to the secondary school stage, Vischer hoped to ensure that those coming to school with the aim of learning just enough to obtain lucrative clerical posts as quickly as possible were, despite themselves, well grounded in all the elementary and primary subjects first." The popularity of the initial school led to expansion throughout much of the north. These Nassarawa Schools became Britain's model for colonial education in Muslim Africa (Graham, 1966, 137).[3]

The Portuguese government, in ruling over Angola and Mozambique, felt more threatened by English and French – disseminated by traders and missionaries – than by the vernaculars. In 1903, the colonial government forbade the use of English in Angolan schools. Most of the Catholic Mission Society schools were run by the French, but to assuage government fears the French Catholic fathers presented themselves in Lisbon pretending to be Portuguese.

Once English and French were marginalized, however, Portugal challenged the growth of the vernaculars. Overriding the missionary tribal divisons that gave each denomination the right to a specified language group, Portuguese-government education, once it got under way, emphasized immersion in Portuguese. Decree no. 77, published in 1921, prohibited the use of native languages in all schools and prohibited the publication of anything in the vernacular, except as a parallel text to Portuguese. As in the French colonies, knowledge of the colonial language was the key criterion for citizenship. After the Second World War, the government took greater control over education, and in 1950 Portuguese was established as the medium of instruction in all schools (Henderson, 1979; Newitt, 1987).

Germany's experience in imagining a massive colonial state in Mittelafrika, stretching from Southwest Africa to Tanganyika – which would replicate Germany's position in Europe – was short-lived. After Germany's defeat in World War I, the two colonies became League of Nations mandates, governed by South Africa and Great Britain. In Southwest Africa, German administration had been run exclusively through the German medium and required the indigenous population and the Dutch settlers to communicate with officials in German. The colonial episode was marked by the murder of a large percentage of the indigenous population, but those who survived had little cultural or linguistic contact with their German rulers. Use of the German language was limited to the settler community. In Tanganyika, on the other hand, assiduous efforts were made to administer the colony solely in Swahili.

German administrators were not permitted to take their posts unless they had passed a proficiency examination in Swahili. Here, two motives – German romantic idealism (that all peoples have, in Hegel's formulation, a language through which to reach their destiny), and the desire to administer the vast colony at low cost through a language that was widely understood – supported the policy of promoting an indigenous language (Iliffe, 1969). German administration in Swahili influenced future decisions, by the British-mandated authority and the Tanzanian government, to rely on Swahili for government administration.

Belgian goals in the Congo had a special flavor, in that the colonial power itself was importing to the Congo its own language wars between French and Flemish speakers. In the most sophisticated monograph on colonial language policy in Africa now available, Fabian (1986, 48–9) enumerates Belgian state goals, going back to the Colonial Charter of 1908, as being to: (1) avoid multilingualism, if possible, because it is a threat to order; (2) if this is not possible, rank all languages hierarchically, with French at the top; and (3) help indigenous languages develop in a rational way, because evolutionary development will encourage order. The result of these principles was a policy that created a three-tier system. First, it promoted French as a link language; next came four regional lingua francas (called "vehicular" languages in Belgian colonial discourse), used as official media in different parts of the country; finally came the local vernaculars, which stood below the vehiculars.

CHRISTIAN MISSIONARIES

Christian evangelization was as diverse in Africa as are African cultures themselves. With the establishment of Freetown in Sierra Leone as a home for the slaves "recaptured" from the British naval blockade inaugurated in 1791, the Church Missionary Society actively taught "establishment English," but as its missionaries moved toward the hinterland the society became a strong advocate of vernacular development. The Wesleyans relied on English in their early years in the Gold Coast; the Basel Mission relied on the vernaculars (Spencer, 1971, 13–20). There are many descriptions of missionary language practice, mostly by missionaries, but there has been little systematic work exploring general patterns.[4] However, the following principles can serve as a starting point for assessing missionary preferences.

First, the missionaries needed to survive personally in a demanding environment. The strategy of Sigusmund Wilhelm Koelle, a missionary educator in Freetown under the CMS, became for many a model for directed activity. Koelle wrote transcriptions of 283 words and phrases in 156 languages spoken by the freed slaves there and these transcriptions were the basis for his seminal work *Polyglotta Africana,* published in 1854. Acquainting oneself with the local languages and writing useful grammars and dictionaries became part of the missionary's daily regimen. The fruits of these labors constitute the earliest examples available of some African languages being written (Welmers, 1971, 559–69).

Second, missionaries sought to win souls. The best way to do this was not absolutely clear. But by the 1830s, when most Protestant denominations were already relying on vernaculars, missionaries began justifying those policies in Hegelian terms. For example, a missionary in Central Africa stated, in the respected London journal *Africa,* that "by taking away a people's language we cripple . . . its soul. . . . [T]he vernacular . . . is the vessel in which the whole national life is contained and through which it finds expression" (Broomfield, 1930, 516–22; see also Schmidt, 1930).

Third, missionaries sought to win converts. This goal – since it was quantifiable – usually overrode the second. Often potential converts saw job prospects coming from education and identified with the mission that opened up such opportunities. In light of this fact, Protestants in Igboland who favored vernacular development began to operate in English when rival Catholics achieved popularity by promoting English (Nwoye, 1978). In Dar es Salaam, Catholics offered the vehicular Swahili in their educational institutions, and when vernacular-using Protestants began losing market share, they too moved to Swahili (Barton, 1980, 181). In the face of Muslim encroachment in Gambia, English-medium missionaries switched to Wolof (Bowcock, 1985, 128ff.).

The political battle for converts and market share reached epic proportions in the Congo Free State, ceded to Belgian King Leopold in the Berlin Conference of 1884 (Yates, 1978, 1980). Protestant missionaries were already operating in traditional villages, relying on vernacular education. The Catholic mission stations adopted a different strategy. They set up shop near plantations and taught the children of conscripted workers and redeemed slaves. These schools, given their diverse constituencies, relied on regional lingua francas.

Meanwhile King Leopold feared that the Protestant presence would undermine his colonial sphere of influence. None of the nine Protestant societies which taught more than half of the forty-six thousand pupils in 1908 was Belgian, and none was dependent on government subsidy. The Berlin Act, which gave the king his sphere of influence, mandated that he had to permit missionaries of all denominations to proselytize, and he therefore could not keep out non-Belgian missionaries. Fearing that the "foreign" (mostly English) missionaries would turn the Congo into an extension of southern and eastern Africa, and hoping at least to influence the French-speaking Catholic missionaries, Leopold's Education Act in 1890 decreed that French was to be the language of missionary instruction.

But Leopold's strategy failed. The Parti Catholique was in power in Brussels, and the king relied on Parliament for extensive loans to support his Free State. Edouard Kervyn, pro-Catholic director of the justice and education departments in Brussels, pointed out to Parliament the dangers of relying on French. It would induce students to avoid manual labor; they would become déclassé, even anarchists. And when the Catholic missions in the Congo refused to comply with Leopold's decree, the king had no recourse. It took years before French appeared in the Congo curriculum, and even then only in the upper levels. This battle illustrates many themes – among them the paternalism of the missions, and the tension between government and mission – but the struggle to win converts among the Christian denominations was a fundamental part of this battle. The Catholics, standing behind the vehicular languages of the Congo, were able to establish a protected market in conversions, even if those converts were of little use to the growing administrative apparatus, which had to look elsewhere, mostly to western Africa, for linguistically compatible servants.

Fourth, Christian missionaries, due to the highly bureaucratic structures within which they worked, were under intense pressure to mark the geographical scope of their missions (Harries, 1988). In fact, they wanted to expand that scope in a clearly defined way, so that their prayer books and Bible segments could reach larger audiences than the village station in which they worked. This pressure helps to explain why missionaries spent great effort in seeking to standardize dialect sets and to give these dialect sets names (Itebete, 1970). It also helped push for vehicular languages, or lingua francas, above local dialects (Fabian, 1986, 75–8). Today, this kind of work, which focuses on identifying language zones and codifying "standard" languages from a set of diverse dialects, is known as "corpus planning."

Fifth, missionaries were always on the brink of financial disaster. They were often able to get colonial government subventions to run their schools, if they met certain criteria in the curriculum. This helps explain why so many missions, deeply committed to vernacular development, began to provide basic education in the European language of the colonial state (Fabian, 1986, 75–8).

Missionary motives were complex in regard to languages in Africa. The missions' ambivalent relations with the colonial state induced them to provide limited education in European languages, and their schools consequently became the principal training ground for access to European languages. But many mission schools reflected a strong commitment to teach and preach through the medium of the indigenous languages, irrespective of the preferences of the colonial government. In regard to indigenous languages, missionaries played a fundamental role in naming and describing these languages, sometimes even inventing them. They promoted some, yet rejected others. Reward will come to the intrepid scholar who writes a monograph on missionary linguistics in Africa.

MUSLIM MISSIONARIES

Muslim missionaries in sub-Saharan Africa had a highly differentiated approach toward language, depending on functional domain.[5] In regard to prayer, there was complete agreement that lessons in the Qur'an be presented in Arabic, as prescribed in the Hadith, the traditions of the Prophet. No matter where one travels in Muslim Africa, people have a general knowledge of the key suras in classical Arabic. Often this is the limit of local knowledge of Arabic. In vast areas of Islamic practice, such as Somalia, Ethiopia, and Nigeria, the Arabic language remained an archaic tongue, reserved for religious practice (Trimingham, 1952, 1962, 1964; Bujra, 1974). North of the Sahara, of course, Arabic has had a much wider role, serving as a vernacular and a language of state. And even in areas of Chad and the southern Sudan, Arabic dialects have already replaced indigenous languages (Heine, 1970, 115–19). But these dialects are so distinct from classical Arabic, or even the Modern Standard Arabic of Cairo, that they are often treated as separate elements of a language repertoire (Ferguson, 1959).

In regard to trade, some African Muslims developed minimal facility in colloquial Arabic which helped them to participate in the Arab trading system. But there are few records of Arabic writing south of the Sahara that would suggest that the Arab trade in Africa relied on extensive bookkeeping. This is probably because this trading system was already in international decline when Islam began spreading south of the Sahara (Chejne, 1969, chap. 4).

As a lingua franca for interethnic communication, Arabic has served only a limited role. Rarely is Arabic reported as a lingua franca in sub-Saharan Africa. African Muslims, in heterogeneous environments – for example, at Haile Selassie University in Ethiopia – have relied on Arabic as the basis for communication with Muslims of different vernaculars (Bender et al., 1976). But there are few examples of Arabic's use in this way in other sub-Saharan African settings.

If Muslim missionaries did not actively cultivate the use of Arabic in a wide arena of social interactions in sub-Saharan Africa, they indeed recognized the threat of the spread of European languages for the future of Islam. They sought to discourage their adherents from studying in mission or colonial schools, even with the promise that Muslim students would be exempt from Christian prayer (Mazrui, 1971; Behrman, 1970, 54–5; Gbadamoshi, 1967). In Somalia, greater adhesion to fundamentalist Muslim views in the north held back the spread of missionary education during the colonial era; the more secular south put up fewer blockades to secular education and gained an educational advantage, at least in terms of the number of students in school in the colonial era (Laitin, 1977, chap. 3).

The result of the Muslim approach to Arabic in Africa is that in North Africa, where Islam and the spread of Arabic coincided, there is a strong commitment to the promotion of Arabic, transcending remaining vernaculars, but in sub-Saharan Africa Muslims have done far less well than Christians in securing bureaucratic employment, and we can say that they have a lower capital investment in an international language than do the Christians. This helps explain why Muslim legal traditions have strongly influenced politics in Nigeria but the language of the Qur'an has had no such influence.

In the mid-1970s, when OPEC countries were collecting colossal rents from petroleum sales, the Arab Gulf states invested substantially in the development projects of African countries with significant Muslim populations. Pressure was put on recipient countries to encourage education in the Arabic language. (Since these countries were short on foreign exchange, books donated from the Gulf states were virtually the only ones available for sale in book shops.) Somalia, which had recently instituted a rationalization program in Somali but which received much Arab aid (and had become a member of the Arab League) enhanced the level of Arabic education in government schools and elevated Arabic to co-official status with Somali. In Chad, President Hassan Habre made Arabic a second official language as part of his courtship of Saudi Arabia to help him fight the Libyan forces which were giving military backing to

Habre's challenger. And Mauritania, a recipient of massive aid from the Gulf states, has also made an educational investment in Arabic-language instruction. The vast pilgrimage to the holy sites in Saudi Arabia, perhaps the most organized tourist industry in the world, also works to spread Arabic among Africans of different countries as a lingua franca. The rather weak eighteenth- and nineteenth-century influence of Arabic in Africa may well be surpassed by these more recent events.

AFRICAN NATIONALIST LEADERS

Many nationalist leaders who rose to power as heads of political parties that courted support for independence and votes in remote villages were strong adherents – at least in public rhetoric – to the doctrine of the replacement of European languages with the languages of the people. The nationalist political parties, such as the Kenya African National Union in Kenya (Rhoades, 1977, 16), the Tanganyika African National Union in (today's) Tanzania (Polomé and Hill, 1980, 144–6), and the Somali Youth League in Somalia (Laitin, 1977, chap. 4), usually had strongly recommended the enrichment, development, and official use of indigenous languages. Their leaders were in agreement. Kenya's legendary nationalist leader, Jomo Kenyatta, in his first speech to Parliament as president in 1964, spoke in English, but concluded his address in Swahili, explaining,

Mr. Speaker, I want to say a few words in Swahili because I personally think that the time is not far away when we will be able to speak Kiswahili, which is our own language, in this House . . .
Now that we have full independence we don't have to be slaves of foreign languages in our affairs, and consequently brothers, I wanted to make this point, because everything has to begin somewhere. If I had left this House without uttering a word of Kiswahili, I would have felt somewhat humiliated. (Quoted in Gorman, 1970, 3)

In a similar vein, Julius Nyerere, leader of the Tanganyika African National Union and first president of Tanzania, was an ardent advocate of Swahili development. In his Republic Day speech of 1962 to Parliament, which was the first parliamentary address he gave in Swahili, he said, "I believe that culture is the spirit and essence of any nation. A country which lacks its own culture is no more than a collection of people without spirit which makes them a nation" (quoted in Polomé and Hill, 1980, 145). Nearly thirty years later, in his final speech as leader of Tanzania's sole political party, Nyerere admitted mistakes, but on the language issue he remained committed to Swahili. "Making Kiswahili Tanzania's language helped us greatly in the battle against tribalism," he preached. "If every Tanzanian had stuck to using his tribal language or if we had tried to make English the official language of Tanzania, I am pretty sure that we would not have created the national unity we currently enjoy. [Applause] Although I am personally of the opinion that we should continue teaching English in our schools because English is the Kiswahili of the world, we have, however, an enormous duty to continue to promote and enhance Kiswahili. It is a great weapon for our country's unity" (reported in the Foreign Broadcast Information Service, 21 August 1990, translated and transcribed from the Dar es Salaam Domestic Service in Swahili, 16 August 1990).

Haile Selassie, too, spoke of "the growth and development of a national language [as] the prime foundation of the greatness of a[n Ethiopian] nation" (Taddese, 1970, 2). And King Hassan of Morocco, seeking to overcome French hegemony, advocated an educational system in 1958 that was "Moroccan in its thinking, Arabic in its language, and Muslim in its spirit" (quoted in Sirles, 1985, 69).

That the use of an indigenous language as the official language is an essential element of political independence was hardly questioned by the first generation of postcolonial leaders.[6] This was definitely not because of self-interest. Kenyatta, Nyerere, Selassie, and King Hassan all had had classical European educations and possessed excellent facility in English or French. Rather, their interest in African languages was based on their roles as leaders of national movements. As representatives of "new nations" they felt that it was rhetorically important to highlight the cultural inheritance, if not unity, of those nations.

In the 1960s, inertia, an overburdened development agenda, the need for technical personnel, and bureaucratic resistance pushed the issue of language off the national agenda in most African states. Realism set in. President Milton Obote of Uganda lamented, in 1967,

We find no alternative to English in Uganda's present position. When I move out of Kampala to talk to people, I have to talk in English. Obviously I have no alternative but I lose a lot . . . Some of the greatest and most dedicated [party] workers are those who do not speak English and yet the Party leader cannot call this great dedicated worker alone and say, "thank you" in a language the man will understand. It has to be translated. (Quoted in Scotton, 1971, 21–2)

President Léopold Senghor of Senegal made no apology for reversing his stance on French. Despite the fact that he had argued in 1937 that French could never capture "our soul," in 1963 he developed a convert's commitment to French, "a language of politeness and honesty." Making

French the language of Senegal, he reasoned, would help French become a truly universal language (Markovitz, 1969).[7]

The second generation of leaders, usually soldiers, brought a new perspective to the language issue. The first African presidents, Mazrui observed, "were disproportionately good public speakers in the language of the colonizer." The colonial soldiers, however, were "semi-literate or illiterate," and therefore these "soldiers might prove to be greater agents for the re-Africanizing of Africa than their civilian predecessors" (Mazrui, 1978, 16–18). Yet, ironically, most of the military juntas were indifferent to the issue of national languages. They came to power in the wake of interethnic political tensions and economic mismanagement. Many of these early military leaders, in Ghana, Nigeria, and Mali, sought to downplay themes of Africa's cultural heritage in an effort to consolidate rule in states that had many nationalities. In Togo, for example, the overthrow of President Sylvanus Olympio by the military and the ceding of government to Nicholas Grunitzky, in 1963, reflected this change in ideological orientation. Under Olympio's nationalism, Ewe and Hausa had served with French as official languages. But after the 1963 coup, French became the sole official language. The older policy had stirred up ethnic tensions; the new one could ensure order (Kozelka, 1984, 70–1). In 1984, in Guinea, the Comité Militaire de Redressment National made Sékou Touré's policy of promotiong indigenous languages the scapegoat for educational and economic failures, and the military junta reverted to French-medium education (Treffgarne, 1986, 160).

Despite this realism, the issue of language has too much symbolic power to be ignored by leaders seeking votes, popular support, or legitimacy. In 1972, the military regime of Maxamed Siyaad Barre in Somalia carried forward the ideal of the Somali language becoming the country's official language. His regime's success in resolving the interminable script war that had delayed the implementation of this much-desired reform gave President Siyaad a residue of public respect that helped him weather a number of devastating ecological, economic, political, and military disasters until his overthrow in February 1991. In a similar manner, in 1976, President Ahmadou Ahidjo sought to resuscitate his standing in Cameroon by inaugurating a cultural revolution in which he demanded that his National Council of Cultural Affairs "investigate the manner in which it is necessary to revalue our languages" (Gandji, 1976, 3–4). In Zaire, the symbolic manipulation of language issues has reached epic proportions. General Joseph Mobutu boasted, in the 1960s, that the Congo "represented the second French-speaking country of the world" (Champion, 1969, 1). The president switched gears in the

name of "authenticity," and his office "africanized" many geographical
names (including "Zaire," the new name of the country – a term, critics
like to point out, of Portuguese origin) and other names (including his
own, which became Mobutu Sésé Séko). An official publication
(Sumaili, 1974), which opens with numerous quotations from Mobutu
on how language relates to authenticity, is devoted to the technical
definition of terms – in French – for use in the legislature. Meanwhile,
the government is producing pamphlets filled with government ideology,
written in Lingala or Kikongo. (See the ephemera collection on Zaire in
the Library of Congress.) If for civil servants, as we shall see, the issue of
African languages is one best forgotten, for political leaders, concerned
with legitimacy and with connection to the "people," the issue cannot go
away.

AFRICAN CIVIL SERVANTS

Unlike nationalist leaders, African civil servants (those people broadly
defined by Markovitz [1977, chap. 6] as members of the "organizational
bourgeoisie") have developed a firm belief, commensurate with their
investment in a European language which provided them with a secure
salary, that the vernacular languages are not equipped to handle technical matters.[8] During the constitutional debates of 1967–8, a Ugandan
government minister said,

. . . official language . . . need not delay us. The official language of the Government of Uganda shall be English. Now I hope that people will not spend a large
expense of time on asking the Minister of Education when he is going to be
teaching Swahili and Zulu: I do not know what other language! We are concerned here only with the Official Language not with teaching another language
altogether, which is altogether strange. [Interruption] Yes, if you teach Swahili,
you might as well teach Gujerati [a language of the principal Indian immigrant
community in Uganda]. Swahili is no nearer to the language of the Hon. Member than Gujerati. I want to challenge him on that. No nearer. He might as well
learn what they speak in Paraguay as learn Swahili. (Quoted in Whiteley, 1969,
98)

Even in Tanzania, where the political imposition of Swahili was popular,
an insider in the Cabinet reported that senior ministers believed reliance
on Swahili would add "significantly to the difficulty of running efficient
cabinet meetings." They argued that "the use of English made acceptable a more bureaucratic and more structured style of decision making"
(Pratt, 1971, 104). In a spirited critique of bureaucratic ideology in
Zambia, Chishimba (1986, 170) writes: "One of the main arguments that

have been made against the use of Zambian languages as media of instruction is the untested claim that these so-called vernaculars do not have the lexical potency and the 'vehicular load' to handle classroom knowledge. . . . This is a flimsy argument to camouflage the fact that Africa's elite has become so Europeanized and preoccupied with affairs of 'internationalism' that they have forgotten that their own languages have names even for a grasshopper's organs."

Observations of bureaucratic language use – whether at the long bar of the New Stanley Hotel in Nairobi or in the elite neighborhood of Victoria Island in Lagos – demonstrate professional civil servants' preference for European languages. In administrative assignments outside the capital, the European languages play an even more compelling role. Consider the following: During World War II, a British army unit stationed in Waajeer, in northeastern Kenya, built, somewhat wistfully, a limestone building shaped like a ship in the middle of the desert, some two hundred fifty miles, as the crow flies, from the sea. It was fondly called the Royal Waajeer Yacht Club. In the 1970s, when I visited it during my field research, it served as a club for the civil servants stationed there. Mostly Luo, they transacted business with the Somalis during the day through Swahili, the lingua franca of British colonialism in this part of the territory. But among themselves in their offices, and in the club when drinking beer or throwing darts, their language was English. This was the language in which they had made a capital investment, and it separated them in status from the people they administered. These civil servants had a clear interest in relying on English for their official duties. The French West African *fonctionnaire* relied on the French language in rural assignments for similar reasons (Cruise O'Brien, 1975, 101). I have observed English or French used as the standard language in government offices in Nigeria, Ghana, and Senegal. One can surmise that the specter of the masses able to penetrate the reserve for those educated in colonial settings upsets many African civil servants. They would be glad to emphasize the difficulty of developing African languages, in order to maintain the status quo.

EDUCATIONAL OFFICIALS

One segment of the organizational bourgeoisie has an interest that diverges considerably from the others. These are the people within the educational establishment. In the early years of independence, the professoriat, educated in European languages, usually in mission schools, was strongly in favor of continued reliance on European languages as media of technical information (Mwanakatwe, 1968, 213). Kenya and Zambia, where the British had introduced vernacular education at the primary level, moved toward immersion programs in English. In Senegal, which had long had French as the sole medium of instruction, vernaculars remained untaught and unused in the school system. But researchers within the educational ministries began to find problems with European-language immersion. They reacted by advocating a new pedagogy, in which, as summarized by a teacher from Thiés, in Senegal, "The mother tongue would become an ally instead of being an obstacle" (Rosse, n.d., 31). Kenyan and Zambian officials reached a similar conclusion, as they felt ever-greater pressure within their ministries for better curriculum development relying on vernaculars as the medium of instruction in the primary years. In the early 1980s, the government of Zambia announced the formation of a National Language Committee to work with the Ministry of Education and Culture. This move suggests that the government was increasingly frustrated by the failures of the English-medium curriculum (Gorman, 1974, 447, on Kenya; Ohannessian, 1978, 272–91, Chishimba, 1986, 155, and Serpell, 1978, 432–3, on Zambia).

REGIONAL ELITES WITHIN STATE BOUNDARIES

It is conventional wisdom that elites from linguistically unified regions are strongly opposed to the naming of a language from a different region as the official language of the state. In Nigeria, during debates on the proposal that Hausa serve that role, Chief Anthony Enahoro, an Edo speaker, stood up in the House of Representatives on 21 November 1961 to say,

> . . . as one who comes from a minority tribe, I deplore the continuing evidence in this country that people wish to impose their customs, their languages, and even their way of life upon the smaller tribes. . . . My people have a language, and that language was handed down through a thousand years of tradition and custom. When the Benin Empire exchanged ambassadors with Portugal, many of the new Nigerian languages of today did not exist. (Quoted in Allan, 1978, 398)

These feelings are surely widespread among minority-language groups in the face of perceived language imposition. The assumption that minority elites mobilize their followers is accepted wisdom in African studies. Yet, in regard to the issue of national language choice, we know very little about the role of the leaders from minority-language groups. The assumption of their outright opposition has neither been demonstrated nor refuted. (For some typical attributions of blocking influence to regional elites in Gabon and Gambia, see Richmond, 1983, 18, 47–8.) Do minority elites combine together to assault proposals for the imposition of a language representing a core-language group? Do these elites mobilize the masses of people in their region against such proposals? Or does the mere specter of arousing the masses send such fear through leaders that no serious attempts at imposition have ever been made? The considerable negative power and parochial preferences of regional groups in regard to language have been widely assumed in African political linguistics but not adequately demonstrated. Their potential opposition is of some importance to anyone making recommendations for language rationalization.

INTERNATIONAL ORGANIZATIONS

International organizations have played a vital role in the development of African languages and in supporting interest in their continued use. (How comparable these efforts are to the international wildlife lobby is worthy of some speculation.) From 1922, when the quasi-independent Phelps-Stokes Commission reported on the "right" of all Africans to learn their own language (Gorman, 1971, 20), international organizations have lobbied for this right in the name of African freedom. In 1953, UNESCO restated this position unequivocally, and it remains a core aspect of UNESCO ideology: "We take it as axiomatic . . . that the best medium for teaching is the mother tongue of the pupil" (UNESCO, 1953).[9]

Another international organization that has played a vital role in supporting language-planning activities is the Ford Foundation, which became interested in cultural issues such as language in the early 1970s. (See Sutton, 1971, and Prator, introduction to Ladefoged et al., 1971, 4.) In the 1970s, the foundation dispersed $1.3 million to support national-language surveys in Kenya, Tanzania, Zambia, Ethiopia, and Uganda, from which many of the findings reported in this book have been drawn.[10] Whatever the direct result of the surveys, an important indirect result was to give further legitimacy and status to both African languages and the linguists who study them.

Foreign governments have continued to influence Africa's language situation, even after independence. The French, in particular, have played a dual role. They are deeply interested in maintaining the "purity" and integrity of the dialect of Ile-de-France (Mayer, 1963; Weinstein, 1976). Yet French officials have begun to recognize that as a mass language in Africa, French is likely to degenerate into unintelligible (to

Frenchmen!) dialects. Their remedy is to support mass education in the vernaculars, with an elite corps of teachers providing French at higher levels. Thus French funding goes to a variety of intergovernmental organizations (such as the Conference of the Ministers of Education of French-speaking States, and the Agency for Cultural and Technical Co-operation). One goal is the "affirmation, safeguarding and promotion of cultural identities through the revalorization of national languages." (The other goal is to develop French as a second language.) (See CONFEMEN, 1986, 365ff.). The Comité Linguistique Africaine à Dakar (CLAD) was created and funded by the French government to safeguard the integrity of the French language in West Africa. In 1965, recognizing the linguistic realities, they began to produce educational material that took into account the mother tongues of potential pupils. This necessitated linguistic research on the structure of African languages (Treffgarne, 1986, 147). Nearly all the sociolinguistic surveys of francophone African states have been funded by French sources and have had French nationals as principal investigators.[11]

The Summer Institute of Linguistics (SIL) has a fascinating history, but its activities have as yet only scratched the surface of African languages. The organization has two branches, a domestic branch, the Wycliffe Bible Translators (WBT), which raises funds in the United States, and SIL, which carries out mission work abroad. SIL's founder, William Cameron Townsend, a Protestant missionary, worked among the Cackchiquel Indians of Guatemala. Because he did not know Spanish, he took no interest in the Spanish Bibles he was supposed to sell. Instead, he spent the next fourteen years of his life translating the Bible into Cackchiquel. One day he was transformed by a vision revealing to him that it was his mission to bring the Word to Bible-less tribes. He got no support from his Central American mission, and it was not until the early 1930s that he created Camp Wycliffe, in Arkansas, where he offered his first Summer Linguistics course. Because foreign missionaries were not welcome in Latin America, he cleverly changed the image of his project there, describing it as linguistic and cultural. To raise money at home, he played missionary; to get visas abroad, he played linguist. This explains the dual branches, created in 1942. SIL has expanded impressively and now has 3,700 persons working on 675 languages in 29 countries. In 1975, WBT / SIL had a reported income of $16.9 million and was the sixth richest Protestant missionary organization based in the United States. It describes itself as conservative, evangelical, and fundamentalist. Most of its missionaries are whites from the Midwest and South. Their ideology suggests that Satan and Communism are one and that God, whites, and Americans are on the other side. Shop is set up in remote areas, young translators are hired from the indigenous population, and a modern, middle-class mission is organized. The indigenous translators, more often than not, become the first converts and bilingual teachers. Once the translations are completed, the SIL team leaves. It does not create an institutionalized church but seeks to promote indigenous churches. Most of SIL's resources have gone into the study of Indian populations in Latin America (Hvalkof and Asby, 1981, 10–14).

SIL's work in Africa has been circumscribed. It entered Ghana in 1962, with President Kwame Nkrumah's support. By 1978, thirteen SIL groups had entered and forty-six people were employed. A Ghana Institute of Linguistics is now slowly taking full responsibility for the development of the project (Bendor-Samuel and Bendor-Samuel, 1983). In Nigeria, a group was established in 1962 at Nsukka and Ahmadu Bello University. Twenty-two groups had come, and there were seventy-one personnel, by the time work was terminated by the government in 1976. But the SIL-advised Nigerian Bible Translation Trust now occupies the former SIL center at Jos and works in fifteen to twenty languages (Hvalkof and Asby, appendix). In Cameroon, a SIL group entered in 1967, under contract with the University of the Cameroon. It was led by missionaries who had been displaced by the Nigerian civil war and went across the border. A new contract was signed in 1975, expanding activities (Gastines, 1986). Programs are also developing in Togo, Ivory Coast (Turcotte, 1981, chap. 4), Burkina Faso, Ethiopia, Sudan, Kenya, and Chad. Explorations to locate field sites have been completed in Zaire and Central African Republic (Hvalkof and Asby, 1981, appendix). SIL is a model of international influence on Africa's language future. SIL translators have the power to name discrete languages and have an interest in preserving those languages in the social and political life of the places where they are spoken.

It is only in the modern era that foreigners have developed such a keen interest in the life and death of languages. When viewed on the international dimension, language shift is usually portrayed as merely the incentive for Africans to learn and use European languages. But, as we see here, international organizations have their own interest in naming and preserving Africa's "traditional" languages.

CONCLUSION

This *tour d'horizon* of social and historical forces has focused on the interests and preferences of actors who have sought to influence Africa's language situation. We have, for the most part, looked upon these actors in isolation from their strategic situation. At times – for example, in the discussion of the second-generation African rulers since independence, or of the conflict between the Catholic missions and King Leopold – we caught a glimpse of preferences rubbing against one another or against politicoeconomic realities. The strategic model demands that we now examine the interaction of these actors.

PART III

Strategic theory applied

6

Strategic theory and Africa's language future

What sort of nation-states will be characteristic of Africa in the coming century? Will they follow in the footsteps of their western European and east Asian predecessors and develop language communities commensurate with political boundaries? If so, will the rationalized languages be those of the overseas conquerors, like in the Americas and Oceania; or will they be indigenous, as in Indochina? Or is the multilingual model of Switzerland or the Soviet Union more applicable to the African states of the future? And if multilingual, what sort of language demands will such a state put on its citizens? What sorts of language repertoires will be necessary for Africa's future citizens if they hope to take reasonable advantage of opportunities available in their country? In this chapter, some preliminary answers are provided.

In formulating these answers, I shall seek to avoid two methodological and ideological errors. The first is to examine Africa as if it were a continent marked only by distinctiveness. I have therefore sought, as have many others, to integrate African studies into a comprehensive world history.[1] In political linguistics, it is too often assumed that, due to the extreme heterogeneity of society within the boundaries of African states and the very arbitrariness of African state boundaries, African nation builders have had a historically unique set of constraints facing them in the development of a coherent language policy. My political-linguistic vignettes of France, Spain, and Japan in Chapter 1 demonstrate, however, that in early periods of state building among states that are now linguistically rationalized, there was considerable language heterogeneity. Moreover, the boundaries of European and Asian states have been as historically contingent as are the boundaries of current African states. My belief that African history is part of a common world history explains why a book about Africa employs a universalistic logic embedded in strategic models and provides illustrations from all over the world.

The second potential flaw is to ignore the distinctiveness of Africa or the vast differences that exist within the African continent. To see all of Africa as merely "peripheral," or racked by "tribalism," or merely "post-colonial" is to miss sociologically important differences within the continent. This second point explains why our attention in Chapters 3 and 4 has been on the particularities of and differences within the African experience.

Our task in social science, in avoiding these two methodological flaws, is to determine what is sociologically distinctive about Africa, or about particular segments of Africa, and to determine how that distinctiveness matters for social, economic, and political outcomes. Distinctiveness without a difference has little sociological meaning; distinctiveness must be tied to outcomes that are important, either to the actors or to the analysts.

Building on some of the observations about the contemporary language scene in Africa and the preference orderings of social, political, and economic groups, it is possible to envisage certain trends concerning African national development. The exercises in this chapter can be considered only preliminary. Some key forces discussed earlier – for example, differential missionary and colonial experience – are not systematically included in the models that follow. Future models of African language politics must factor in a wider array of interests. In Chapter 7, when I put flesh on the game skeletons presented in this chapter, some of the variables ignored in this chapter's models will come into play as part of the larger political context. Although they are insufficient to analyze the full array of interests, the models proposed here give sharp definition to some basic language trends.

EUROPEAN LANGUAGES WILL NOT LOSE OFFICIAL STATUS IN MOST AFRICAN STATES

Language rationalization for most African states will not occur as it has in Western Europe and East Asia, in large part because postcolonial bureaucratic elites have invested heavily in European languages and do not want to lose the benefits of that investment. To give this point both a formal and substantive rationale, consider the conflict in Kenya over English (Kenya's official language) and Swahili (Kenya's national language).[2] Commentators have often noted the ambiguity of the distinction between an "official language" and a "national language" that is made in many postcolonial states but have not provided a cogent explanation explaining why such contradictory signals are sent from the newly formed governments to the population at large (Das Gupta, 1970).

The key to understanding the ambiguous distinction between a national language and an official language is the conflict of interest between nationalist leaders and civil servants. The former have equated a rationalized indigenous language with national independence; the latter have equated European languages with precision, order, and economic advance. This conflict manifests itself practically in Kenya's political and administrative organs. The leading political party, the Kenya African National Union (KANU), has long preferred increasing the importance of Swahili in Kenya's official life. In the late 1960s, fearful that the ideology of cultural independence was being forgotten by the government, the secretary general of KANU got the National Governing Council of the party to give formal recognition to Swahili as the national language of Kenya. While he acknowledged, in his justifying remarks, that English was still a necessary tool for Kenyan citizens, he pressed for greater testing of candidates' competence in Swahili before they could get promotions in government service (Gorman, 1974a, 446). Civil servants, however, prefer to use English. This elite service corps, anxious to attract international organizations and businesses to Kenya, has self-consciously sought to make Kenya an environment suitable for international elites (Leys, 1975, 196–7). Landing the United Nations Environmental Program for Nairobi, for example, was considered a major coup for Kenya's bureaucratic elite. That official life in Kenya is dominated by English is surely not the cause of the United Nations' decision, but the widespread use of English in Kenya certainly reduces the cost to international organizations of operating there. Kenyan civil servants resist party pressure to swahilize administration by pointing to the heavy transition costs of change. For example, the Kenyan minister of state in the president's office, ignoring the success achieved by Tanzania in this regard, pointed to "the unsurmountable practical difficulties in translating our laws and other legal and quasi legal documents into Swahili" (Gorman, 1974a, 438).

To be sure, the boundaries between the political and bureaucratic elites are fluid, with many elite Kenyans moving easily between the two. The argument here is that when acting in their roles of senior bureaucrats, parliamentarians, or party officials, Kenyans will more likely represent the interests of their political organization. In this "role" conflict between party and bureaucracy, KANU elites care more about a united political class (and therefore the ability to govern) than do the civil servants (who would prefer linguistic division within the government to

Matrix 6.1. Party–bureaucrat language game in postcolonial Kenya

| | KANU: language of politics | |
Civil service: language of administration	Swahili	English
English	3, 2	4, 3*
Swahili	2, 4	1, 1

swahilization of the bureaucracy). Matrix 6.1 illustrates this conflict and shows why the civil servants have a strategic advantage in reserving pride of official place for English.

Let us review the choice situation. In the northwestern cell, KANU gets Swahili to become Kenya's national language, used for politics and public ceremony, while the civil service conducts state business in English. In the northeastern cell, both political and administrative life are conducted in English. In the southwestern cell, both political and administrative life are conducted in Swahili. Finally, in the southeastern cell, English is the language of political and ceremonial life while Swahili is the language of state business.

For the bureaucrats, the preferred situation, choice 4, would be where English becomes the sole language of politics and official business. This would help to rationalize the state and would protect their capital investment in a language of high international esteem. Second best (choice 3) would have English as the language of administration while Parliament conducts its business solely in Swahili. This would be inefficient from a bureaucratic point of view, but at least it would ensure bureaucratic continuity in a high-status language. Third best (choice 2) would be a rationalized state where Swahili is the sole national and official language. Indeed, the bureaucrats' expertise in English would lose value (for example, in promotions), but at least there would be societal "order," another value held by bureaucrats. Worst for them (choice 1) would be where they shifted to Swahili, only to find the political class relying on English. That would be a bitter irony for the bureaucrats.

For KANU, first choice (4) would be agreement by all parties on Swahili as the official language of Kenya. This is the great goal of a political party rooted in African nationalist politics. Its second choice (3), given its preference for unity in the country, would be a situation in which administration and politics is in English. Third choice (2) would be a situation where there is a division within the elite: Parliament and daily politics in Swahili, administration and the university in English. Finally, a situation where KANU supports English but the administration supports Swahili (1) would be as bitterly ironic for KANU as for the bureaucrats.

In this game, the bureaucrats have a dominant strategy: Knowing this, KANU, which does not, can only choose between English dominance or a divided central elite. The outcome of this game in Kenya – as in so many postcolonial African states – is continued official dominance of the colonial language. This matrix explains the choice of colonial languages as the sole official language. Because they lose the official-language game to their bureaucrats, politicians can recoup their losses only symbolically, outside of the parameters of the game. This is the reason they move to declare an indigenous language, or a set of indigenous languages, as "national" ones and rely upon them for symbolic occasions.

FOR SOME SMALL STATES THERE WILL BE RATIONALIZATION

That there is strategically powerful interest in support of maintaining colonial languages as official media of discourse does not imply that there will be no examples of successful state rationalization in indigenous languages. In some African countries, such as Somalia, Botswana, Lesotho, Swaziland, and Tanzania, rationalization is likely to succeed. There are two consequential considerations, however. First, there needs to be a single indigenous language which serves as a focal point, so that there are no other languages that can compete with it as obvious choices for official status.

Second, the political elite must exert revolutionary pressure on the civil service so that it complies with indigenization decrees. If the country's ruler chooses to make the national language the sole official language of the state, given the situation described in Matrix 6.1 it remains rational for the bureaucrats to subvert the order. If so, they get a score of 3, whereas they would get a 2 if they complied. Furthermore, in cases where rationalization has been pursued by African rulers, as in Somalia and Tanzania, it was justified by an attention to services to the localities rather than mega-projects in the cities. Awareness of grass-roots concerns, it was argued, is facilitated by an indigenous-language politics. But this concern compounds the conflict between rulers and civil servants. The civil servants had become comfortable, in the waning colonial years, in their capital-city offices; an ideology of grass-roots concerns was perceived by bureaucrats as a threat to their life-style.

It is in this sense that language rationalization in Africa has a different dynamic from the state-rationalization game analyzed in Matrix 2.3. In the state-rationalization game, the players were "rulers" and "lords," and the conditions were of societal multilingualism. In the African case, the players are "nationalists" and "bureaucrats," and the conditions are of societal diglossia. In the state-rationalization game, the equilibrium outcome supports language uniformity. In the politician–bureaucrat game, strategic rationality supports rationalization at the official level but leaves open for politicians the opportunity to subvert that equilibrium by giving symbolic support for a national language or a set of national languages. Only revolutionary action, outside the framework of the game, can yield the rationalization outcome.

This point is illustrated nicely in the case of Somalia, where nearly all citizens consider Somali to be their primary language. In 1960, three foreign languages – English, Italian, and Arabic – served as means of official communication, and the Somali language had no official role. One might have expected that with political independence this reliance on foreign languages would have been curtailed and that Somali would become the sole official language of the state. This appeared to be an ideal situation for the successful rationalization of Somali. Yet a prolonged battle over the proper script to use for writing Somali held back rationalization for over a decade. In my research on this "script war," I found that Somali civil servants emphasized the costs of the transition to the use of Somali (in whatever script) in order to protect their investment in foreign languages (1977, chap. 5). It took a revolutionary regime to compel the society to adopt a script for its language and to employ that language in administration. This episode reflects the powerful forces supporting the language status quo, even under perfect conditions for the officialization of the most widely spoken language in the country. Language rationalization is indeed possible in Africa, but conditions are favorable for it only in a few countries, and even in those it takes committed leadership to succeed.

NATIONAL LANGUAGES WILL GET ONLY DIFFUSE SUPPORT IN MULTILINGUAL STATES

To demonstrate the fate of national languages, the case of Swahili in Kenya is most illustrative. Swahili has been chosen to represent national values that will, as in the admonition "Harrambee!", "pull the country together." Given Swahili's role as Kenya's national language, the postindependence government has sought to promote a Swahili curriculum for the schools. But it has also been under pressure to promote English and the vernaculars. Everything cannot be promoted at the same time; choices must be made. How can we analyze the choice situation in Kenya?[3]

Let us consider the choice situation as a strategic game between the government of Kenya and the parents of schoolchildren. Government reports at various times have discussed many language curricula; here we shall examine four of them: (1) English only; (2) Swahili only; (3) English medium with compulsory Swahili; and (4) vernacular medium, as a bridge to English medium at higher levels. Meanwhile, parents have sought to influence their children's language repertoires. Three of the prominent strategies are as follows: (1) Learn English at all costs; (2) Encourage development of vernaculars, but use English as a language of wider communication (LWC); and (3) Accept national values and assimilate into a Swahili-speaking environment. These choices, when juxtaposed in a matrix, yield twelve possibilities.

To figure out the equilibrium outcome of this complex configuration, we will need to examine the preferences of each player. For the Kenyan government, we can assume that there is a preference for rationalization. But, as we have already seen, the civil servants, who favor the continued use of English in elite domains, are in a strategically advantageous position compared to the party elites, who favor the rapid expansion of Swahili. So far, English rationalization is preferred over the widespread use of an indigenous language. Finally, from the viewpoint of the center, the promotion of nationalism is of greater value than the promotion of the various vernaculars. These preferences can be reduced to the following ordering:

A   (4 points)   "Efficient rationalization," that is, both the government and the citizens can communicate in English;

A– (3.5 points) Less efficient rationalization, that is, both the government and the citizens can communicate in Swahili;

B   (3 points)   No waste in educational effort, that is, government and citizens agree on education in a single language;

C   (2 points)   Nationalism is promoted: That is, the government teaches Swahili, and the citizens seek to learn it;

D   (1 point)   Indigenous culture is promoted: That is, the government develops educational material in the vernaculars, and the citizens seek to learn it.

These values are reflected in the scoring in Matrix 6.2.

Now for the Kenyan parents. The discussion of the micro dynamics of language choice in Chapter 4 gives us some clues as to the parents'

Strategic theory applied

Matrix 6.2. Government values in language-of-education game

	Government policy			
	Swahili and English	English and vernaculars	English only	Swahili only
English immersion	A (4)	A (4)	A, B (7)	(0)
Swahili immersion	A−, C (5.5)	(0)	(0)	A−, B, C (9.5)
Vernaculars with English as LWC	A (4)	A, D (5)	A (4)	(0)

preferences. They recognize the status of English and would hardly want to deny it to their own children. They rely quite often on Swahili, but only to neutralize complex interactions. It is seen as a tool for neighborhood or market interaction but not for status and mobility. Finally, vernaculars are regarded as an important clue to membership and identity, not to be squandered frivolously. In light of these observations, I postulate three goals, in descending order of preference, for Kenyan parents:

A (4 points) Social mobility for their children into elite domains is made possible. (This is a short-term assessment and is based on the current value of English.)

B (3 points) Their own culture is promoted by government, and fellow citizens take advantage of it.

C (2 points) If National values are promoted, and their fellow citizens take advantage of it.

These values are indicated on Matrix 6.3. The data in Matrix 6.2 and Matrix 6.3 can be combined to form Matrix 6.4, which gives cardinal scores for both the Kenyan people (first score) and the government (second score). Neither player has a dominant strategy, but to reach the unique equilibrium we shall use the game-theoretic technique of "iterated deletion of dominated strategies." This means that a player is assumed to eliminate a choice if he or she can do better with another choice no matter what the other player chooses. We assume that players will know that one of their choices is dominated by another and that the other player will know, as well, that it would be irrational for the opponent to chose a dominated strategy. We are therefore assuming considerable rationality and perspicacity, but given that learning another language is very costly and that people think a lot about it, this is not wholly unrealistic.

Matrix 6.3. Citizen values in language-of-education game

Kenyan people seek for their children:	Government policy			
	Swahili and English	English and vernaculars	English only	Swahili only
English immersion	A (4)	A (4)	A (4)	A (4)
Swahili immersion	C (2)	(0)	(0)	C (2)
Vernaculars with English as LWC	A (4)	A, B (7)	A (4)	A (4)

Matrix 6.4. The education game in Kenya

Kenyan people seek for their children:	Government policy			
	Swahili and English	English and vernaculars	English only	Swahili only
English immersion	4, 4	4, 4	4, 7	4, 0
Swahili immersion	2, 5.5	0, 0	0, 0	2, 9.5
Vernaculars with English as LWC	4, 4	7, 5*	4, 4	4, 0

In this game, the people's second choice, Swahili immersion, is dominated by both the first and third choices, so it is eliminated from consideration. If that is eliminated, the government's fourth choice, Swahili only, is dominated by the first three choices. (Note that it would not be dominated if the people's second choice remained.) At this point, the people have a dominant strategy: to choose "vernaculars, with English as a LWC," because that will always do as well or better than English immersion. Given that rational choice, the best the government can do under the circumstances is to choose education in English and the vernaculars.

This game shows that choosing Swahili as the language of education is not a rational strategy, however much its promotion would serve diffuse goals, and even though the government would get its highest score if it promoted Swahili and got full citizen compliance. It is little wonder that in Kenya's schools, where Swahili is still taught, most children and their parents refuse to take it seriously. If this were the only language game being played, and if a rational equilibrium is achieved, the model would predict Swahili's elimination from the future Kenyan curriculum. We can deduce from this exercise that languages which symbolize national unity but have no strong local support nor strong bureaucratic support will be marginalized in Africa's educational systems of the future.

A 3 ± 1 OUTCOME FOR AFRICA'S LINGUISTICALLY DIVERSE STATES

The 3 ± 1 outcome is a likely outcome for many of Africa's more diverse states. The mechanisms, given Africa's distinctive history, will be somewhat different from those in India, but much of the reasoning is the same. What follows is an outline of the political logic of Africa's 3 ± 1 language outcome.

Diffuse support for an indigenous national language

At independence, there was diffuse support for indigenous language(s), with a coordination problem as to which could serve as the official language of the state. Nationalist leaders and their parties were, as we have seen, committed to the development of indigenous African languages and were opposed to the continued use of the language of colonial administration. Many African languages, used by missionaries, colonial governments, and international organizations, are sufficiently developed for easy incorporation in technical domains (Heine, 1970, 42–43). The promotion of these languages is quite a popular political stance, in general. But when the policy begins to get specific, coming down to actually choosing which vernacular will be promoted, or relying upon it to teach chemistry or mathematics, or demanding that government forms be filled out in it, the general support gives way to specific objections.

Consider this statement, by a prominent Zambian official:

> On political grounds alone, it is clearly impossible to adopt any one of the official vernaculars as a medium of instruction in primary schools without exciting tribal passions and creating serious discontent and unrest. In making tactful inquiries, the author had heard confessions from even the most extremist tribal adherents that an imposition of their own language on the rest of the country would be disastrous. (J. M. Mwanakatwe, quoted in Abdulaziz and Fox, 1978, 6)

The role of Swahili in Kenya demonstrates the validity of this principle, even with the choice of a politically neutral lingua franca. In the school system, Swahili is a compulsory subject (reflecting the nationalist desire to have an indigenous lingua franca), but success in Swahili has not been necessary for job promotion (reflecting the bureaucratic belief that Swahili is not to be taken seriously). In a large survey ($n = 2,480$) of Kenyan secondary school entrants, Gorman found attitudes consistent with this diffuse support (1971, chap. 5). There was substantial agreement to the proposition that "I will be sorry if the tribal languages used in Kenya begin to die out, but this is necessary if we are to build one nation." However, he found stronger majorities agreeing to the proposition that "all children should be taught to read and write their own mother tongue before they are taught to read and write English and Kiswahili." Eastman (n.d., 4) made a related observation in regard to Nairobi: "Even though official language policy . . . calls for setting up Swahili teacher training programs and language learning workshops, there is little demonstrated interest on the part of students [at the University of Nairobi] to major in Swahili or to answer the nation's call in this regard."[4]

Specific regional support for the vernaculars

Meanwhile there has been specific support for the regional vernaculars within the bureaucratic and educational establishment, for a number of reasons: (1) missionaries had defined them and provided grammars and books in them; (2) indirect rule in the colonial period gave political reality to the missionaries' cultural boundaries; (3) international organizations have given continued support to development of the vernaculars; and (4) under conditions of centralized political rule in the postcolonial period, organization against state authority has often relied upon the bonds created by sharing a common vernacular.

The specificity of support for vernaculars versus the diffuseness of support for lingua francas has a clear logic (illustrated by the case of Varenasi in Chapter 4). Often, although individuals vote for the promotion of a national language (showing diffuse support for it), in their personal lives they act in a way that subverts that vote. In many cases they enroll their children in schools where access to the former colonial language is ensured and, at the same time, demand equal favor for their vernacular. In the sardonic words of the Tunisian general secretary of secondary public education, "We do not cease to repeat 'Arabization, Arabization,' all the while sending our children to the schools of the MUCF [French private system]" (Sirles, 1985, 236–7).

The political trend may thus not be toward vehicular lingua francas but rather toward well-defined vernaculars. In a clairvoyant research note, Hans Wolff (1967, 24) reported that among the hinterland societies in the eastern Niger delta, the various language groups began, in the nineteenth century, to learn the language of the coast and to assimilate words and phrases from the coastal languages into their vernaculars. The changing political landscape in independent Nigeria altered the course of language shift, toward a "greater awareness of ethnic identity and a growing trend . . . away from national or even regional unity and towards diversity and particularism." There has been a concomitant attempt in some of these hinterlands to replace official (foreign) place-names with older (local) names and to make the local vernacular the principal medium of communication. To be sure, this article was written just before the outbreak of civil war. But the specific interests in vernacular development have emerged in many states as a dialectical response to national policies promoting an indigenous lingua franca.

The rationalization of vernaculars within regions presupposes, as was demonstrated with regard to India, clearly demarcated language regions. This situation, however, rarely is found in Africa. Consider the case of Gambia. Gambia is one of many countries that has faced pressure by regional groups to promote their vernaculars, in large part a response to efforts to give special status to either Mandingo (spoken by about 60 percent of the population) or Wolof (the lingua franca of the capital city). In a survey of schoolteachers in rural Gambia, Bowcock found considerable resistance to the criterion of "geographical area" for determining the medium of instruction (1985, chap. 5). As one teacher noted, "The idea of different geographical areas for specific tribes and languages is not applicable considering the rate of migration" (357). This study reminds us that "language regions" are only vaguely defined in Africa, quite a different situation from that of India. Still, evidence from Kenya shows that the seventeen separate language programs have been staffed "into provinces, districts and divisions" (Richmond, 1983, 41). There is therefore an incentive in the administration of language programs to draw sharp boundaries. To the extent that clearly bounded regions, each representing a language group, are delineated in the political process, then the 3 ± 1 outcome is more likely to emerge.

Given the specific support associated with them, the vernaculars have been appropriated politically to serve a range of functions. Opposition groups in Senegal relied on Wolof for their propaganda, in part to embarrass President Senghor, who had once argued for the importance of the restoration of African languages. In Kenya, Ngugi wa Thiong'o relied on the use of the Kikuyu language in the theater to mobilize opposition to the political authorities. Meanwhile the regime, especially under Kenyatta, gave support to Swahili as a national language and to vernaculars as folkloric languages in order to maintain a nationalist fervor.

Rapid growth in the use of pidgins, urban argots, and lingua francas

Massive urbanization and government failure to meet the social needs of the people have created an environment conducive to the rapid growth of lingua francas that are far from the standard languages recorded by missionaries. Languages such as West African pidgin, Sango in Central African Republic, Shang and other popular dialects of Swahili in Kenya, Akan–English code switching in Ghana, and a popular Lingala in Zaire are well-known examples of language innovation. Meanwhile the spread of the European languages has been uneven. In the schools, the teaching corps does not have the language capabilities to transmit standard European languages. And in urban families, there is little evidence of children being brought up as monolinguals in the official language of the state, showing that few families see a European language as the sole language of political and social life of the future. Growth of argots and slow spread of colonial languages represent the present situation.

A populist language program

Should there be an opening for free political expression, perhaps in a new era of elections in Africa, there is a political logic for a strong populist leader winning over the capital and other major cities by advocating some form of the urban lingua franca as the real national language. Linguists and authors could then be mobilized to provide a standard for the expanded official use of the proclaimed national language. With their political victory, this populist group would be opposed by bureaucrats who would defy the program, thereby creating a dual official language at the political center.

The populists will have no easy victory. Promotion of popular urban languages, when people hold them in nearly universal disregard and even deny that they speak them, will require a complete status reversal. Sometimes exemplary literary figures, "language strategists" (Weinstein, 1979), can create a language out of a low-status speech form in the public's mind: A Noah Webster can, by his own lexicographic efforts, establish an *American* English, or a Bishop Crowther, through his biblical translation, a *standard* Yoruba. To do this for popular Swahili in Uganda, or Sango in Central African Republic, or pidgin in Nigeria, would take revolutionary literary action, almost what it took Henry V to promote the language of Falstaffian carousing as the "king's English." In a judicious set of lectures, entitled "Language and Nationhood," in

Ghana, Professor R. F. Amonoo showed open-mindedness about all Ghanaian languages save the code-switching variety that is so prevalent in his Legon (University of Ghana) surroundings. He used the word "contamination" to describe the effect of the Legon speech on the proper languages of Ghana (1989, 32). If populist leaders can succeed in legitimizing popular speech, however, they will have a powerful mobilizational tool in their hands.

National politicians with regional bases of support would quickly see the challenge and opportunity associated with the new populism. They would see that demanding promotion of their regional language for regional politics, in the context of the lingua franca serving the role of language for the central state, would serve their interests in two ways. First, use of vernaculars would solidify their support in their regional constituencies; second, use of vernaculars would promote federalism, which would give regional leaders a high degree of local patronage. Regional-language promotion would also keep migrants from other regions out of the newly formed regional bureaucratic job market. The regional leaders would therefore be able to build on the work of the nineteenth-century missionaries and the twentieth-century international organizations that helped standardize and reduce to writing a large number of vernaculars. Vernaculars that were codified in this way will have a reasonable chance of getting local political support for their expansion.

Voters under populist politics would be cross-pressured. On the one hand, they might want to support the populist program for its promises of national renewal. On the other hand, they might still want their children to receive the best European-language instruction possible. But a coalition of the political forces to support both a lingua franca *and* the regional languages will seek to close off opportunities to enroll children in schools where a European language is the only medium of instruction. This has happened elsewhere: English schools in Quebec and German schools in French communal Switzerland – even on the private level – have largely been banned. Rationalization will be more demanding on the regional level (to keep out migrants from job opportunities in the regional bureaucracies) than on the national level. Yet the power of the central bureaucracy should act as a constraint against a move by the regional politicians to ban education through a European-language medium. In India, while regional leaders decry Hindi, they have never (as regional leaders) sought to eliminate English. Populism could thus achieve the promotion of a national populist language for many official functions, live with the simultaneous promotion of the vernaculars for regional education and administration, and be forced to accept the continued bureaucratic use of European languages in highly technical domains.

(Slow) death of (some) unrecognized languages

There will be a slow death of small languages without a defined regional base. Speakers of these languages will slowly, over the generations, assimilate the titular language of the region in which they live or specialize in the national language and seek their futures in being assimilated nationals.

The 3 ± 1 result

The result will be a modified 3 ± 1 language outcome. Citizens will need to know (1) a European language, which will continue to be used in certain domains where the central bureaucracy or educational establishment is especially tenacious; (2) the national language, which will replace the European language in a wide array of language domains and will be a required subject for educational advancement throughout the country; (3) their own vernacular, which will be the medium of instruction for the initial years of their education, and also the language of administration in their home region. Those citizens whose vernacular is the same as the lingua franca will need to learn only two languages. Migrants from one "titular" state living in another will feel compelled to learn a fourth language, especially if they feel nativist pressures in their new homes that might lead to their exile. This is an equilibrium outcome, because no party will have a clear interest in challenging it.

Could long-term social, economic, and political change upset this equilibrium? Some plausible scenarios: (1) Vast economic growth in the capital area might give populist leadership an interest in challenging its bureaucracy and demand the supremacy of the lingua franca. If more jobs are available in the lingua franca, then the power of the bureaucracy can be reduced. If new and highly remunerative jobs become available for literates in the lingua franca, this would send signals to the regions that the lingua franca is beginning to dominate both the colonial language and the regional vernaculars. If citizens throughout the country respond to these incentives by specializing in the lingua franca, the seeds of language rationalization would have been planted. (2) Economic dynamism in one of the regions could lead to migration pressures there and to vast assimilation into the language group of the dynamic region. Leaders here can pursue an imperialist policy of incorporation of the peripheries, maybe made up of zones of a few states, into a new national state. This is the Prussian model, and it too would lead to rationalization. (3) Proliferation of federal states might occur within a country, so that the number of vernaculars that are official increases. This would reduce fewer languages to death and might reduce the significance of the lingua franca. A two-language outcome might then be reached.

Despite these possibilities, the 3 ± 1 outcome will most likely become institutionalized (raising the costs of any transition) well before the changes mentioned here will have a strong impact on language outcomes. So even with these changes, the likelihood of a long-term 3 ± 1 language outcome is high.

A 2-LANGUAGE OUTCOME WHERE THERE IS NO POTENTIAL NATIONAL LANGUAGE

This logic does not apply to states in which there is no obvious vernacular, lingua franca, or pidgin that could serve to symbolize national values, remain politically neutral, and be widely understood. In situations of this sort, due to the nationalist–bureaucrat game, the European language is likely to remain the interregional link language. But there will remain open the incentive for regional elites to press for cultural autonomy within their regions of power. The cost for the central bureaucracy of avoiding regional secession could well be agreement on language autonomy in the region, in the context of a "national" communications network in a European language. If these conditions hold, then an individual would be able to get a government job within his or her region by being literate in the local vernacular and to get a job in the national capital by being literate in the international language.

The source of stability of this model remains to be investigated. The power of the vernacular promoters in India, and probably in the emergent 3 ± 1 countries in Africa, originates in the language ambiguity at the center, for regional politicians can gain autonomy from the center when the center itself is divided. But with no challenger to the colonial languages, the center will remain united, leaving less political space for regional interests. Whether regional leaders will be able to nurture the development of languages spoken only in the region remains to be seen.

CONCLUSION

In this chapter, we have built upon three earlier discussions: (1) the game-theoretic models of language outcomes in Chapter 2; (2) the discussion of the sociodynamics of language use in contemporary Africa in Chapter 4; and (3) the analysis of language interests in African history in Chapter 5. The most important general finding of the game-theoretic analysis is that the "players" involved in state construction are different over the centuries, leading to differently constituted language games and different equilibrium outcomes. The nature of the postcolonial bureaucracy has made it a key independent player in African state building, able to subvert the language goals of political leadership. Also, the involvement of the state in mass education has brought school administrators and parents into the arena of language policy, interests that state builders of earlier centuries never encountered. New players and newly unleashed interests have led to newly constituted games. The dynamics of these games have pushed many African states not toward rationalization but toward a 3 ± 1 multilingual outcome.

More specifically, this chapter has analyzed the likely political logic of Africa's language future. It has been shown that for most African countries (1) the European languages will not disappear; (2) the indigenous lingua francas will play an important role but will rarely dominate the European languages in official discourse; (3) the regional vernaculars of reasonable size will gain in function and will likely become languages of administration in carefully bounded regions internal to the states; and (4) the speakers of African languages spoken by few people, or by groups that are geographically dispersed, will face great pressures to abandon, at least intergenerationally, their languages. Some of these languages, especially those named and codified by missionaries or other international organizations, will become protected minority languages. The prediction of the 3 ± 1 and the 2-language outcomes means that multilingualism will remain the norm for most African citizens throughout the state-building period.

7

Case studies from independent Africa

Each of the three patterns of African national development that has been identified necessitates a distinct language repertoire. Citizens of states where there has been language rationalization need to become equipped to read and write in the official language of state business. And what about those who do not speak it? In Africa, few states with significant language minorities will carry out a rationalization program. But for those minorities, bilingualism will persist, perhaps for centuries. Nonetheless, if everyone within the state's boundaries becomes fluent in the state language, speakers of the nonchosen languages will find that they use them in a decreasing number of social domains. Intergenerationally, this situation pushes toward assimilation into the language of the state by all social groups. To be sure, historical memories of the language will remain, and some social strata – for example, religious diviners, or *griots* – will seek to maintain those memories. These memories will serve the interests of a counterhegemonic project, or regional revival, if conditions allow.[1] Also, many citizens involved in technical work or international commerce will need to learn an international language. But for most purposes citizens will need to know but one language to fulfill themselves within the national arena.

For citizens of states that settle on a 2-language formula, each person will need to identify him- or herself with a regional language group. Interregional job mobility within the country will be somewhat constrained, because parents will find it difficult to get an education for their children in their own language outside of their geographical zone. Yet interregional and region–center communication will be maintained through the use of a highly formalized international language, most probably the language of former colonial control.[2] In a state with language rationalization, citizens will be able to learn any number of foreign languages for the purpose of international contact, as there will be no internal coordination problem. In countries of the 2-language formula, however, all citizens will need to know the same international language.

The 3 ± 1 outcome states will put a distinct constraint on their citizens. Citizens will need to learn the official language, which will most likely be the language of colonial control. Second, they will need to study, and probably pass an examination in, the national language. Third, they will need to maintain literacy in their vernacular, which will be the official language of their region and the medium of instruction for at least the primary years of schooling. These three languages will be standard parts of most citizens' language repertoires. Those whose vernacular is the same as the national language will need to learn only two languages (3 − 1), and those who live outside their home area and get protected-minority status will receive basic education in their primary language and will therefore need to maintain four languages (3 + 1).

The purpose of this chapter is to breathe some political life into these formulas, while not forgetting the strategic analysis that led to their designation. The best way to do this is to provide vignettes illustrating various language policies in African states. Because the outcomes described in the formal models are emergent, rather than fulfilled, these vignettes will be both history and projection.

EXAMPLES OF THE EMERGENT 3 ± 1 LANGUAGE OUTCOME

The 3 ± 1 outcome is a null set in today's Africa. Yet, like India, many African states manifest a conflict of interest between civil servants and party leaders. Furthermore, we have identified a conflict of interest between educational authorities and parents in regard to the medium of instruction. These conflicts portend a language future for a number of African countries similar to India's, where a 3 ± 1 outcome is rapidly becoming institutionalized. In Chapter 6, I used the case of Kenya to discuss the pressures toward a 3 ± 1 outcome in Africa. In this section, I shall discuss trends in five other countries – Nigeria, Zaire, Senegal, Zambia, and Ghana – to demonstrate the wide applicability of the model.

Nigeria

Nigeria, because of its federal structure, is farthest along the line in consolidating a formal 3 ± 1 framework. In the colonial period, Nigeria's Northern Region was administered largely in Hausa, while in the

East and West, English became the language of administration. With some four hundred distinct languages throughout the country and a different "majority" language in each of the three regions, the 1954 constitution named English as the official language. Already families in the East and West were in a race to see how many qualified civil servants they could produce to run the country when the British handed over power. They sought English education for their children. In the East, people demanded that missionary schools stop seeking to reach their souls through the Igbo medium and start helping their pocketbooks through English (Nwoye, 1978, 63). Banking on cocoa resources, Chief Obafemi Awolowo instituted universal primary education (in English) to help the "sons" of the Western Region capture many of the senior civil service jobs (Achebe, 1966; Abernethy, 1969).

Despite the incentives for individuals to learn English for career success, Nigeria did not move toward language rationalization in English. The pressures were toward a 3 ± 1 outcome. Politicians understood that there was a longing for a Nigerian national language. Successive Nigerian governments invested in planning activities to make possible the transition toward a (set of) national language(s). In 1977, the federal National Policy on Education required that every school child learn either Hausa, Yoruba, or Igbo, the three major Nigerian languages. In the 1979 constitution, certain legal changes were adopted. To be sure, since the document was originally published in English, it tacitly maintained the preeminence of English as the official language, but it permitted the use of Hausa, Igbo, and Yoruba for public business in the National Assembly. Thus the three vernaculars with the largest number of speakers were beginning to be recognized as indigenous "national" languages.

A second pressure towards the 3 ± 1 outcome has been a result of Nigeria's federalism, which has sustained an interest in the development of a number of vernaculars as "state" languages. (To keep my terminology consistent with actual political debate, for the Nigeria case I shall refer to rationalization at the level of the separate states as "state rationalization." Rationalization at the level of the federation will be called "federal rationalization.") During the civil war of 1967–70, in which the eastern region sought to secede, the three-region framework was deemed to be a contributing cause of the conflict, and a greater number of states was recognized. Minority-language groups in the three-region scheme became majority groups in the newly created states. Under the 1979 constitution, states were given the right to promote local languages as they saw fit. Thus vernaculars different from the major languages now had states interested in their promotion.

Subtle pressures within the federal framework encouraged states to differentiate themselves culturally. The 1979 constitution stipulated that appointments to the federal bureaucracy and the leadership of political parties must both reflect Nigeria's federal character, which meant that political jobs had to be distributed to people from all states. To implement this goal, it became necessary to determine everyone's "state of origin," which was not necessarily the state in which he or she had been born. Federal contracts and other state largess were to be distributed fairly to all parts of the federation. These policies clearly unleashed pressures for the creation of new states, since every minority in one state wanted to become the majority within its own state. The federal government has developed strict procedures for the creation of new states, fearing that chaos would result if each of Nigeria's four hundred language groups had its own state apparatus. Nonetheless, in August 1987, two new states were recognized. One of them, Akwa Ibom, with a large number of Ibibio speakers, was defined in order to make boundaries commensurate with language group (Brann, 1989, 50). In discussions leading to the draft for the 1991 constitution, twelve regional languages, which Nigerians call "network languages," were considered as federally sponsored state languages. Nigerian federalism, then, has substituted rationalization at the state level for the lack of rationalization at the federal level.

In 1990, A. Babs Fafunwa was named Nigeria's minister of education. As a professor of education and a prolific author, Fafunwa was a strong advocate of indigenous-language instruction. He played a crucial role in the development of Yoruba-language materials for primary education in the southwestern states of Nigeria that constitute Yorubaland. "It is only those of us who are products of colonialism," he reported to *New York Times* correspondent Kenneth Noble (23 May 1991), "who are forced to go to school in a language different from our own." Lagos's *Daily Times* has been a severe critic of Fafunwa's vision. "The least luxury we can afford in the last decade of the twentieth century," it editorialized, "is an idealistic experiment in linguistic nationalism which could cut our children off from the main current of human development." The forces supporting the status quo are strong; but the logic of an indigenous-language policy, with a concomitant policy of language zoning, remains powerful. Fafunwa's tenure can only help to aid states in their language-rationalization projects.

Nigeria therefore faces pressures for a national language and for rationalization of vernaculars within states. But there is yet another pressure which could help to consolidate the +1 part of the formula. Since the adoption of the 1979 constitution, the right of all Nigerians to defend themselves in the criminal courts in their own language has been recognized. Thus minority languages within states must be protected (Brann, 1980). To the extent that protection of some minority languages is built into law and practice, the elements of the 3 ± 1 formula would be in place.

Still, the 3 ± 1 situation in Nigeria remains emergent. States that provide education with the state language as the medium of instruction (for example, Cross River State, in Efik) do not have provisions for teaching linguistic minorities in their vernaculars. The common perception that state governments have been unhospitable to their minorities is not mere paranoia. During the Constituent Assembly debates preceding the adoption of the 1979 constitution, one speaker said, with regret, "People tend to think that once a new State has been created, nonindigenes of the State should pack bag and baggage and go." Justice Udo Udoma, the assembly chair, agreed that this was indeed "the common man's view" (quoted in Bach, 1989). The common man's view, however, has implications for people's decisions as to whether it is better in the long term to live in one's state of origin. The constitution, perhaps unwittingly, lowered the expected utility of internal migration. If most states become linguistically homogeneous, then few Nigerians will require a 3 + 1 repertoire.

A second constraint to the fulfillment of the 3 ± 1 logic has to do with the linkages between the center and localities. Commensurate with the move in 1991 to give federal support to states, there has been considerable effort by the military regime under President Ibrahim Babangida to give funds directly to localities, bypassing state governments. If this sort of centralization continues, it could undermine the patronage power of states, the only power which can provide economic support for the state languages.

But the biggest stumbling block that could prevent Nigeria from attaining a 3 ± 1 equilibrium has to do with the choice of a national language. Because having three national languages (Hausa, Yoruba, and Igbo) is cumbersome for interregional communication, there is little incentive for speakers of minority languages to learn one of the three major languages adequately. In a situation with English sharing official status with three regional languages, any official communication in, say, Hausa, has to be translated into English, for Yoruba and Igbo speakers. An Efik speaker consequently can "free-ride" on the translation into English, whether it is from Hausa, Yoruba, or Igbo, without having to pay the cost of learning one of them.

The lack of an obvious national language in Nigeria does not, however, constitute a fatal blow to the 3 ± 1 outcome. The continued appeal for such a language – in the press, in public discourse, and in academic treatises – shows a pervasive desire to agree on a single national language. Onuigbo Nwoye's sophisticated dissertation, for example, made a strong appeal for mother-tongue education, on pedagogical grounds, and an equally strong appeal for an "endoglossic [i.e., indigenous] national language," on political grounds (1978, chap. 6). While he did not designate one, he developed interesting criteria for its choice. Implicitly using a form of welfare economics, he sought a choice in which costs and benefits might be equally distributed among geographical areas. If Hausa were chosen, he argues, it would provide an affirmative-action program for northerners in the civil service, an arena of power where they have been less successful for a half-century, due to their lower level of English education. If Efik were chosen, it would be easily learned throughout the country because it is used extensively as a trade language, yet it would not be seen to be the language of a group that could dominate Nigeria. The key theoretical assumption in Nwoye's analysis, albeit implicit, is that "losers" in the choice of a national language need to be compensated for their loss by the "winners." Educational fees, licenses, job opportunities, and tax savings can all be used to induce language losers to accept more easily another group's language as the official language for state business. The pressure for a choice of a national language may not forever fail.

Whether this sort of bargaining can work when the choice of a national language is at stake remains a dubious proposition. During the 1989 debates by the Constituent Assembly concerning the 1991 constitution, the assembly decided to retain English, Hausa, Igbo, and Yoruba as the languages for its own business. The debate became heated and emotional, and Lagos radio reported that "a few members from the minority ethnic groups walked out of the assembly in protest" (Foreign Broadcast Information Service, 13 January 1989, 29). The choice of any one of these languages is likely to engender deep opposition.

It is for this reason that Biodun Sofunke (1990) rejects the principle of the three major languages having a special pan-Nigerian role. His criterion for an all-Nigerian link language is one "which can adequately serve as the cultural, political, and linguistic bridge between the cultural north of Nigeria and the cultural south" (p. 43). He argues that Igala, a language spoken in the zone in Nigeria's "Middle Belt," has linguistic properties that help tie together the north and south. Furthermore, in that it is a language of a small minority of Nigerians, he argues that the choice of Igala will not threaten any other group's position in Nigeria. He suggests that the language be enriched with words from Nigerian and international languages, and that it be called "Nigerian." Although this proposal is a serious one, I fear that it will not unleash creative energies among Nigerian writers to produce a new literature in Nigerian. Without a large culture-producing industry that relies on Nigerian, few people will have the incentive to learn to use it well. It will be a language that is likely to fall into desuetude.

A more likely choice of a national language would be the Nigerian version of pidgin English. Although northerners would feel that such a choice discriminated against their region, and many well-educated people from all over the country would be appalled by the idea, it is clear that pidgin is widely known, dynamic, Nigerian, and politically neutral. It might take a century before pidgin English would play a serious role in official documents, but educational authorities would have little difficulty in inducing Nigerian writers to prepare material for literature courses in pidgin. Nigerian writers, as we saw in the discussion of Ken Saro-Wiwa and Wole Soyinka in Chapter 4, have already begun to incorporate pidgin into their works. The expansion of pidgin into official roles has already been proposed by a professor of English at Ahmadu Bello University in northern Nigeria (Gani-Ikilama, 1990). The choice of a language that has emerged from the multicultural life of the newly constituted state could well provide the missing link for Nigeria's 3 ± 1 formula.

Nigeria's language dynamics, in large part due to the lack of an obvious national language, are therefore different from India's, where the full logic of the 3 ± 1 outcome has played itself out. Surely the game tree developed for India (in Chapter 2) cannot be applied without modification to the Nigerian situation. In Nigeria, the game between bureaucrats and nationalist politicians was hardly played at all, because the politicians had no agreed-upon language that they could propose to counter the legitimacy of English as the language of the newly independent state. Nigeria's federal structure, however, gave incentives for regional politicians to emphasize the cultural distinctiveness of their states. Expansion in the number of states has unleashed a process of a greater number of language / ethnic groups claiming a state of their own. The number of states has expanded, as has the degree of language homogeneity within each state. This process of heightened decentralization has given local politicians incentives to emphasize (in education and in adminstration) the majority language of the state. First, this legitimates their claim to need separate administration; second, to the degree that local languages are used, civil service jobs can become fiefs of native sons. Although this process of promotion of state languages is in its infancy, the incentive structures suggest that the process will expand. If it does, politicians whose constituencies are national will see a need to promote "Nigerian" values as a way to prevent future secessions. A shared indigenous language would be a symbolic element in a national compound. In India, then, an "obvious" national language provoked a regional reaction; in Nigeria, the development of regional consciousness could provoke the identification of a "truly Nigerian" national language. Thus I see a second path to the 3 ± 1 outcome.

Zaire

In Zaire, the 3 ± 1 logic is also emergent (Ndoma, 1977; Polomé, 1982, chaps. 2–4; CONFEMEN, 1986; Fabian, 1986). The French language, despite the best efforts of missionaries to sidestep it, became the language of elite discourse in colonial Congo. In 1962, amid civil war, presidential order no. 174 declared French the language of education at all levels. And despite fifteen years of seeking to implement an "authentic" language regime, the status of French is rising, if anything. Bisima Nthawakuderwa, an applied linguist who seeks to phase out French as a medium of instruction in Zaire, acknowledges that "recently, in Zaire, there has been an upsurge of interest in learning French. . . . This vested interest in French will continue to grow so long as both parents and pupils realize that the Zairian education system can only lead to an elitist type of society in which good knowledge of French plays an important role" (1986, 120). The logic here is the same as that concerning Hindi in Varenasi, described in Chapter 4: Even if parents agree with Nthawakuderwa, they would be irrational to ignore French for their children unless all other parents did the same. This coordination problem cannot easily be resolved when the state bureaucrats, who are the only ones able to implement a program to overcome the coordination problem, have an interest in the maintenance of French as the language of official business.

Nonetheless, the colonial legacy, which defined four languages as "vehicular" and gave them special roles, continues to influence language debate in Zaire. These four languages (Kingwana, the Zairian dialect of Swahili; Lingala; Kikongo; and Ciluba) divide the country linguistically. As of today, Zairians who seek to play a role in the modern sector need to know not only French but also the vehicular language of their region. There is some indication that the lingua francas are facing strong resistance from vernacular interests (Polomé, 1982, 54–5), but I have not read any studies showing local politicization of the language issue pressing for vernaculars over vehiculars. (But see Sesep, 1978, 7, who records debates in Zaire within the general group seeking "authenticity" by reducing the role of French. There are supporters of both vernaculars and vehiculars.) As the politics of language in Zaire unfold, it is likely that some of Zaire's two hundred fifty vernaculars will get official support equal to that for the vehiculars, and designated boundaries for their promotion.

Meanwhile there has been a concerted effort by President Mobutu, with the support of many intellectuals from Lubumbashi, the center of Zaire's university system in Kinshasa, to raise the status of Lingala by selecting it as Zaire's national language. In 1974, a conference of Zairian linguists was asked by the government to develop a language plan for education. During that conference there was general agreement that in each designated region a vehicular language should become the language of instruction, supplanting French, through the first two years of secondary school. This agreement was the source of the 1974 Lubumbashi Plan, which instituted the vehiculars as authorized media of instruction.

Although no consensus was reached at the Lubumbashi conference in regard to a national language, a group of linguists seeking to implement Mobutu's policy of "authenticity" tried to get general agreement on selecting Lingala as the national language. In the words of Eyamba Bokamba, a prominent linguist whose research (Bokamba, 1984) has pointed to the relationship between education in French and high student dropout rates, "Ironically, while . . . Mobutu . . . has successfully dismantled one colonial monument after another, and has attempted to efface other vestiges of the colonial past, [he] has left one important monument thus far untouched, viz. French" (Bokamba, 1976, 29). Bokamba favors Lingala (although he calls for more demographic data to assure himself that this is a good choice), because it is widely spread throughout the country, in use by the army, people of the capital city, and in nearly 70 percent of Zaire's popular music. Like pidgin English in Nigeria, Lingala is Zaire's language of popular culture.

Another linguist, part of the group of Lubumbashi intellectuals supporting Lingala, is Tshimpaka Yanga, whose University of Texas doctoral dissertation (1980) contains a spirited defense of Lingala as Zaire's national language. Lingala's great past, its expanding present, and its promising future lead Yanga to speak of its role in providing "spiritual unity" to Zaire. By emphasizing the mainstream development of Lingala in Zairian cultural life, he argues, and by "minimizing the particular, regional and tribalistic connotations, the present project is a definite step in the *emancipatory* direction" (emphasis in original, 225).

By 1984, the supporters of Lingala had made some official progress. The ministry of education had developed a pilot program relying upon Lingala as the medium of instruction from kindergarten through two years of secondary school, even in regions where it is not the mother tongue of the pupils. The pupils' mother tongue is taught as a subject in these schools.

If Lingala gains support as Zaire's national language, it would stand in a balance-of-power relationship with French. It would be irrational for any Zairian parent to abjure French in his or her child's education, yet it would be necessary, at least in order to pass school examinations, to learn Lingala. And the regional legacy should persist, giving speakers of at least the three other vehiculars a region in which their language would serve educational and administrative purposes, with jobs going to adepts. This is a 3 − 1 language outcome. To the extent that protection for minority languages is built into the plan, the outcome would move toward 3 ± 1.

Senegal

Senegal, too, has tendencies that point to a 3 ± 1 outcome. President Senghor's decision to promote French was made at a time when no more than 15 percent of the population spoke French (Alexandre, 1972) and when 65 to 85 percent of the people spoke Wolof. Anti-Senghor populists within his party seized the political opportunity to begin publishing a newspaper called *Kadu* ("speech," in Wolof), inducing the Ministry of Culture to respond with an official bilingual journal, *Léeb* (also "speech," but with the connotation of it being slow, even nonchalant). Still, the government has restricted Wolof's use by setting strict orthographic requirements for its presentation (Richmond, 1983, 17). Such restrictions had no import in the Medina, the migrant African community in Dakar, where it became necessary for all children to "se woliphisent" (Morin, 1967). It is in Dakar and other heterogeneous environments that there is latent and diffuse support for Wolof as a true national language. Meanwhile, speakers of six vernaculars (Wolof, Peul / Fulani, Serer, Diola, Malinke, and Soninke) make up 86 percent of the population, and each language has a well-defined geographical zone. In 1965, these six languages achieved official recognition, and they are now used in primary school, on television, in the theater, on radio, and in literacy campaigns (CONFEMEN, 1986, 291–2).

Given this configuration of forces, should a populist program supporting the full recognition of (popular) Wolof as a national language gain
ground – in the same way that Lingala has become the hegemonic project of those seeking "authenticity" in Zaire – the model of language
dynamics presented here would predict a strong regional response to
protect the five other national languages to be used, for example, as
media of instruction. Such a move would only mobilize minorities to
demand instruction in at least some mother tongues not now officially
recognized. Should this scenario play itself out fully, Senegal would
reach a 3 ± 1 outcome.

Zambia

Zambia, too, appears to be facing a political linguistic dialectic moving it
toward a 3 ± 1 solution. As with all countries with emergent 3 ± 1
language situations, the language of colonial control (English) is the
official language, for use as a medium of instruction in schools (especially higher education), for administration, and for important business
correspondence. In 1965, a new educational curriculum promoted English as the sole medium of instruction for Zambian primary school
students. This policy caused considerable controversy, and supporters of
the vernaculars demanded its reassessment. In 1976, the Ministry of
Education, recognizing the ambiguous results of the curriculum, reintro-
duced the vernaculars as media of instruction for the first four years of
school. Seven (Bemba, Kaonde, Lozi, Lunda, Luvale, Nyanja, and
Tonga) out of some seventy-two distinct languages have been officially
promoted for broadcasting, literacy campaigns, and dissemination of
government propaganda (Kashoki, 1978, 19–21; Ohannessian, 1978,
272). This policy, albeit implicitly, is officially encouraging the death of
sixty-five living languages. Meanwhile, two languages – Bemba (spoken
by some 56% of the population) and Nyanja (42%) – are widely spoken
lingua francas (data from a Mass Media Audience Survey, reported in
Kashoki, 1978, 32). There has been no popular movement to enshrine
either of these languages as Zambia's national language.

Mubanga Kashoki, a distinguished sociologist, language planner, and
now university administrator, has pressed for a policy that would effectively consolidate the present language situation, a 3 ± 1 formula. He
would like to see "Nyanja and Bemba . . . emerge as national resources
and not as the exclusive property of particular ethnic groups" (1977c,
19). Further, he proposes a general policy of "language zoning" (Kashoki, 1975) in which the other national languages serve as media of in-

struction in their particular region. But flexibility demands that mother-tongue education be provided to minorities within a region, which would at minimum temporarily strengthen the sixty-five living languages that have gotten no official support. The key, for Kashoki, is recognition that the future citizen of Zambia will be multilingual, employing "(1) a dominant local dialect, (2) a Bantu lingua franca and (3) English." Most important, Kashoki claims that this policy reflects "realistic trends . . . phenomena and developments that at least bear some resemblance to reality" (1977c, 17). These trends, even though they push for two national languages, rather than one, point in the direction of a 3 ± 1 outcome.

Ghana

In Ghana, English was assumed to be the official language, and in some of the country's constitutions this was explicitly acknowledged. In the 1969 constitution, which heralded the Second Republic, a member of Parliament was required (in Article 71 [d]) to be "able to speak and, unless incapacitated by blindness or other physical cause, to read the English language with a degree of proficiency sufficient to enable him to take an active part in the proceedings of the Assembly." Although there has never been an explicit decree naming English as the official language of Ghana, its status is quite high, and speaking it well is a clear sign of having been properly educated. Nonetheless, despite some stormy debates and losing votes, a variety of parliamentary efforts to substitute Akan (which, in one estimate is spoken by 44% of Ghanaians as a first language and perhaps 20% more as a second language) for English have been initiated.

Ghana has, therefore, a far clearer opportunity in regard to a single national language than does Zambia, but still its situation can only be described as an "emergent 3 ± 1." (See Kropp Dakubu, 1988, for a linguistic survey of Ghana.) There is little doubt that some standardized form of Akan is widely recognized by Ghanaians of all language groups to be the only reasonable choice for a national language. It is also widely believed that English is deeply entrenched in the civil service, business, and higher-education sectors. A choice of Akan as Ghana's national language would not, then, supplant English in a variety of official roles.

While many Ghanaians might support in general the development of Akan as a national language, they would, in dialectical opposition to that policy, demand greater recognition of the regional vernaculars. In Reginald F. Amonoo's lectures on the subject, he judiciously gave up the goal of a single official language for Ghana and advocated the promotion of virtually all of Ghana's languages, along with their merging, standardization, and development (1989, 54).

Perhaps this proposal is being implemented with the new system of local councils developed by President Jerry Rawlings in the late 1980s and early 1990s. The newly developed district-assembly system, under the Rawlings government, has put the issue of indigenous languages back on the political agenda. In an attempt to reduce the power of Ghana's ten regions, the government enhanced the power of the districts and increased their number from sixty-five to one hundred ten. Nearly all districts are linguistically homogeneous. In the first elections for district assemblies, candidates who had no facility in English were permitted to run. Consequently political debate in the assemblies, especially in rural districts, takes place in indigenous languages. Debates have been lively and participation active. This is the most important official use of indigenous languages in modern Ghana.[3] Clearly there is now an interest in the development of district languages for official use.

But what about Akan as the national language? Evidence concerning language use in Ghana demonstrates that the vernaculars throughout much of Ghana are interdependent with Akan (Johnson, 1973; Kropp Dakubu, 1981), suggesting that if Akan is named Ghana's national language it will be easy for many non-Akan speakers to learn. Furthermore, given Forson's (1979) data on code switching, the national Akan will be a mixed language and therefore more politically neutral than, say, Asante, a leading Akan dialect connected with a particular tribe. Furthermore, to the extent that Akan gets promoted in a serious way (something that has not happened), it will not be at the expense of English, which will continue to play a bureaucratic and educational role parallel to that of Akan. If anything, this language division at the center will induce regional politicians to promote local vernaculars. A 3 ± 1 situation would be the result.

These vignettes do not demonstrate the 3 ± 1 language outcome in any African country. Rather they give some flesh to the skeletal frames of the rational-choice models. The models provide the clue as to where to search for pressures and conflicts, but unless there are real-world applications the models have only an abstract existence. These examples have shown that there are social and political forces in a number of African states whose interests and actions have, so far, corroborated the model's prediction that many African states will move towards a 3 ± 1 equilibrium.

EXAMPLES OF THE 2-LANGUAGE OUTCOME

In a significant number of African states, an exogenous international language can serve as a symbol of national unity. Here are two examples. In southern Africa, English is a "national" language, because it is not Afrikaans; in Mozambique and Angola, Portuguese is a "national" language, perhaps because many of the anticolonial revolutionary leaders there were of mixed Portuguese and African descent. When an exogenous language can serve as a national symbol and there are different regional languages, a 2-language outcome can be expected, rather than rationalization. There appear to be two complementary reasons why rationalization in the European language might be forestalled. First, under conditions in which any regional group feels threatened by the dominance of another group, it is likely to seek regional autonomy by using language as the symbol of difference. If any region claims the right to use its language for official discourse (thereby securing a civil service made up of "sons of the soil"), other regions will likely follow, protecting the job opportunities of their language group. When language rationalization occurred in Europe, the imposed national language inexorably replaced regional languages in an increasing number of domains. Under conditions in some African states, rationalization in a European language was a fait accompli at independence, but the promotion of regional languages, although at first only in domains of low official importance, can begin a slow counterhegemonic dynamic. While the domains of regional European languages seemed to decrease during their period of state building, the domains of regional languages in Africa appear to be establishing a beachhead. While Europeans living in regions could risk the abandonment of their primary language for their descendants, Africans in this situation will see a need to hedge their language bets.

There is a second reason why rationalization in European languages will be forestalled. Under conditions of welfare-oriented politics in which ministries of education or health seek to maintain communication with rural folk, there will be a state interest in promoting regional languages as instruments of basic literacy. These ministries, given what I argued concerning education and late state building, will sustain a state interest in giving material support for local languages, even under conditions where local politicians are not mobilizing on their behalf. The expectation that the role of regional languages will grow and the particular conditions linked with late state building both work to make the state rationalization logic less powerful for regionally diverse African states than it was for regionally diverse European states some centuries earlier. Now let us examine cases from Zimbabwe, Portuguese Africa, southern Africa, and the Maghreb.

Zimbabwe

Zimbabwe has two major vernaculars that account for 85 percent of the population: Shona (70.8%) and Ndebele (14.6%) (Ngara, 1982). During the independence struggle against the white-controlled Ian Smith regime, the armies of these two groups were not integrated, and tensions between them were played down because of the common enemy in war. These tensions became manifest soon after independence; a contributing cause was the suggestion in official circles that Shona, the majority language, ought to become Zimbabwe's national language. Many Shonas, sensitive to the cultural situation in Zimbabwe, were as critical of this idea as were the leading Ndebele speakers. Meanwhile, English is the lingua franca that unites the elites of these two groups; neither Shona nor Ndebele has played a role as an important lingua franca.

Great support within the two regions of Zimbabwe for vernacular development suggests the following dynamic: (1) gradual death of the minor languages; (2) rationalization of Shona and Ndebele in Zimbabwe's two regions, itself a complex project of choosing a standard dialect and promoting it; and (3) consolidation of English as Zimbabwe's official, intraelite, and international language. This fits the model of the 2-language outcome.[4]

Portuguese Africa

Mozambique (and presumably Angola) also face pressures toward a 2-language outcome (Mozambique, 1982). The particular nature of Portuguese colonialism, in which a besieged administration and a foreign missionary contingent both supported Portuguese language use led to a situation where Portuguese was well understood among elites throughout much of the colonial territories. Nationalist elites (perhaps because so many of them came from mixed African and Portuguese parents) never seriously questioned Portuguese's dominant role. In 1981, in Mozambique, the Peoples' Assembly approved a document with an objective "to spread, by the means of education, the use of the Portuguese language, [in order] to contribute to the consolidation of national unity." Accordingly the legislators recognized that Portuguese would "continue to be the only language of instruction at all levels of education." Yet party and educational officials in Mozambique are well aware that Portuguese is not widely understood in the countryside, and officials are working toward a program to develop a "positive form of bilingualism." This has not been outlined, but it will inevitably yield recognition of a number of vernaculars for special promotion in specified domains. Mozambique's leadership, despite its socialist rhetoric, has not shown a strong interest in the implications of its language policy for rural people. But bureaucrats in the education ministry and the rural-development ministry will continue to recognize the usefulness of the regional languages and thereby will hold back pressures for full rationalization in Portuguese.

Southern Africa

South Africa and Namibia both will face strong pressures toward a 2-language outcome. For both, English is likely to become the interregional language which all citizens learn, and citizens will also be zoned according to their choice of available vernaculars. But, as we shall see, the route to equilibrium in these two states will not be straightforward.

(1) The African vernaculars. Because of the Bantustan policies implemented by the Afrikaners, vernacular education is associated politically in southern Africa with oppression. In Namibia, the opposition to the Bantustan policy which compelled Africans to study through their own mother tongue led many Nama parents to send their children to the German schools which still existed to serve the descendents of the German settlers. Others sent their children to other African countries (Kleinz, 1984, 36). When the Democratic Turnhalle Alliance came to power in 1978, even though they were clients of the Afrikaner authorities, they instituted English as a major medium of instruction in Southwest African schools, thereby reducing the rate of the brain drain. In a 1985 survey of schoolteacher trainees in Windhoek, the great majority rejected vernacular education and claimed, according to Harlech-Jones (1986, 392), that mother-tongue education would reinforce separate identities and that this was harmful for Namibia's growth.

Despite the negative associations that Africans presently hold between vernacular education and political freedom, the Bantustan policies of the colonial period have given names to languages, standardized grammars, and delimited geographical boundaries to indigenous language groups (Kloss, 1978, 21, 28–9). This policy ensured that no African language has been permitted to serve as a lingua franca, and a choice of any language (e.g., Xhosa or Zulu, in South Africa; Oshiwambo or Kavango, in Namibia) by a nationalist elite would create a majority against it. To be sure, Fanagalo – sometimes referred to as Tsotsi Taal (Heine, 1970, 47–52) – a Bantu language originating from Zulu – European contact in Natal in the wake of the Chaka wars and spread through migrants working in the mines and through Indian merchants in regional trade, could well have emerged in South Africa as Swahili did in East Africa. But its use as a language of command to subordinates, and the Bantustan policy of promoting the separate vernaculars, meant that Fanagalo has had no political support from either the white settlers or the black nationalists. A radical antiapartheid activist, sensitive to language dynamics, has speculated that a consolidated Bantu language, which he calls "Nguni," might one day replace English as South Africa's lingua franca (Alexander, 1990, 202). Although his analysis of the overall language dynamics is consistent with my exposition, on this point he is quixotic and presents no evidence of the popular merging of the various Bantu tongues. An indigenous lingua franca, a necessary component for the 3 ± 1 outcome, is not likely to emerge in free South Africa.

(2) English.   Ideological support for English grows. Respondents to Harlech-Jones's survey in Namibia separated the issue of mother tongue from nationalism and argued that "English is the language of the future" (1986: 392). The movement away from vernacular education has been supported by the major mining corporations, which have set up technical colleges and adult training programs that operate in English. Black intellectuals have set up clubs and societies in churches and community centers to spread English as well (Tieber, 1990, 28–30).

(3) Afrikaans.   Afrikaans is widely used as a lingua franca. In Namibia, it is estimated that 70 percent of the whites and 92 percent of the Coloureds have Afrikaans as their mother tongue (Kleinz, 1984:30). And its spread among the African population has been rapid, many Africans now having it as their primary language. Civil service jobs and military service during the war between South Africa and Angola (in which Namibia was a staging ground and recruitment area for South Africa's army) all required Afrikaans. In a survey completed in 1982, 28 percent of Namibian respondents regarded Afrikaans as the most important language in Namibia (Cluver, 1991).

   In South Africa, the Afrikaners and many Coloureds (people of mixed European and African heritage) consider Afrikaans as their mother tongue, and it plays a crucial role in the mines, in the African townships, and in popular culture. Astounding his supporters and critics, Nelson Mandela, when, after initial negotiations with President F. W. de Klerk, he sought to publicly reassure the Afrikaner population of the good intentions of the African National Congress, did so in part by addressing them in Afrikaans (*New York Times,* 3 May 1990). Nonetheless, Afrikaans is ideologically unacceptable as a national language for an independent African state. The outbreak of violence in Soweto in 1976 was ignited by a proposal to increase Afrikaans at the expense of English in the schools of the black townships; this was anathema to the students of Soweto, who spontaneously rioted against the proposal (Hirson, 1981). In light of these strong popular feelings, no nationalist elite would reward the Afrikaners with an official language that cedes to them a strategic language advantage.

What can we make of the political dynamic of this complex situation? Majority rule will inexorably lead to the naming of English as the official link language of government business. The Afrikaners will not strongly object, due to their nearly universal Afrikaans–English bilingualism. At most, the Afrikaners will probably get, in a constitutional compromise, the right to teach their own people in Afrikaans and to rely upon English, as they now do, as a second language. The special rights given to Afrikaners could well provoke other nationalities to demand the same for themselves. The Inkatha, headed by Chief Mangosuthu Gatsha Buthelezi, might well demand vernacular education in Zulu. As African school officials learn about the difficulties of English immersion in the African context, they too might push for language zones in which African languages play a key role as media of instruction in early education. But local politicians will also recognize the patronage possibilities of a regional administration that operates in the local language, and they could ally with school officials to support a politics of regional languages. In the cities, the principle of "personality" (choose the mother-tongue school of your identification) could be promoted, as is presently the case in Brussels, Belgium. In Namibia and South Africa, with English as the official link language and official status given to regional or group languages such as Afrikaans, Zulu, Xhosa, and Ovambo, a 2-language outcome could be the result.

The Maghreb

Morocco and Tunisia, despite strong nationalist calls for rationalization, are also moving toward a 2-language outcome (Gallagher, 1968; Abassi,

1977; Hammoud, 1982; Grandguillaume, 1983; Sirles, 1985). The dilemma of Arabic is well presented by Grandguillaume:

> Arabization in the Maghreb . . . constitutes an intangible dogma, an incontest-
> able objective of national construction. . . . But to this strong affirmation of the
> legitimacy of a national language corresponds a dilatoriness in putting it to work
> [and] the experience of extreme difficulty in breaking from French. . . . Arabi-
> zation is often presented, by responsible officials and by ideologues, as the
> cultural face of independence, a complementary element of political and eco-
> nomic independence. . . . Under this rubric, the objective of arabization can be
> proposed to citizens with the same absolute character as that of independence.
> (29–34)

There are circumstances that might act as constraints against the fulfillment of the cultural component of political independence. (1) The civil
service and other elites in the Maghreb have been largely educated in
French. (2) There are rather significant dialectical differences among
classical Arabic (the language of the Qur'an), Modern Standard Arabic
(the language of modern intra-Arab communication, as well as of any
teachers hired in the Maghred to replace the French), and local Arabic.
(3) There is a Berber-speaking population, which was cultivated by the
French to help administer the country and to resist the development of
Arabic.

Arabic rationalizers maintain their activities in the Maghreb. Perhaps,
as we shall discuss, the possibility for rationalization of Arabic is greater
in Algeria. But in Morocco and Tunisia, ideologically inspired programs
to increase the use of Arabic in elite domains, and careful efforts to
develop, through a form of scientific planning, a viable Arabic standard
have faced strong setbacks. In Morocco, when Mohammed al-Fassi, as
minister of education, tried to introduce Arabic as a medium of instruction, he encountered the rigid opposition of his own teaching corps.
When French teachers began to emigrate, the government opened a
loophole, enabling an elite private (and French) system to survive.
Meanwhile, in the public sector, the high failure rates in examinations
administered in French led to riots in 1965. The new minister of education retrenched and promised that arabization would not "be seriously
considered for another ten years" (Sirles, 1985, 235).

The likely long-term outcome for Morocco and Tunisia is that some
dialect of Arabic, and eventually a standardized Berber language will
become important languages of education and cultural life, but French
will remain the language of intraelite contact. Thus, again we have a 2-
language outcome. However, if Modern Standard Arabic becomes the
"national" language, with Berber and local Arabic becoming standard-

ized regional languages, these Maghreb states might find themselves in the 3 ± 1 dynamic.

EXAMPLES OF EMERGENT LANGUAGE RATIONALIZATION

State rationalization such that citizens will have few incentives to maintain multilingual language repertoires will not, as I have emphasized, be the norm for Africa. Nonetheless, some African countries are on paths leading to rationalization. This does not mean the elimination of international or regional languages; rather it means that the business of rule will be conducted in a single language. These trends toward rationalization are pushed by three different logics. First, in countries that are linguistically homogeneous (or have a single lingua franca that is known throughout the country) but are economically weak, there are few opportunities for urban social mobility. The expected utility of relying on an international language (except for migration) is low. Under this condition, it has been feasible for rulers to give official status to the national language, despite bureaucratic resistance. Second, a revolutionary nationalist party that is intent on forging a coalition against colonial interests can – at the cost of severely weakening the state bureaucracy and the educational system – elevate a single indigenous language as official. Finally, in a state that is highly penetrated by international business and in which there is considerable heterogeneity of indigenous languages, a political project to develop the language of the colonial state as the language of state rationalization becomes feasible. I shall discuss Tanzania and Central Africa as examples of the first path. Somalia's situation was highlighted in Chapter 6 and will not be repeated here. It should be remembered, however, that due to its situation of relying on three foreign languages during the colonial period and having a single indigenous language, it was in an ideal situation for rationalization, yet the process was long and difficult, requiring revolutionary action. This should be lesson enough that state rationalization of language in Africa is not a likely general outcome. The other two paths do not have many cases either. Algeria will be discussed as an example of the second, and Ivory Coast as an example of the third.

Tanzania

Tanzania is the most celebrated case of language rationalization in Africa, in large part because of the brilliant defense of Swahili by President Julius Nyerere, especially in his influential document "Education for

Self-Reliance" (Nyerere, 1968). Tanzania is not linguistically homogeneous: There are as many as eighty-nine vernaculars among its 24 million people. But because the leading fifteen languages are the primary languages of perhaps 35 percent of the population, there are no powerful regional groups. Furthermore, Swahili has a special role in Tanzania. Some 90 percent of the population speaks Swahili; in virtually no place is it not known; and no group is excessively chauvinistic about its promotion. Finally, Swahili was well developed as a lingua franca by the Germans (who colonized Tanganyika), the missionaries, and eventually the British.

Rationalization began in 1964, when the government declared Swahili the national language (Whiteley, 1969). In 1967, it was made the official language of state as well. Primary education is now transmitted in Swahili, and nearly all government business is executed in Swahili. Evidence from rural Tanzania (W. O'Barr, 1971) suggests that knowledge of Swahili is widespread there as well and that Swahili is replacing the vernacular in a variety of domains. The last holdouts are the local courts, where the use of the vernaculars for testimony remains important (Kavugha and Bobb, 1980), and in higher education, where the professoriat remains committed to the protection of its investment in English. If this rationalization program were similar to that which occurred in France and Japan, we would predict that these holdouts could not last, especially with Swahili's prestige rising and with English falling into desuetude in some elite domains (Hill, 1980; Abdulaziz, 1980).

It must be remembered, however, that the model of rationalization applied to Africa does not predict an equilibrium in favor of the nationalist elite and that, even under ideal conditions in Somalia, rationalization has not unfolded smoothly. This should alert us to the forces in Tanzania weakening the drive toward language rationalization. Here is a country that has relied principally on foreign donations to meet basic recurrent budget requirements, and it has therefore remained closely tied to Europe, despite the ideology of self-reliance. Tanzanians who desperately want to keep these contacts alive hold onto English as a resource of inestimable value. This is why the government is facing popular pressure from students to provide secondary education in the English medium (and, indeed, the government has retreated on this issue); this is also why civil servants and university faculty are so unwilling to accept Swahili as their sole means of intranational communication.

Meanwhile, the sociodynamics of language in Tanzania are quite different from what would be expected from the choice of the prestige Zanzibari dialect as the official standard. In daily life, code mixing has infused Swahili with a great deal of English. In the rural areas, courts and communities tenaciously hold to their vernaculars and pass them on intergenerationally. Multilingualism seems as prevalent in Tanzania as elsewhere in Africa.[5] The macro dynamic toward rationalization is not inexorable; it will take considerable political effort by Nyerere's successors to ensure Swahili's integrity and development as Tanzania's sole official language. But there remains the possibility that Nyerere's rationalization strategy – supported by historical circumstance and assiduous political effort – will succeed and that Swahili will be the only necessary language for communication, education, and occupational mobility throughout Tanzania.

Central Africa

Central Africa's situation with regard to Sango is not too different from Tanzania's with respect to Swahili (Samarin, 1955; Heine, 1970, 131–8; CONFEMEN, 1986, 117ff).[6] Sango is a pidgin / creole that was heavily infused with vocabulary from the vernacular of the same name, and it became a lingua franca in the Ubangi Valley in the context of intraregional trade. The full commercialization of the river trade by the French, and the missionary presence, stimulated Sango's development. Like Swahili, it is considered the mother tongue of only a minuscule percentage of the republic's population, but it is known by virtually all Central Africans (Jacquot, 1961; Déchamps-Wenezoui, 1981). In a survey of a multiethnic quarter in the capital city of Bangui, every single respondent reported facility in Sango, 51.6 percent reported Sango as their "first language," and more than 20 percent could not speak the vernacular of their tribe. Sango has developed an élan for these respondents. "In our opinion," reports the survey director, "even in the villages and especially among the young, Sango is a symbol of modernity and 'evolution' [a term dating from the French colonial period; those Africans who 'evolved' qualified for French citizenship]" (Déchamps-Wenezoui, 1981, chaps. 1–2). Sango's role in Central Africa's life has, like Swahili's in Tanzania, expanded in the postindependence period. It is estimated that Sango is now used on the national radio for 65 percent of broadcast time. Also, religious tracts written in Sango have begun to appear in market stalls. In 1964, Sango was declared Central Africa's "national language"; in 1984, for the second time, it was declared to be, with French, a medium of instruction in all public schools.[7]

But there are differences from Tanzania as well. Here the different colonial experiences come into play, for France gave no support and provided no official domains for the use of any African vernacular. In consequence, French remains Central Africa's official language, and Sango remains a language reserved for "lower" functions. The bureaucracy holds tenaciously to use of French, as do radio journalists, who do their serious reporting in French. Nearly all writing is in French, and Déchamps-Wenezoui reports that respondents were incredulous when asked if they would prefer to write in Sango (116).

The logic of rationalization remains to be put in motion. Given Central Africa's colonial experience, rationalization would require a quasi-revolutionary populist regime that seeks to marginalize the francophiles and to invest heavily in the development of materials in Sango. World opportunities for many Central Africans would therefore be lessened, because the cost of maintaining French would rise. But the opportunity is there for a political entrepreneur to exploit. A rationalization program would be popular, even though many of its supporters would seek to subvert it, individually, once it was instituted. Even if instituted, as in Tanzania (and in France, for that matter), the vernaculars will maintain themselves in the hinterland. But if the national language were to become the only necessary language for public life, this would signal the success of language rationalization.

Algeria

The logic of rationalization in Algeria, if it ever manifests itself clearly, will have very different parameters from rationalization in the relatively poor and economically isolated states of Somalia, Tanzania, and Central Africa. Like Tunisia and Morocco, Algeria's elite citizens are typically triglossic, in standard Arabic, French, and a mother tongue (local Arabic or a Berber language). As we have seen, bureaucratic resistance to the imposition of Arabic throughout the Maghreb, combined with local attachments to the mother tongue, has overwhelmed the widespread diffuse support for state rationalization in Arabic.

But Algeria, according to Grandguillaume (1983), has a configuration of forces somewhat different from its Maghreb neighbors, making rationalization of Arabic more likely. Because of the length and intensity of Algeria's colonial experience and France's insistence, in a 1938 law, that Arabic is a "foreign" language in Algeria, the radical army of the National Liberation Front (NLF) joined with the 'Ulama during the independence struggle to demand the "restoration" of Arabic as Algeria's official language. Once independent, and building on France's jacobin tradition, the Algerian governments, under Ahmed Ben Bella and

Houari Boumediene, pushed for the introduction of Arabic in the schools and as a condition for promotion in the bureaucracy. Although bureaucratic resistance was strong, the ministries of education and defense became largely arabized by the mid-1970s. To be sure, opposition from Berber students, from French-educated functionaries, and from commercial elites restrains rationalization. Yet the jacobin revolutionary style of Algerian politics favors the fulfillment of an ideological, and apparently impractical, program. Perhaps more important, in Grand-guillaume's assessment, Algeria, unlike Morocco and Tunisia, does not have a unified aristocratic elite, capable of articulating "national" symbols without having to rely on Arabic. Algerian elites are groping for symbols of unity. Not the Arabic of the Qur'an, perhaps, but rather Arabic as translated from the French is one of the few symbols available to the legitimacy-seeking lower strata at the helm of the Algerian state.

The Arabic language may be the symbol of the jacobin possibility in Algeria, but there are indeed pressures for pluralism. In December 1989, Ocin Ait Ahmed, a former leader of the FLN who had been exiled after years of imprisonment, returned to Algiers. He hoped to reconstruct a democratic Algeria. *El País* (Madrid) reported that he declared himself "in favor of the official recognition of the undervalued language and culture of the Berbers" (16 December 1989). The jacobins fought back. In December 1990, with a free election on the horizon, the government sought public support by legislating again for the expanded official use of Arabic, requiring total arabization of the central administration by 1992 and of the university by 1997. Although the law faces considerable public resistance (among civil servants and Berbers), official arabization is an issue that remains central to Algeria's political agenda (Lévy, 1991). If the jacobin style wins out, Algeria could have rationalization in Arabic; if not, it will likely join the 2-language pattern of the other Maghreb states.

Ivory Coast

The Ivory Coast has a configuration of forces that should have promoted a 3 ± 1 outcome (Turcotte, 1981; Djité, 1988). It is a country with four distinct culture zones – Akan, Krou, Voltaïque, and Mandé – each, in turn, containing a number of language groups. A Mandé language, Dyula, is widely spoken throughout the country, with perhaps 65 percent (CONFEMEN, 1986, 151) of the Ivoirians able to speak it. With some sixty-five distinct languages in the country, there could hardly be a coordinated effort to block Dyula's acceptance. One can easily surmise from these data, from our game models, that many of the languages would disappear, perhaps in centuries, with a standardized language becoming dominant in each region. Regional languages would act as a complement to Dyula, which would serve as a national language having a quasi-official status, like Hindi in India. French would remain official for "serious" business. This is the 3 ± 1 configuration.

But, as in the case of Tanzania, political leadership can alter the course of a country's history. President Houphouët-Boigny's linguistic vision, though dialectically the opposite of Nyerere's, is ideologically just as tenacious. The first article of the Ivoirian constitution states, "La langue officielle est le français." From the early years of independence, Houphouët called French "notre langue nationale" but rarely spoke about the language issue. He has refused to meet with leaders of movements to promote vernaculars and has refused as well to fund academic institutes interested in developing indigenous languages. From this policy, is rationalization in French at all possible?

Perhaps it is. More than a quarter of the residents of Abidjan are foreigners, most of them technical personnel who are French speakers. This gives the capital city an aura of being a French outpost. Partly as a result of this urban culture, and partly due to the unequivocal official support for French, an increasing number of Ivoirian youth are reporting that French is their "mother tongue" (Turcotte, 1981, chap. 2, using unpublished data gathered by Suzanne Lafage). It may take centuries before the vernaculars face extinction in the Ivory Coast; it may be that a new generation of populist leaders will identify with Dyula; it may be that a pidginized French, known as "Sabir Franco-Ivoirien," could replace French as an Ivoirian national symbol (Djité, 1988); but the country is now on a linguistic track not dissimilar to France in 1539, when François Ier issued the Edict of Villers-Cotterêts, establishing Francien, the dialect of Ile-de-France, as the only official language of state. Some dialect of French could well become the sole necessary language for social, political, and economic life in the Ivory Coast by the late twenty-first century.

CONCLUSION

In this chapter, I have described the political dynamics that will likely lead to each of three outcomes as African states consolidate: the 3 ± 1 outcome, the 2-language outcome, and finally, state rationalization. The principal finding is that the 3 ± 1 formula, which had been modeled formally and shown to have empirical reference in India, has applicability to a wide array of African states. The illustrations of the 3 ± 1 dynamic, along with the processes leading to the other two outcomes, are of considerable methodological importance. The language survey work cited in this chapter should be better appreciated by Africanist scholars in general. The patterns are few enough so that there are many exemplars of each, yet numerous enough to allow for intra-African comparative research to assess the causes and consequences of difference. The sociology of language up to the present has therefore provided a great opportunity for comparative research on patterns of African state development.

PART IV

Conclusion and policy recommendations

8

Shaping the 3 ± 1 language state

Nationalist movements in most African countries achieved their goal of political independence a generation ago, yet cultural independence remains elusive. Africa's failure to assert its cultural autonomy manifests itself most sharply in language, since facility in the language of the former metropole remains a key to elite status throughout much of Africa. Meanwhile, the primary languages of nearly all Africans, while socially viable, continue to have low status in education, administration, and big business. In light of the feeling of dependency that follows from their linguistic situation, not to mention despondency at the fact that high linguistic barriers separate the citizen from the state, African policymakers, intellectuals, and ordinary citizens have asked themselves, throughout the last quarter-century – as I have asked throughout this book – What might be the role of indigenous languages in modern Africa?

A genre of recent writings by African intellectuals demonstrates these deep-seated feelings about the role of languages in modern African society. The best-known of this genre is Ngugi wa Thiong'o's *Decolonising the Mind: The Politics of Language in African Literature* (1986), where this master of the English language renounced any future creative work in the language of the colonial state. But the themes that Ngugi raised are pervasive ones in intellectual discourse within Africa. A continuing theme in the annual conferences of the Linguistic Association of Nigeria for three consecutive years, 1985 (in Zaria), 1986 (in Maiduguri), and 1987 (in Port Harcourt), has been the passionate search for a single indigenous national language but in the context of preserving all indigenous languages as well as multilingual repertoires (Emenanjo, 1990, vi). In the postindependence period, proposals for language reform from planners, linguists, intellectuals, chauvinists, and patriots

This chapter is based largely on my article "Can Language Be Planned?" (*Transition* 54, n.s. vol. 1, no.4, 1991, pp. 131–41).

have fallen on deaf ears. But the question of national language does not leave Africa's policy agenda.

Prevalent in the discourse about African language policies is the model of a single language unifying a modern state, such as English in the United Kingdom, Japanese in Japan, Spanish in Spain, French in France, and Chinese in China. Djité (1985) assumes the importance of a single national language. He opens his well-regarded dissertation on language planning in the Ivory Coast by claiming that that country, "like many other nations in Africa, faces the problem of choosing *a* national language. *The task* is difficult. . . ." I emphasize the words that reveal Djité's assumption that there ought to be one national language and that it is a single task to impose it. Yanga (1980), as we saw in Chapter 7, emphasizes the spiritual aspect of sharing a national language, seeing it as part of the route toward emancipation. Nwoye (1978) is more technocratic. He advocates the choice of "a national language" indigenous to Nigeria, since "it is more efficient to use a single language in the administration of a country" (161). All of these authors share a vision of language uniformity as the basis for a powerful nation.

A related genre (Kodjo, 1987, 243) seeks to prepare the way for a united and powerful continent through pan-African language rationalization. Proposals to coordinate intercontinentally the learning of languages such as Swahili and Hausa speak to a profound hope that African language unity is the key to political and economic progress.

These intellectuals are yearning for the rationalization of their homelands, in their quest to be citizens of a strong state. It should be remembered that Max Weber, who wrote extensively about rationalization, did not see it as a joyous goal but rather as a necessary component of modernity, which would force us all into an "iron cage." Many African intellectuals clearly want to foster cultural unity among their peoples and increase the power of their countries by emulating models of successful rationalization, even if they and their people would wind up, like their former colonial masters, in iron cages.

The game-theoretic analysis developed in this book should make us wary of any attempt to envision a collective good such as rationalization that is not built upon strong individual motivations. While it might be good if all West Africans were fluent in Hausa, it would be irrational for anyone to choose to become the first Igbo or Akan in the locality to learn it. Leaving aside such utopian dreams, more modest questions – asking, for example, if indigenous languages can play any useful official role, or if any sort of rationalization is possible – need to be addressed.

LANGUAGE PLANNERS AND REFORM-MONGERS

The field of "language planning" has sought to answer these questions in a systematic way. Language planners, however, seem to be unaware of the fate of their brethren in urban planning and economic planning (whether of the French "indicative" type or the Soviet "centralized input–output" type), where lofty goals have long been subverted by grim realities. Departments and schools of "planning" have given way to schools of "management" and "public policy." This change reflects an understanding that market forces determine a great deal of social behavior and that the best policies are those that recognize the power of market-induced equilibria. With such knowledge, technocrats can have considerable power in altering incentives and changing behaviors of individuals and groups. To call these technocrats "planners," however, would be a misnomer. In the words of a development economist of some repute (Hirschman, 1963), they might best be called "reform-mongers."

So we can answer the question asked by Rubin and Jernudd (1971) in a pioneering volume in the language field – Can language be planned? – rather simply: Rarely in the way planners thought it could be. The questions of "choosing" a lingua franca; of agreeing upon a national or official language; of raising the status of a dying language; of adapting a language for modern usages – the core questions asked by language planners – presuppose an understanding of market forces, individual incentives, and language equilibria.

Consider the case of Somalia, which I discussed in Chapter 6, from a somewhat new angle. As we saw, Somalia is a country in which virtually all citizens speak Somali. Yet the country had, when it became independent in 1960, three official languages – Arabic, English, and Italian – each of them of foreign origin. Somali could not be the official language, because of disagreement as to the proper orthography to use for it. In 1972, after the script war entered its twenty-fifth year, a revolutionary government decreed that a modified Latin script would be used and that Somali would be the official language of the state. The announcement was made amid the anniversary celebration of political independence from colonial control, with air-force planes dropping Somali-language grammars from high in the sky, as if from Allah. There was general euphoria, and no one questioned the extensive opportunities afforded by an educational and administrative system that relied upon a common language. Adult literacy programs immediately became feasible, and national literacy rates soared.

Yet elite Somalis feared that the educational system they were so strongly favoring worked against the interests of their own children. These elites were literate in Italian, English, and Arabic, all languages of international communication. It was clear to them that those Somalis who had the best skills in international languages would have a great advantage in commerce and politics. The scarcer the skills in international languages in the national "market," they reckoned, the more an investment in a foreign language would be worth. The market for private instruction in international languages and in sending children to Egypt (to English- or Arabic-medium schools) intensified.

This anecdote – along with the case of Varenasi and the Hindi language, discussed in Chapter 4 – illustrates a curious phenomenon, best called the "private subversion of a public good." Everyone agreed that Somali-language dominance was a public good, but those with private resources found it individually beneficial to circumvent the very system they found so satisfying. If everyone does what is individually rational and has no incentive to change his or her own behavior, economists say the outcome is in equilibrium. The equilibrium outcome of this phenomenon, in the Somali case, is, we can infer, the growing competition to learn languages that were generally thought to be worth eliminating from the school curriculum.

Djité (1985) observed the same phenomenon in Abidjan. While politicians talked about the promotion of national vernaculars, the ordinary citizens he questioned for his surveys were suspicious. "The claims of authenticity, the advertised need of national unity do not . . . convince the people," he writes. "The dream of being able to speak Standard French one day and finally achieve higher social status is coupled with the suspicion that the officials are trying to rob them of that one opportunity. They argue that while the officials are making promises about the new language policy, they are sending their own children abroad so that they do not have to suffer from the change. Thus, the national language is seen only as a lure to self-destruction" (76).

The private subversion of a public good is a phenomenon that serves as grist for the mill of the satirist. Will Rogers is said to have commented that the people of Oklahoma would continue to vote for Prohibition as long as they could stagger to the polls. Voting for the promotion of local languages and subverting that goal through one's daily behavior is a phenomenon well known to distress language activists elsewhere. In Catalonia, where a language-revival movement has been quite successful, private subverters would buy an inferior newspaper written in Catalan, but not really to read. Instead they would use it to hide the

Spanish-language newspaper that was placed inside. They avoided public humiliation, without having to pay the private cost of reading an inferior paper. The result of such actions, if they become prevalent, is to sustain the reality of Spanish-language dominance that these readers had already voted to counter.

Public support for indigenous languages, even if all citizens in an African country could agree on which indigenous language to promote, is therefore not enough to bring about language independence, nor is the identification by planners that a certain language policy would bring the greatest benefit to all. The sum of incentives to develop individually rational language repertoires can override the best-laid plans of ideologues and planners. In light of this, perhaps we can turn our attention to language equilibria in Africa to better understand how reform-mongers might have an impact on the language scene.

For many African countries, as we have seen, market forces are working towards a 3 ± 1 language outcome. No African country has yet attained as clear a 3 ± 1 outcome as India has reached. But Nigeria, Zaire, and Kenya may well be on that road. In Kenya, for example, English is the language of bureaucratic and other technical domains. Swahili is the national language, with official status, and is a required school subject. Meanwhile, activists in support of vernacular development for such languages as Kikuyu, Luo, and Maasai have demanded official recognition of these languages in their particular geographical zones. Should these groups get recognition for geographically specified zones, the central state will be pressured by minorities within those zones to provide educational opportunities for their children as well, through the medium of their mother tongue. Should this dynamic unfold, Kenya would have a 3 ± 1 language situation. The 3 ± 1 outcome was not identified because it is necessarily desirable; rather it was identified because an equilibrium logic predicts that for a number of populous African countries, this is the outcome if everyone seeks to maximize his or her own language interests.

A particularly good example of the power of the 3 ± 1 equilibrium can be observed in the 1990–1 constitutional debates in Uganda.[1] Given the tribal conflicts of the 1960s, "federalism" is a dirty word in Uganda, and no aspiring politician would propose it. Yet the local district-council system established by President Yoweri Museveni's government is quite popular. These councils have the right to tax and can also monitor the activities of the chiefs. Although many of these districts are incommensurate with language zones, a new sort of federal structure may well emerge through the back door. Rationalization of boundaries, to make them more commensurate with language groups (and to model each from the case of the powerful Batoro, whose territory has not been carved up), could well follow from the successful institutionalization of the district-council structure.

If federalism was a dirty word in Uganda because of the conflicts of the 1960s, "Swahili" is a dirtier word, because it is associated with the brutal dictatorship of Idi Amin, whose soldiers were known to beat, and even murder, civilians who did not answer their questions posed in Swahili. Yet those Ugandans who have begun to trade in the national market find Swahili to be essential, and even though people deny knowing it, its usefulness as a lingua franca is undeniable. The potential for a 3 ± 1 outcome, with English, Swahili, and the regional languages playing their separate roles, is powerful. Historical forces (such as experience with federalism and with Amin) could well block its development, but this does not negate its potency.

THE PRAGMATICS OF LANGUAGE PLANNING

In light of this market-equilibrium or interest-oriented model, what can language strategists or reform-mongers do? Reform-mongers in countries that have the potential for a 3 ± 1 outcome might think of facilitating it, in order to reduce the high political and economic costs of slowly and painfully finding the way toward this equilibrium outcome. How can this be accomplished? Clearly, the 3 ± 1 formula requires the choice of a national language. But how is that to be done, and isn't that an insurmountable problem?

It might not be insurmountable if it is done in the context of setting up specified language regions. Each region would have control over the medium of instruction for primary education and the language for official services. (Regional elites would have to promise to protect minority-language rights for language groups that constitute a pre-set percentage of the population in their region. Minority groups would be given specified procedures to use in applying for regional status.) With the possibility of regional language centers, opposition to an indigenous national language would be somewhat assuaged.

Yet which language gets chosen as official? Yanga (1980) has his own political project in mind, in his passionate espousal of Lingala as an all-Zairian language. His passion, however, can only unleash counter-passions for alternative choices. Nwoye (1978), as we saw in Chapter 7, suggests that the criterion of choice be that of equal burdens. This notion is surely on the right track, but, as I pointed out, perhaps Nwoye should have thought more about African creoles and pidgins as national languages, in the context of vernaculars serving as official languages of regions.

Standardization and enrichment of "West African pidgin" would not threaten anyone today, and, as we saw in Chapter 4, pidgin can hardly be identified as a nonindigenous language. Over time, it would become ever more localized in its lexicon and syntax. Required courses in its structure and literature would, over some generations, lay the basis for an indigenous language playing a truly national role. Language planners elsewhere – for example, in Norway – have despaired of trying to get writers to use the standardized languages as defined in newly established official grammars (Haugen, 1966). With West African pidgin, writers would be asked to develop material in a language in everyday use and commonly used within standard literary works. The market forces in Africa today are creating lingua francas that enhance levels of intergroup communication. A language plan that relied on these forces, instead of seeking to block them, should have a greater chance for success.

In regard to the development of new languages, Forson (1979) has presented innovative data with a novel idea. His study, analyzed earlier, was a technical one on the role of code switching in Akan–English bilingualism. Rather than see this repertoire of using English within Akan speech as a symbol of decay, or contamination (Amonoo, 1989, 32), Forson sees it as the development of a "tongue," with its own rules and grammar. While most educated Africans see pidgins, creoles, street argots, and switching as examples of societal disarray, within the context of a 3 ± 1 language formula choosing one of these languages as the national language might have considerable merit.

Under a language regime of this nature, energies from within the society would be unleashed to fulfill the plan rather than subvert it. The "corpus planning" (standardization and modernization) of the national language would not be taking place against the interests of vernacular groups but rather in conjunction with dynamic popular culture. Vernaculars would be promoted not merely to pay lip service to tradition but to make citizens qualified to dispense services within their region, as well as to communicate in writing with regional leaders. Speakers of minority languages could assimilate into a regional group or demand similar status as regional groups. Once parents sense that the language formula is in equilibrium, they would begin to adjust their educational strategies for their children to maximize benefits from the new language regime.

Reform-mongers would, in the context of implementing a 3 ± 1 plan, surely recognize that, as with all policies, certain people will feel themselves to be losers, especially members of language groups that are split between different regions or that are too small for recognition by the state. And so, while some African languages will be given the support to thrive as living languages in the century to come, many languages and dialects will have their social foundations undermined. International language trends show that the modern world has been harsh on languages with few speakers. If the 3 ± 1 formula reaches stability, it could well be that many African languages will be defunct within a century or two.

The question is whether reform-mongering politicians can help some indigenous languages survive as viable modern languages through the twenty-first century. Speakers of nonchosen languages will clearly be the losers. Other citizens will be winners. Those who need to learn only two languages (Swahili speakers on Kenya's coast, for example) would have lower language-learning costs than those who need to learn four (Kamba speakers living within a Kikuyu region). Reform-mongers might consider welfare payouts to those citizens who have to pay higher language costs or who feel pressures to assimilate. These payouts can be in the form of scholarships, affirmative-action rights in the job market, or the use of a "curve" to score civil service examinations. Elugbe (1990, 19) has suggested that special scholarships be given to Nigerian students who study as their major field an indigenous national language that is not their own.

The idea of compensating the victims of language policies may seem like a perfect solution, but it faces serious obstacles. There is the problem of determining how much compensation should be paid and out of whose pocket it should come. As soon as an agreement has been reached in principle to let those whose languages are made official compensate all others, the former will naturally begin to underestimate their gains, and the latter will begin to overestimate the losses they suffer, so as to skew the amount of compensation to serve their interests. And who is to say how much compensation would be fair, when the costs, which involve learning, loss of prestige, feeling like a foreigner in one's own country, are largely subjective?

Recent work by Pool (1991) has formally modeled this problem and for the first time has demonstrated that under some conditions a clever reform-monger could (in principle) invent a foolproof scheme that lets the language groups disclose their own costs. The scheme would be so designed that no group could be overcompensated as a result of exaggerating its costs. Pools's model, however, applies only when a country contains two distinct language groups, each capable of making a single cost statement for learning the other language. These assumptions severely restrict the real-world relevance of this scheme, as Pool recognizes.

Even if it were possible to get a fair and objective compensation scheme, there is yet another obstacle. Language may possibly be too emotional an issue, with people loving their mother tongues too much to accept welfare payments to give them up. Brouhahas in India, in Canada, in Estonia, and in Soweto surely demonstrate that people often are willing to riot rather than calculate the costs when it comes to language issues.

Language chauvinism, however, may be far less powerful in Africa than is often assumed. In his 1985 survey, Djité found considerably less language stereotyping than he expected. Ivoirians were learning Dyula in great numbers, without intertribal hatred. Bawlé speakers, who constitute a plurality in the Ivory Coast, showed no desire to impose their language on others. And Dyula speakers favored the promotion of their language not in order to attain power but rather in recognition of the sociolinguistic reality that Dyula is widely understood as a second language. Bargaining over a single national language would not, in Djité's judgment, drag the Ivory Coast into a civil war. In fact, Djité argues that the unstable governments, economic chaos, and civil wars in so many African states are due to the fact that political elites rely on languages that do not effectively reach the masses. Indigenous-language policies would not destabilize African countries, Djité reasons, but strengthen them (Djité, 1991, 124).

In a preliminary survey of Ghanaians that I and Edward Mensah made (1991), we reached the same conclusion as Djité. We found losers willing to learn indigenous languages other than their own for official purposes, if they were compensated for doing so with job security or welfare distributions. There is no reason why speakers of minority languages should continue to bear the whole burden of translation in communicating with the powerful, as has been the practice in virtually all states. A 3 ± 1 language policy should be sensitive to Nwoye's call for equal burdens.

The 3 ± 1 policy that I have outlined here differs in some respects from the proposals of Mubanga Kashoki (1977c). Kashoki recognizes that individual and societal multilingualism is a fact of African life and believes that no policy could or should seek to eliminate the diversity of language repertoires within most African contexts. Kashoki has emphasized the equal rights of all languages and suggests that all citizens, in whatever part of the country they live, have the right to education and services in their own language. Similarly Okon Essien, part of a group of

Nigerian linguists who seek to promote a national language for Nigeria, insists that all minority groups have a right to the use of their language as media of instruction and for other official interactions (Essien, 1990, 163–4).

My own proposal has a harsher reality to it than Kashoki's or Essien's. It recognizes that regional leaders, who will be given considerable (but not complete) autonomy within their boundaries, will become strong language rationalizers themselves. If we think again about the Swiss experience, for example, we will remember that although there is great toleration for language diversity between regions, there is an equally great insistence on the hegemony of the communal language within each commune. The 3 ± 1 policy therefore projects language conflict between the rationalizers among regional elites and the spokesmen for minority languages within each region. If the balance of regional power develops into an equilibrium, few languages that are not official in any state will survive, outside of limited social domains. The national state will set limits to this conflict and will require compensation for losers but cannot be in the business of promoting all indigenous languages equally. There indeed will be conflict in the implementation of a 3 ± 1 formula; the question is whether the status quo, in which the weak are not being compensated for their burdens and educational systems are in disarray, is better. I believe the 3 ± 1 formula merits consideration not because it will end conflict but because it will make hard choices that can be implemented.

To help focus debate on its merits and problems, let me briefly summarize the development of a 3 ± 1 language policy as a six-point program:

1. Language "states" or "regions" are designated, and procedures are established by which the people of the region can set an official state language for use in a range of functions, specified by regional leaders but constrained by the central state.
2. An administrative court at the federal level is constituted to hear demands for boundary rectification and state creation, with the authority to implement its decisions.
3. A national language is designed by the federal government which all citizens are required to know for educational advancement, government promotion, and civil service employment.
4. The language of the former metropole is maintained as co-official, and all citizens are given the right to use it in their dealings with the state.
5. A federal code of minority-language rights is legislated, and a branch of the administrative court is empowered to enforce the code. Individuals and groups both have the right to make appeals to it.
6. A cabinet-level ministry of language is set up to design programs such that the language policy does not put unequal burdens on citizens. It will have the power to formulate affirmative-action and other burden-sharing programs.

Reform-mongers, even if they implement this program with great political skill, will not bring harmony; political strife will undoubtedly be present. But the status quo remains intolerable to many, especially those who recognize that after thirty years of de jure metropol-centric language policies, knowledge of French and English in Africa remains thin. Djité (1985), for example, regrets that the irreversibility of the preeminence of French in education sustains the continued high illiteracy rate in the Ivory Coast. Education and communication between state and society suffer immensely. The 3 ± 1 language program is one that holds the promise, for some African countries, of allowing them to acknowledge their African heritage without suffering the penalty of technological backwardness. Indeed, conflict will occur in the wake of such a program's implementation, but not necessarily the debilitating conflict of tribal hatred and civil war.

ECONOMIC GROWTH, DEMOCRACY, AND HEGEMONY

In Chapter 3 I asked whether language outcomes really matter and whether it is worth our sociological energies to model language dynamics at all. No conclusive answer was provided in that chapter. Yet some speculation on these matters, in light of the specification of the 3 ± 1 outcome as one that merits reform mongering, is in order. Of special importance are the questions of economic growth and political democracy, two goals that have been elusive in postindependence Africa. The methodological problem for social science of evaluating performance in attaining these goals is that there is insufficient variation among the African states in realization of democracy and economic growth – nearly all have suffered egregiously on both fronts – for any explanatory variable to carry much weight.

On economic growth, for example, the quantitative data show no convincing evidence correlating language situation or language policy, conventionally understood, with economic performance (Morrison et al., 1989). Since the categorization offered here – rationalization, the 2-language formula, and the 3 ± 1 outcome – represents only emergent outcomes, there is no evidence of economic trends suggesting that one language outcome is better positioned for economic advance. Similarly with democracy: The variation in "democratic-ness" is so limited that language situations can hardly explain the marginal differences. And the emergent language outcomes, since they have not been consolidated in any African state, cannot be seen as causal agents at this time.

Yet some speculations about the likely impact of the 3 ± 1 outcome

for multilingual African states are worthwhile. Consider first the proposition that human-rights abuses might be partially remedied by the language zoning that is part of the 3 ± 1 language policy. In contemporary
Africa, the leviathan state may be lame in many policy areas (Callaghy,
1987), but its police tentacles are hardly weak. They reach into most
regions, and arbitrary arrests are possible everywhere. If an African
regime identifies a citizen as a threat, his or her only recourse is exile.
Under a 3 ± 1 regionalist scheme, every citizen will be under two systems of authority: the regional government that operates in his or her
language, and the central government that operates in an indigenous
lingua franca and an international language. If a particular group faces
discrimination at the political center – for example, if it had once controlled the presidency but no longer does – many of its members will
surely face security crises in the country's capital. Under a regionalist
scheme, these citizens can "escape" to be under the protection of their
regional government. With competition for clients, both regional and
central leaders will have incentives to be less arbitrary in their dealings
with citizens. Citizens who are in a better negotiating position with
leadership are more powerful, and more powerful citizens are better
able to check the arbitrary rules of a potential dictator. The chance for
democracy is thereby enhanced – but by no means ensured – under conditions of devolved authority that the 3 ± 1 outcome implies.

This relates directly to the issue of economic performance. It would be
mistaken to make too much of the argument about cultural distinctiveness and economic takeoff – the argument made in Chapter 3 in regard
to dissociation and innovation. Yet it would be equally mistaken to
argue that Yoruba, or Luo, or Ga as the medium of instruction would
put a brake on technological innovation. The possibility of radical innovation in a language of the periphery must be weighed against the cost of
maintaining an educational system in a language that few of the teachers
can speak with fluency.

There is yet another consideration in regard to economic performance
and the 3 ± 1 language outcome. Perhaps the most grievous horror in
postcolonial nationalism has been the treatment of minorities. It might
be said that what Africa has best produced in the postcolonial era has
been refugees. Minorities have always been the source for economic
entrepreneurship, whether it be Jews in medieval Europe, Gujeratis in
East Africa, or Lebanese in West Africa. Constraints on the free commercial operation of minorities has been a hallmark of twentieth-century
Third World nationalism.

We might thus ask: Under conditions of 3 ± 1 regionalism, will refugees be produced at the same level as today? Perhaps so, given the pressure for linguistic homogeneity in every region. But an alternative scenario is one in which regional governance permits separate economic-development programs. After cultural predominance is ensured, those regional elites who make bargains with entrepreneurial minorities and international capitalists will outperform their neighbors. An implicit bargain – that the indigenous population would have a near-monopoly on civil-service jobs and migrants would have opportunities for capital accumulation – a bargain that has worked moderately well in Malaysia, may reduce the antagonism between the indigenous population and the new bourgeoisie. Economic growth in one region could serve as a catalyst for other regional leaders to copy the winning formula. Regional competition within a state could well be a motor for economic growth.

Growing regional economic disparity, with some regions in a country taking advantage of growth possibilities and others not, could also be a prescription for civil war. Not even clever reform-mongered redistribution schemes can ensure regional peace during periods of asymmetrical economic growth. I grant this possibility; reform-mongerers should not deny the potential costs of their visions. But the 3 ± 1 program was not designed to make all political conflict disappear: It was designed to make language conflict more political, and therefore more open to compromise than to war. As for the ideal of "balanced growth," in which economic development occurs evenly throughout the continent, that is a chimera of more optimistic days. Economic development in Africa, like everywhere else in the world, will build from pockets of economic dynamism. Wherever this dynamism emerges, hostility from losers – as well as migration of losers into those pockets – will follow. If the 3 ± 1 formula hastens the day in which there are in Africa some areas of regional economic dynamism, that would be a good thing. Economic dynamism would be better than the current situation, in which African successes are barely keeping real GNP per capita at the level it was a generation ago. All African states will one day have to deal with growing regional disparities of wealth. I would argue that the 3 ± 1 language states will not be in a worse position than their more unitary neighbors in the effort to work out these conflicts politically rather than militarily.

The possibilities for democracy and economic growth can well be enhanced by the official recognition and promotion of multilingualism, if done with a reform-mongerer's eye. What sort of states will then emerge? What does this mean for African cultures? These questions raise again the issue of hegemony.

I have described hegemony as "the political forging – whether through coercion or elite bargaining – and institutionalization of a pattern of group activity in a state and the concurrent idealization of that schema into a dominant symbolic framework that reigns as common sense" (Laitin, 1986, 19). In late nineteenth-century France, the French language, which had dominated at least since the sixteenth century, began to be seen by both speakers and nonspeakers of French as the commonsense common language of all citizens. The establishment of language hegemony in France was not smooth or always peaceful, nor did it eliminate possible counterhegemonies in the symbolic repertoire of regional challengers. But as long as the Occitan, Catalan, and Provençal separatists are popularly seen in France as merely utopian, as charlatan visionaries, French-language hegemony persists.

The hegemonic framework in most of Africa, largely as a result of the nature of colonial control and boundary creation, has been a framework that has recognized and even reified "tribes." The criterion for a tribe's separate identity was politically forged with evidence based on the existence of a distinct language. Colonial control strategies, combined with the legitimacy that the tribal framework already had enjoyed, surely strengthened the ideological power of tribal identities in African politics. A core pattern of group political activity – except for some short periods during anticolonial struggle – has been based on tribal affiliation. Although some have predicted its demise and others have scorned its tenacity, the mobilizational power of tribal identities in Africa has not been diminished in the postindependence generation.

The 3 ± 1 outcome will undoubtedly reaffirm the hegemony of tribal differentiation. In the hopeful 1960s, when many Africans believed that their political kingdoms could be made anew, any proposal to reaffirm colonial hegemony would have been seen as backward, as antimodern. Indeed that is how the devolutionary ideology of the Kenya African Democratic Union – which articulated a political formula that gave cultural rights to the separate tribal groups of Kenya – was treated by commentators from within and outside Africa. But African independence is now in its second generation, and these issues can and should be examined freshly. The advantage of an institutionalized pattern of group political activity – even if based on tribal identities – is that it is better than no group political activity at all. If political action based on tribal identities is treated by African leaders as illegitimate and other forms of political mobilization are difficult to organize, then there remains a politics without a civil society. There will only be the government and its retainers. As an alternative to the present situation of empty centralization, the recognition of a hegemony of reified tribal boundaries might well be acceptable to many citizens of African states. Perhaps it will be seen as preferable to the arbitrary dictatorship of a former staff sergeant, colonel, or general who espouses "national" values and jails opponents for their lack of (his) national perspective.

CONCLUSION

African intellectuals often demonstrate a deep-seated anxiety concerning the national-language question. While language is not a burning issue now in most African countries, it has the potential for becoming one. Should military despots and International Monetary Fund salvation teams give way to elected representatives, perhaps then politicians and voters will express concern about the language of politics, education, business, and administration. Although some analysts will call this a return to "primordial" issues, in reality it will be a return to the politics of participation, of identity, and of meaning.

A resurgence of language politics does not necessarily mean the breakdown of frail multinational states into tribal homelands. If the historical record establishes anything on this matter, it is that while language issues have brought down fragile governments in countries such as Belgium, Canada, and India, these issues have not, until now, eroded the integrity of state boundaries there. Concessions on language autonomy in these nations have not automatically snowballed into uncontrollable demands for separate sovereignty.

"Politics" is not a dirty word. Opening up the possibility for "language politics" means only that language *interests* will be pursued; the pursuit of language interests implies the recognition by all parties of some serious conflicts of interest. The purpose of politics is to reconcile conflicts of interest without violence. Giving language conflicts over to politics may not exacerbate violence; it may defuse potential violence. In this book, equilibrium analysis has been used in order to see how language conflicts might become politically and peacefully resolved in the African context. A number of trends were identified.

First, the colonial heritage has had a critical impact on Africa's linguistic situation: European languages, in a variety of forms, will persist in Africa, but in most countries colonial languages will in no way substitute for African vernaculars in family life, religious life, and local courts. Second, most African languages, although they continue to be used in a wide spectrum of social domains, will not play a role in technical, educational, business, and administrative domains. Third, multilingual repertoires will be normal for most Africans, and those who have access to a variety of languages will be highly valued members of the community in which they live. Fourth, in the dynamic urban centers of Africa, pidgins and creoles are being enriched and serve as key elements in supratribal communication.

Many others have identified these trends, but still they hold up a historically unrealistic model of a linguistically rationalized state. Due to the early consolidation of African civil services, compared to nationalist parties, and the engagement of the new states in mass education, most African ruling groups will not be able to achieve rationalization of language at the level of the political center, even if it were desirable. A new historical era of state building poses different challenges and holds new opportunities.

The question for African language planners is how best to acknowledge the force of these trends yet still fulfill some of the goals of the independence movements, such as the development of powerful states, respect for African cultures, and the promotion of political participation in the government. For language planners, these goals entail the promotion of some African languages for expanded roles in official communication. In this book, I have argued that there are reasonable formulas to meet these goals, ones which will unleash creative and powerful forces from within African society. It remains a challenge for Africans to develop plans that do not limit the opportunities of their citizens but expand them. The status quo is intolerable to many, because so much of Africa's heritage is being ignored and even scorned, while the spread of standard European languages is frustratingly slow. The outcome identified here – the 3 ± 1 formula for those African countries that are linguistically heterogeneous yet have a basis for an indigenous lingua franca – promotes some African vernaculars, accepts societal multilingualism, relies selectively on colonial languages, and legitimizes the inventiveness and communicative value of pidgins and creoles, all in the framework of a coherent program.

Nurturing a 3 ± 1 outcome for Africa's multilingual states captures much of the hope of African language visionaries but gives up from them what is unattainable. It paints a language future for Africa in which the multilingual repertoires of the people are used to advantage. Also, it is consistent with a pattern of cultural politics that provides incentives for democratic and growth-oriented politics. But the real promise of the 3 ± 1 formula for many African states is in the cultural domain itself: Their citizens, artists, and intellectuals will have language repertoires that encourage free expression and cosmopolitan contact, and live in states that respect human dignity.

Notes

Chapter 1. Language repertoires as political outcomes

1 See also Hymes, 1962; Blom and Gumperz, 1971; and Gumperz and Hymes, 1972, for the seminal papers in the "ethnography of speaking" research program.

2 Gumperz (1971a, 157) hypothesized that rules about switching speech forms ("co-occurrence rules") are more rigid in multilingual than in monolingual situations. Recent studies (e.g., Forson, 1979) would dispute this hypothesis. Nonetheless, ethnographers of speaking such as Gumperz have recognized that counting the languages in a repertoire is easier than counting the whole set of speech forms.

3 I am referring to Weber's notion of "formal" rationality. See Weber, 1968, 71 (economic rationalization); 1108 (educational rationalization); 655, 809–38 (legal rationalization).

4 See Weber's discussion of language, the nation, and the state, in Gerth and Mills, 1958, 177–9, which deals indirectly with rationalization.

5 On language rationalization in Spain, see Linz (1974), Vallverdú (1981), and Laitin (1989b).

6 For this section I have relied on translations done for me by Kaoru Okuizumi from the following works: Akira Matsumura, *Nihongo no Sekai* (1986), vol. 2; Jissen Kokugo Kenkyu Kai, *Kokugo No Chishiki* (1963); Munemasa Toku-gawa, *Nihongo No Sekai* (1981), vol. 8; Y. Iwabuchi and R. Asuda, eds., *Nihongo no Rekishi* (1975), vol. 4; Haga Noburu, *Edogo No Seiritsu* (1982); and Maruyama Rinpei, *Nihongo: Jodai Kara Gendai Made* (1975). The best source in English is Masayoshi Shibatani, *The Languages of Japan* (1990), which is cited with the references.

7 This section is derived from the excellent study of the language issue in Switzerland by Kenneth McRae (1983).

8 This entire section draws on Laitin (1988).

9 The specification here of the 3 ± 1 outcome is based upon, but somewhat distinct from, the formulations by Brann (1981) and Abdulaziz (1972).

10 Ferguson (1966, 309) defines a "language situation" as "the total configuration of language use at a given time and place, including such data as how many and what kinds of languages are spoken in the area by how many people, under what circumstances, and what the attitudes and beliefs about

languages held by the members of the community are." In this book, the unit of analysis – Ferguson's "area" – is the contemporary African state.

11 I rely on J. Greenberg's (1966) classification. See also D. Westermann and M. A. Bryan (1952); A. N. Tucker and M. A. Bryan (1956); M. Delafosse (1952). Alexandre (1972), chap. 3, provides a succinct summary of the historiographical and methodological debates.

12 Nearly all sociolinguists who study language facility and language use – unlike those linguists who study language classification – rely on state boundaries for their classifications. This choice shows – at least implicitly – how important "stateness" is as a variable explaining language shift.

13 Dankwart Rustow (1967) – a political scientist – develops a typology that similarly overemphasizes the importance of a language as a given. Instead of languages with "Great Traditions," Rustow focuses on languages with, or without, "substantial literary traditions."

14 The most comprehensive typologies are those by Alexandre (1961), Heine (1970, 1976), Reh and Heine (1982), and Kloss (1968).

Chapter 2. Three theories explaining language outcomes

1 It derives as well from his experience as a young activist in post–World War I eastern Europe, where the intense nationalism of the time clearly influenced his research agenda. As a matter of intellectual history, one might say that Deutsch took Otto Bauer's influential work on eastern European nationalities and rewired it in a cybernetic net.

2 Readers may want to examine Deutsch's brilliant discussions of human purpose and will in *The Nerves of Government* (1966, chap. 11 and elsewhere). But in his writings on nation building and language shift, these ideas are not developed. My sense is that cybernetic theory can account for human purpose but is not well equipped to develop these notions theoretically, because it gives priority to channels of communication rather than to the substance of what is communicated.

3 Fabian's earlier work on lexical borrowing (1982) focused more on the poetic and creative bases of semantic expansion. Again, this is a critique of simple cybernetic or evolutionary models, but it is less political than Fabian's later work. For an excellent discussion of the political sources of language change, see Scotton (1965).

4 Alexandre's (1972, 60) discussion of the retreat of Creole in Senegal and Wolff's (1959) discussion of the "vanishing intelligibility" of Urhobo by Isoko speakers both rely on a form of expected-utility analysis to explain the loss of lingua-franca facility.

5 For empirical support of Scotton's theory of "markedness," see Kariuki (1986).

6 I relied upon a strategic theory of state construction in "Language Games" (1988). The discussion of strategic theory in this chapter draws upon that essay and a more historically attuned essay on language diversity, "Language Policy and Political Strategy in India" (1989a).

7 Pool's studies (e.g., 1991) rest on a sturdier mathematical game foundation than my strategic theory. I discuss his models in the context of policy analysis in Chapter 8.

8 This criterion of equilibrium represents the basic logic of John Nash's formalization. Game theorists refer to this criterion as the "Nash equilibrium."

9 By a "dominant strategy" is meant that a player will do equally well or better by making a specific choice, no matter what the other player chooses. Here is how to determine whether a player has a dominant strategy for the game represented in Matrix 2.3: Consider first the lord's situation: If the ruler chooses "ruler," the lord does better if he "learns"; if the ruler chooses "lord," the lord does better if he "doesn't learn"; consequently, the lord's best choice is dependent on the choice of the ruler. Now consider the ruler: If the lord chooses "learn" or "doesn't learn," the ruler both times does better by choosing "ruler"; consequently the ruler's best choice is not dependent on the choice of the lord. Only the ruler has a dominant strategy.

10 The following section draws heavily on Laitin (1989a).

11 The number can reach five. The minority in Mysore that speaks Dakkhini Urdu, H. R. Dua reports, has to know Dakkhini Urdu (for family functions), standard Urdu (for religious and some literary functions), Kannada (the state language), and Hindi and English (the All-Union languages) (Dua, 1986). It might be argued that Hindi and the two Urdus are basically the same language, but that is a political rather than a linguistic claim.

12 Politicians and bureaucrats can well be the same people, or from the same family. Nehru, for example (Potter, 1986, 129) had three close relatives in the Indian Administrative Service. When this occurs we can say the individual or family is cross-pressured, for the theory here posits "roles" rather than individuals.

13 See Das Gupta (1976) for material that informs my preference rankings for the bureaucrats; see Mallikarjun (1986, 28–9) for material that informs my preference orderings for Congress party politicians.

14 I recognize that there was considerable debate at the constituent assembly in regard to the question of whether Hindi or Hindustani should be the national language. Hindi is a literary language, close in structure and vocabulary to Sanskrit; Hindustani is the dialect of Hindi that is more popularly understood throughout northern India and heavily influenced by Persian. From the point of view of the 3 ± 1 outcome, this debate is not directly relevant.

15 It should be noted that the Indian Administrative Service numbered only 451 individuals when India achieved independence. But as an elite cadre, its style pervaded the values of the lesser government services.

16 State politicians often were Congress party elites as well. Nonetheless it is possible to disaggregate interests; certain people will be "divided within themselves," which is a phenomenon closely related to being cross-pressured.

17 Preferences are here based on an expected-utility calculus in which the value for using the regional language is multiplied by the probability that other states will choose to rely on their languages.

18 The states were originally in a difficult position, in that they had to communicate with the center and respect the linguistic rights of all minorities in their states (Dua, 1985). But they have had a rare opportunity to develop their languages. State bureaucrats are probably more compliant to their political superiors (because they do not have the long institutional tradition of the Indian Administrative Service) than All-Union bureaucrats are to theirs.

19 In game theory terms, the issues raised by this tree concern "backward

induction," and whether it is possible to find a unique equilibrium at the top of the tree that is built upon rationality at each branch (choice node) on the tree. If so, the solution is "subgame perfect." Without giving up the rationality assumption, game theorists remain puzzled by paradoxes of rationality in the playing of these games. An excellent introduction to these issues is in Rasmusen (1990), chap. 4.

20 The degree to which the vernaculars would have been less developed had the Congress supported English as the sole link language is not entirely clear. After all, the vernaculars have already given way to English for nearly all technical matters. Nonetheless, in Tamil Nadu, Maharashtra, Karnataka, and perhaps elsewhere, movements to increase the realms of normal use for the state language are achieving considerable success, and it is likely that there would have been similar pressure, though not as intense, had there been a united all-English policy at the political center.

21 Game theorists would be reluctant to call the outcome described here an "equilibrium." Why, they could ask, couldn't P switch to English in a subsequent iteration of the game? The answer to this question is in the phenomenon of "sour grapes" (Elster, 1983). Indian politicians now glorify the 3 ± 1 outcome as if it had been their original goal and praise it as consistent with India's historical cultural diversity.

Chapter 3. Do language outcomes matter?

1 Jonathan Pool (1991) has modeled issues of language coordination in a way that is sensitive to individual interests but not based on an empirical reckoning of preference functions. I hold that the issues about preferences that I am raising in this chapter, and of actor interests in subsequent chapters, should serve as an inducement to deductive modelers in Pool's tradition to incorporate – as far as their commitments to parsimony and mathematical elegance will permit – a wider range of utility calculations into their models. Pool's model of choosing an official language will be discussed in Chapter 8.

2 Suppose a parent, in deciding on her child's school, had to choose whether the child would develop facility in a language which could become official. Expected-utility analysis would require her to assess the benefits of having facility in that language, were it to become official, multiplied by the probability of it becoming official; added to this figure would be the benefits of developing facility in that language were it not to become official, multiplied by one minus the probability of it becoming official; from this figure she should subtract the costs of learning the language. The result of this computation is the expected utility of learning that language. Finally, she would want to compare the expected utility of learning that language with the expected utility of alternate courses of action in the time saved from having to learn it.

3 The translation from Italian is mine. (The reader will note that since 1969 I have learned to read Italian.)

4 See Alexandre (1963), who divides African intellectuals into three camps in regard to the preservation of African vernaculars: idealists, realists, and technicians.

Chapter 4. The micro dynamics of language use in contemporary Africa

1 This section draws heavily on Laitin and Eastman (1989).
2 On word borrowing, see also Ansre (1971) and Kirk-Greene (1971).

Chapter 5. Macro forces shaping the contemporary language situation
in Africa

1 This evidence clearly weakens the power of the "least-moves" approach to historical reconstruction, discussed in Ehret and Posnansky (1982). Migrations are reconstructed by assuming that speakers of a language reached their current homeland by moving through a language matrix in the most efficient manner (with the fewest moves) from the point of view of linguistic structure. The problem with this assumption, consistent with cybernetic theory, is that it does not take into account the interests and actions of those historical actors who have wanted to consolidate political authority. To the extent that states were "strong," at least in regard to language shift, the least-moves hypothesis requires some modification.
2 Africanists owe much to Denis Turcotte, whose *Lois, règlements et textes administratifs sur l'usage des langues en Afrique Occidentale Française* (1983) represents a labor of great commitment. Another good source for French-colonial language policy is Hardy (1917), whose title, *Une conquête morale,* describes the author's (a school inspector in French West Africa) thesis.
3 Discussions of British language policy in Africa are available in Bowcock (1985, chap. 4), Ladefoged et al. (1971, 22–3, 88), Spencer (1971, 20), and Gorman (1971). For a good comparison of the colonial language policies of France and Britain, see Labouret (1928). A general survey of colonial language policies in education is available in Kitchen (1962).
4 Even the simple generalization that Protestants favored vernaculars and Catholics the European languages has too many exceptions to be useful. See Klein (1968, 189–90), on Catholic education in the Wolof medium in Sine-Saloum, and de Gastines (1986) on the Jesuits in Cameroon.
5 The best introduction in English to the role of the Arabic language in different functional domains, over time, is that of Chejne (1969). Ferguson (1970) analyzes the spread of Arabic according to functional domain, and I rely here on his categories.
6 The great exception is Houphouët-Boigny, who, as we will see, was Africa's first realist.
7 This was not Senghor's first change of heart. His graduate thesis and his application to become an education official in French West Africa both reflected a desire to enrich Africa with the French language. See Hymans (1971).
8 A crucial stratum within the organizational bourgeoisie is made up of managers of international businesses. Few studies have been done of the relationship between language and international business in Africa. (For an important exception, see Fabian, 1986, chap. 4.)
9 For an example of the programmatic implications of UNESCO ideology in the

1980s in Burkina Faso, see Nikiema, 1980, introduction, and Tiendrebeogo and Yago, 1983, preface, and 59.

10 I am grateful to Melvin Fox and William Carmichael of the Ford Foundation for supplying me with a confidential report on the language survey, written by Mohamed Abdulaziz and Fox (1978).

11 See the lists of sociolinguistic research for each country in CONFEMEN, 1986, part I. See also, Turcotte, 1981, chap. 4, which makes this claim explicitly. J.-P. Caprile, in work funded by the Laboratoire de Langues et Civilisations à Tradition Orale (LACITO), also reflects interest in France in the systematic understanding of the vernaculars. (See the listings for Caprile in the References.)

Chapter 6. *Strategic theory and Africa's language future*

1 Immanuel Wallerstein (1974), through his claim that African states have been economically "peripheral" and thereby face the same constraints as other states on the periphery of the world economy, has been a pioneer in this effort. In political science, Thomas Callaghy's work on state building (1984) has been exemplary in this regard.

2 This section draws from Laitin and Eastman (1989, 62–3).

3 The basic data for this analysis come from the work of Gorman (1974a, b, c). An earlier form of the following model was published in Laitin and Eastman (1989, 63–6). The changes are significant and reflect a now somewhat sharper analytical approach.

4 See Ladefoged et al. (1971, 28–9) for even stronger findings on the low specific support for Swahili. Also Laitin and Mensah, (1991) in a small sample survey, found great diffuse support but weak specific support for Akan among Ghanaians.

Chapter 7. *Case studies from independent Africa*

1 For an analysis of the sources of regional revivals, see Gourevitch, 1979, and Laitin, 1989b.

2 But not universally. Consider Indonesia. Switching of a country's international language from a language with low expected utility (Dutch, Italian, Portuguese) to one with a higher expected utility (English, French) is indeed possible.

3 Interview conducted by David Laitin with Kwamena Ahwoi, secretary for local government, Accra, 29 October 1990.

4 Togo, with Ewe in the south and Kabie in the north, has a similar configuration, with similar prospects, as Zimbabwe. See Brann, 1981:9.

5 The observations of this paragraph come to me from personal communications of Johannes Fabian, Carol Eastman, and Carol Scotton. See also Polomé, 1980, and W. O'Barr, 1971, who have published similar observations.

6 Countries with configurations similar to that of Central Africa include Botswana (Duggal, 1981), Burundi (Verdoodt, 1968), Madagascar (Turcotte, 1981), and Rwanda (Tuska, 1968).

7 I should like to thank R. B. Le Page for supplying me with these recent data, reported to the International Group for the Study of Language Standardization and the Vernacularization of Literacy, York University, Canada, 1988.

Chapter 8. Shaping the 3 ± 1 language state

1 I owe this example to a private communication from Ronald Kassimir, who was engaged in field research in Uganda at the time.

References

Abassi, Abdelaziz. 1977. "A Sociolinguistic Analysis of Multilingualism in Mo-
rocco." Ph.D. diss., University of Texas, Austin.
Abdulaziz, M. H. 1971. "Tanzania's National Language Policy and the Rise of
Swahili Political Culture." In Whiteley, ed., 1971, 160–78.
    1972. "Triglossia and Swahili–English Bilingualism in Tanzania." *Language
and Society* 1:197–213.
    1980. "The Ecology of Tanzanian National Language Policy." In Polomé and
Hill, eds., 1980, 139–75.
Abdulaziz, Mohamed H., and Melvin J. Fox. 1978. "Evaluation Report on
Survey of Language Use and Language Teaching of Eastern Africa." Ford
Foundation. September.
Abernethy, David. 1969. *The Political Dilemma of Popular Education.* Stanford:
Stanford University Press.
Achebe, C. 1966. *A Man of the People.* London: Heinemann.
Adam, Hussein. 1969. "A Nation in Search of a Script." M.A. thesis, University
of East Africa, Makerere.
    1979. *The Revolutionary Development of the Somali Language.* Los Angeles:
UCLA Occasional Papers in African Studies.
Adams, Charles. 1982. "Lexical Accession in Sharamboko: A *Camp* Language
in Lesotho." *Anthropological Linguistics* 24:137–82.
Afolayan, A. 1976. "The Six Year Primary Project in Nigeria." In Ayo
Bamgbose, ed., *Mother Tongue Education: The West African Experience,*
113–34. London: Hodder & Stroughton.
Akinnaso, Festus Niyi. 1983. "The Structure of Divinatory Speech: A So-
ciolinguistic Analysis of Yoruba 'Sixteen-Cowry' Divination." Ph.D. diss.,
University of California, Berkeley.
    1988. "Language Education Opportunities in Nigerian Schools." *Educational
Review* 40:89–103.
Alexander, Neville. 1990. *Education and the Struggle for National Liberation in
South Africa.* Braamfontein, South Africa: Skotaville Publishers.
Alexandre, Pierre. 1961. "Problèmes linguistiques des états négro-africaines à
l'heure de l'indépendance." *Cahiers d'Études Africaines* 6:177–95.
    1963. "Les problèmes linguistiques africains vus de Paris." In Spencer, ed.,
1963, 53–9.
    1972. *Languages and Language in Black Africa.* Evanston: Northwestern
University Press.

Allan, Keith. 1978. "Nation, Tribalism and National Language: Nigeria's Case." *Cahiers d'Etudes Africaines* 18:397–415.

Ambrose, S. 1982. "Archaeology and Linguistic Reconstructions of History in East Africa." In Ehret and Posnansky, eds., 1982, 104–57.

Amonoo, Reginald F. 1989. *Language and Nationhood: Reflections on Language Situations with Particular Reference to Ghana.* Accra: Ghana Academy of Arts and Sciences.

Anderson, Benedict. 1983. *Imagined Communities.* London: Verso.

Andersson, Anders. 1967. "Multilingualism and Attitudes: An Explorative-descriptive Study among Secondary School Students in Ethiopia and Tanzania." Ph.D. diss., University of Uppsala.

Andrzejewski, B. W. 1978. "The Development of a National Orthography in Somalia and the Modernization of the Somali Language." *Horn of Africa* 1:39–45.

Ansre, G. 1971. "The Influence of English on West African Languages." In Spencer, ed., 1971, 145–64.

Apronti, E. O. 1969. "Multilingualism in Ghana." Paper presented to the Week-End Seminar on Yoruba Language and Literature, University of Ife (Nigeria). December.

Armstrong, Robert. 1968. "Language Policies and Language Practices in West Africa." In Fishman, Ferguson, and Das Gupta, 1968, 227–36.

Atkinson, Ronald. 1985. " 'State' Formation and Language Change in Westernmost Acholi in the Eighteenth Century." In Ahmed Idha Salim, ed., *State Formation in Eastern Africa,* 91–125. New York: St. Martin's.

Bach, Daniel. 1989. "Managing a Plural Society: The Boomerang Effects of Nigerian Federalism." *Journal of Commonwealth and Comparative Politics* 27:218–45.

Barbag-Stoll, Anna. 1983. *Social and Linguistic History of Nigerian Pidgin English.* Tübingen: Stauffenberg.

Barnouw, Adriaan J. 1934. *Language and Race Problems in South Africa.* The Hague: Nijhoff.

Barton, H. D. 1980. "Language Use among Ilala Residents." In Polomé and Hill, 1980, 176–205.

Behrman, L. 1970. *Muslim Brotherhoods and Politics in Senegal.* Cambridge, Mass.: Harvard University Press.

Bender, M. L. 1985. "Ethiopian Language Policy, 1974–1981." *Anthropological Linguistics* 27:273–9.

Bender, M. L., et al. 1976. *Language in Ethiopia.* Oxford: Oxford University Press.

Bendor-Samuel, David, and Margaret M. Bendor-Samuel. 1983. *Community Literacy Programmes in Northern Ghana.* Dallas: Summer Institute of Linguistics.

Berry, J. 1971. "Pidgins and Creoles in Africa." In Sebeok, ed., 1971, 510–36.

Bird, Charles. 1970. "The Development of Mandekan (Manding): A Study of the Role of Extra-linguistic Factors in Linguistic Change." In Dalby, ed., 1970, 146–59.

Black, Max. 1959. "Linguistic Relativity: The Views of Benjamin Lee Whorf." *Philosophical Review* 59:228–38.

Blom, Jan-Petter, and John Gumperz. 1971. "Social Meaning in Linguistic Structures: Code-Switching in Norway." In Gumperz, ed. 1971, 274–310.

Bloom, A. H. 1981. *The Linguistic Shaping of Thought: A Study in the Impact of Language on Thinking in China and the West.* Hillsdale, N.J.: Erlbaum.

Bloomfield, Leonard. 1933. *Language.* New York: Holt.

Bokamba, Eyamba G. 1976. "Authenticity and the Choice of a National Language: The Case of Zaire." *Studies in the Linguistic Sciences* 6:23–64.

——— 1984. "French Colonial Language Policy in Africa and Its Legacies." *Studies in the Linguistic Sciences* 14:1–35.

Bokamba, Eyamba G., and Carol Eastman. N.d. "Urban Linguistics: A Cross-linguistic Study of Code Switching." University of Washington, unpublished ms.

Bowcock, Dianne. 1985. "Educational Language Planning in the Gambia." Ph.D. diss., University of Wisconsin. University Microfilms: MBP85-16756.

Brann, C. 1980. "Some Linguistic Implications of the Constitution of the Federal Republic of Nigeria." *Africa (Rome)* 35: 1–15.

——— 1981. *Trilingualism in Language Planning for Education in Sub-Saharan Africa.* UNESCO doc. Ed 91 WS 116. Paris: UNESCO, Division of Structures, Content, Methods and Techniques of Education.

——— 1983. *Language Policy, Planning and Management in Africa: A Select Bibliography.* Publication, H-2. Quebec: International Center for Research on Bilingualism.

——— 1989. "The Indian and Nigerian Polito-Linguistic Configurations: A Comparison." *Journal of Asian and African Affairs* 1:49–55.

Brass, Paul. 1974. *Language, Religion, and Politics in North India.* Cambridge: Cambridge University Press.

Brauner, S. 1982. "Problèmes actuels du développement des langues nationales en République Populaire du Congo." In Brauner and Ochotina, eds., 1982, 99–126.

Brauner, Siegmund, and N. V. Ochotina, eds. 1982. *Studien zur nationalsprächlichen Entwicklung in Afrika.* Berlin: Akademie.

Broomfield, G. W. 1930. "The Development of the Swahili Language." *Africa* 3:516–22.

Bujra, J. 1974. "Pumwani: Language Usage in an Urban Muslim Community." In Whiteley, ed., 1974c, 217–52.

Callaghy, Thomas. 1984. *The State–Society Struggle.* New York: Columbia University Press.

——— 1987. "The State as a Lame Leviathan: The Patrimonial Administrative State in Africa." In Zaki Ergas, ed., *The African State in Transition,* 87–116. London: Macmillan.

Caprile, J.-P. 1978. "L'importance d'une langue peut-elle se mesurer au nombre de ses locuteurs? Essai d'évaluation démolinguistique du Tchad." In Caprile et al., eds., 1978, 73–88.

Caprile, J.-P., et al., eds. 1978a. *Demographie linguistique: Approche quantitative.* Contacts de Langues et Contacts de Cultures, no. 1. Paris: Laboratoire de Langues et Civilisations à Tradition Orale.

——— 1978b. *La situation du Tchad: Approche globale au niveau national.* Contacts de Langues et Contacts de Cultures no. 2. Paris: Laboratoire de Langues et Civilisations à Tradition Orale.

1979. *La création lexicale spontanée en Afrique centrale par emprunt au français.*" Contacts de Langues et Contacts de Cultures, no. 3. Paris: Laboratoire de Langues et Civilisations à Tradition Orale.

1982. *L'expansion des langues Africaines: Peul, Sango, Kikongo, Ciluba, Swahili.* Contacts de Langues et Contacts de Cultures, no. 4. Paris: Laboratoire de Langues et Civilisations à Tradition Orale.

Carroll, John. 1956. "Introduction." In Whorf, 1956, 1–34.

1964. *Language and Thought.* Englewood Cliffs, N.J.: Prentice-Hall.

Certeau, Michel de, et al. 1975. *Une politique de la langue: La révolution française et les patois.* Paris: Gallimard.

Champion, J. 1969. "Native Languages Suggested for African Education." *Le Monde,* Paris, 3 December, pp. 1, 11.

Chejne, A. 1969. *The Arabic Language: Its Role in History.* Minneapolis: University of Minnesota Press.

Chimuka, S. S., et al. 1978. "Language and Education in Zambia." Lusaka: Institute for African Studies, University of Zambia. Pamphlet.

Chishimba, Maurice M. 1986. "Language Policy and Education in Zambia." *International Education Journal* 1:151–80.

Chumbow, Beban Sammy. 1980. "Language and Language Policy in Cameroon." In Ndiva Kofele-Kale, ed., *An African Experiment in National Building: The Bilingual Cameroon Republic since Reunification,* 281–311. Boulder: Westview Press.

1987. "Towards a Language Planning Model for Africa." *Journal of West African Languages* 17:15–22.

Cluver, August D. de V. 1991. "A Systems Approach to Language Planning: The Case of Namibia." *Language Problems and Language Planning* 15:43–64.

Cohen, Abner. 1969. *Custom and Politics in Urban Africa.* Berkeley and Los Angeles: University of California.

Colot, A. 1965. "Notes sur l'entrée à l'école dans l'agglomération Dakaroise." *Psychopathologie Africaine (Dakar)* 1:130–50.

CONFEMEN (Conférence des Ministres de l'Éducation des États d'Expression Française). 1986. *Promotion et intégration des langues nationales dans les systèmes éducatifs.* Paris: Champion.

Cruise O'Brien, Donal. 1975. *States and Politicians.* Cambridge: Cambridge University Press.

Dahl, Robert. 1971. *Polyarchy.* New Haven: Yale University Press.

Dalby, David, ed. 1970. *Language and History in Africa.* London: Cass.

Das Gupta, Jyotirindra. 1970. *Language Conflict and National Development.* Berkeley and Los Angeles: University of California Press.

1976. "Practice and Theory of Language Planning: The Indian Policy Process." In O'Barr and O'Barr, eds., 1976, 195–212.

Déchamps-Wenezoui, Martine. 1981. *Le Français, le Sango et les autres langues centrafricaines: Enquête sociolinguistique au quartier Roy Babe.* Langues et Civilisations à Tradition Orale, no. 48. Paris: SELAF.

Delafosse, M. 1952. "Langues du Soudan et de la Guinée." In A. Meillet and M. Cohen, eds., *Les langues du monde,* 2 vol., 2:737–845. Paris: Champion.

Deutsch, Karl W. 1942. "The Trend of European Nationalism: The Language Aspect." *American Political Science Review* 36:533–41.

1953. *Nationalism and Social Communication.* Cambridge, Mass.: MIT Press.
1966. *The Nerves of Government.* New York: Free Press.
Deutsch, Karl W., and William J. Foltz, eds. 1966. *Nation-building.* New York: Atherton.
Dil, A. 1973. "Towards a General Model of Language Planning Policy." In UNESCO, *Anthropology and Language Science in Educational Development,* 55–8. Paris: UNESCO.
Dimmendaal, Gerrit J. 1989. "On Language Death in Eastern Africa." In Dorian, ed., 1989, 13–31.
Djité, Paulin Goupognon. 1985. "Language Attitudes in Abidjan: Implications for Language Planning in the Ivory Coast." Ph.D. diss., Georgetown University.
1988. "The Spread of Dyula and Popular French in Côte d'Ivoire." *Language Problems and Language Planning* 12:213–25.
1991. "Langues et développement en Afrique." *Language Problems and Language Planning* 15:121–38.
Dorian, Nancy C. 1981. *Language Death: The Life Cycle of a Scottish Gaelic Dialect.* Philadelphia: University of Pennsylvania Press.
Dorian, Nancy C., ed. 1989. *Investigating Obsolescence: Studies in Language Contraction and Death.* Cambridge: Cambridge University Press.
Dua, Hans R. 1985. *Language Planning in India.* New Delhi: Harnam.
1986. *Language Use, Attitudes and Identity among Linguistic Minorities.* Mysore: Central Institute of Indian Languages.
Ducos, Gisèle. 1978. "L'usage du français et des langues africaines en milieu urbain: Le cas de Ziguinchor au Sénégal." In Caprile et al., eds., 1978, 67–72.
Duggal, N. K., ed. 1981. *Toward a Language Policy for Namibia.* Lusaka: United Nations Institute for Namibia.
Eastman, Carol M. N.d. "Language Policy, Language Use, and Kenya's Political Economy." Unpublished ms., University of Washington, Seattle.
1979. Review of Laitin, 1977. *American Anthropologist* 81:380–1.
1983. *Language Planning.* San Francisco: Chandler & Sharp.
Ehret, C. 1980. "The Nilotic Languages of Tanzania." In Polomé and Hill, eds., 1980, 68–78.
Ehret, Christopher, and Merrick Posnansky, eds. 1982. *The Archaeological and Linguistic Reconstruction of African History.* Berkeley and Los Angeles: University of California Press.
Elster, Jon. 1983. *Sour Grapes.* Cambridge: Cambridge University Press.
Elugbe, B. O. 1990. "National Language and National Development." In Emenanjo, ed., 1990, 10–19.
Emenanjo, E. N., ed. 1990. *Multilingualism, Minority Languages and Language Policy in Nigeria.* Agbor, Bendel State, Nigeria: Central Books.
Essien, O. E. 1990. "The Future of Minority Languages." In Emenanjo, 1990, 155–168.
Fabian, Johannes. 1982. "Scratching the Surface: Observations on the Poetics of Lexical Borrowing in Shaba Swahili." *Anthropological Linguistics* 24:14–50.
1986. *Language and Colonial Power: The Appropriation of Swahili in the Former Belgian Congo.* Cambridge: Cambridge University Press.

Ferguson, Charles A. 1959. "Diglossia." *Word* 15:325–40.
    1966. "National Sociolinguistic Profile Formulas." In W. Bright, *Socio-linguistics*, 309–24. The Hague: Mouton.
    1970. *The Role of Arabic in Ethiopia: A Sociolinguistic Perspective.* Mono-graph Series on Languages and Linguistics, no. 23. Washington, D.C.: Georgetown University.
Fernandez, James. 1986. "Lexical Fields: And Some Movements about, within, and between Them." In Fernandez, ed., *Persuasions and Performances*, 130–56. Bloomington: Indiana University Press.
Fishman, Joshua. 1967. "Some Contrasts between Linguistically Homogeneous and Linguistically Heterogeneous Policies." *International Journal of American Linguistics* 33:18–30.
    1971. "National Languages and Languages of Wider Communication in the Developing Nations." First Published 1968. In Whiteley, ed., 1971, 27–56.
Fishman, J., Charles Ferguson, and J. Das Gupta, eds., 1968. *Language Problems of Developing Nations.* New York: Wiley.
Foltz, William. 1981. "Modernization and Nation Building: The Social Mobilization Model Reconsidered." In R. Merritt and B. Russett, eds., *From National Development to Global Community*, 25–45. London: Allen & Unwin.
Forson, Barnabas. 1979. "Code-switching in Akan–English Bilingualism." Ph.D. diss., UCLA. University microfilms: 8007431.
Fougeyrollas, Pierre. 1967. "The Teaching of French in the Service of the Senegalese Nation." Dakar: Comité Linguistique Africaine à Dakar (CLAD) document.
Friedman, David. 1977. "A Theory of the Size and Shape of Nations." *Journal of Political Economy* 85:59–77.
Galaal, M. 1954. "Arabic Script for Somali." *Islamic Quarterly* 1:114–19.
Gallagher, Charles. 1968. "North African Problems and Prospects." In Fishman, Ferguson, and Das Gupta, 1968, 129–50.
Gandhi, K. L. 1984. *The Problem of Official Language in India.* New Delhi: Arya Book Depot.
Gandji, F. A. 1976. "Discours d'ouverture du séminaire sur la 'Promotion des langues nationales.' " Mimeo available in "Cameroon" ephemera box, Library of Congress.
Gani-Ikilama, T. O. 1990. "Use of Nigerian Pidgin in Education: Why Not?" In Emenanjo, ed., 1990, 219–27.
Gastines, François de. 1986. "L'expérience d'enseignement des langues nationales au College Libermann de Douala." Douala. Mimeo available in "Cameroon" ephemera box, Library of Congress.
Gbadamoshi, G. O. 1967. "The Establishment of Western Education among Muslims in Nigeria, 1896–1926." *Journal of the Historical Society of Nigeria* 4:89–115.
Geertz, Clifford. 1963. "The Integrative Revolution: Primordial Sentiments and Civil Politics in the New States." In Geertz, ed., *Old Societies and New States.* 105–57. New York: Free Press.
    1973. *The Interpretation of Cultures.* New York: Basic Books.
Gerth, H. H., and C. W. Mills, eds. 1958. *From Max Weber.* New York: Oxford University Press.

Godfrey, Martin. 1976. "The Outflow of Trained Personnel from Developing Countries 'Brain Drain': The Disengagement Alternative." UN doc., ECOSOC, no. E / CN.5 / L.421. Paris: United Nations.

Gorman, Thomas Patrick. 1970. "Language Policy in Kenya." Paper presented to the Language Association of Eastern Africa, Conference on Language for Development, Nairobi. Mimeo.

    1971. "A Survey of Educational Language Policy." Ph.D. diss., University of Nairobi.

    1974a. "The Development of Language Policy in Kenya with Particular Reference to the Educational System." In Whiteley, ed., 1974c, 397–453.

    1974b. "Patterns of Language Use among School Children and Their Parents." In Whiteley, ed., 1974c, 351–93.

    1974c. "The Teaching of Languages at Secondary Level." In Whiteley, ed., 1974c, 481–545.

Gourevitch, Peter A. 1979. "The Reemergence of 'Peripheral Nationalisms': Some Comparative Speculations on the Spatial Distribution of Political Leadership and Economic Growth." *Comparative Studies in Society and History* 21:303–22.

Graham, Sonia F. 1966. *Government and Mission Education in Northern Nigeria, 1900–1919, with Special Reference to the Work of Hanns Vischer.* Ibadan: Ibadan University Press.

Grandguillaume, Gilbert. 1983. *Arabisation et politique linguistique au Maghreb.* Paris: Maisonneuve & Larose.

Greenberg, Joseph H. 1965. "Urbanism, Migration, and Language." In Hilda Kuper, ed., *Urbanization and Migration in West Africa*, 50–9. Berkeley and Los Angeles: University of California Press.

    1966. *The Languages of Africa.* Bloomington: Indiana University Press.

Guillaume, Henri, and Jean-Michel Delobeau. 1978. "Une Mosaïque ethnique et linguistique en milieu rural." In Caprile et al., eds., 1978, 12–65.

Gumperz, John. 1964. "Hindi–Punjabi Code Switching in Delhi." In H. Lunt, ed., *Proceedings of the Ninth International Congress of Linguists*, 1115–24. The Hague: Mouton.

    1971a. "Linguistic and Social Interaction in Two Communities." In Gumperz, 1971b, 151–76. Reprinted from *American Anthropologist* 66, pt. 2 (1964):137–53.

Gumperz, John, ed. 1971b. *Language in Social Groups.* Stanford: Stanford University Press.

Gumperz, John, and Jenny Cook-Gumperz. 1982. "Introduction: Language and the Communication of Social Identity." In Gumperz, ed., *Language and Social Identity*, 1–21. Cambridge: Cambridge University Press.

Gumperz, John, and E. Hernández-Chávez. 1972. "Bilingualism, Bidialectalism and Classroom Interaction." In C. Cazden, V. P. John, and D. Hymes, eds., *Functions of Language in the Classroom*, 84–108. New York: Teachers' College Press.

Gumperz, John, and Dell Hymes, eds. 1972. *Directions in Sociolinguistics.* New York: Holt, Rinehart & Winston.

Guthrie, Malcolm. "Contributions from Comparative Bantu Studies to the Prehistory of Africa." In Dalby, ed., 1970, 20–49.

Hair, P. E. H. 1970. "The Contribution of Early Linguistic Material to the History of West Africa." In Dalby, ed., 1970, 50–63.

Hammoud, Mohamed Salah-Dine. 1982. "Arabicization in Morocco: A Case Study of Language Planning and Language Policy Attitudes." Ph.D. diss., University of Texas, Austin.

Hardy, Georges. 1917. *Une conquête morale.* Paris: Colin.

Harlech-Jones, Brian. 1986. "An Evaluation of Assumptions Underlying Language in Education in Namibia." In *Language in Education in Africa*, 1986, 383–411.

Harries, Patrick. 1988. "The Roots of Ethnicity: Discourse and the Politics of Language Construction in South-East Africa." *African Affairs* 87:25–52.

Hattiger, J.-L. 1983. *Le français populaire d'Abidjan: Un cas de pidginisation.* Papers of the Institut de Linguistique Appliquée, no. 87. Abidjan: Institut de Linguistique Appliquée.

Haugen, Einar. 1966. *Language Conflict and Language Planning: The Case of Modern Norwegian.* Cambridge, Mass.: Harvard University Press.

1978. "Bilingualism, Language Contact, and Immigrant Languages in the United States: A Research Report, 1956–1970." In Joshua Fishman, ed., *Advances in the Study of Societal Multilingualism*, 1–111. The Hague: Mouton.

Heine, Bernd. 1970. *Status and Use of African Lingua Francas.* Munich: Weltforum.

1976. *A Typology of African Languages: Based on the Order of Meaningful Elements.* Berlin: Reimer.

1978. "The Sam Languages: A History of Rendille, Boni and Somali." *Afroasiatic Linguistics* 6:1–93.

1979. *Sprache, Gesellschaft und Kommunikation in Afrika.* Munich: Weltforum.

1990. "Language Policy in Africa." In Brian Weinstein, ed., *Language Policy and Political Development*, 167–84. Norwood, N.J.: Ablex.

Heine, Bernd, and Wilhelm J. G. Möhlig. 1980. *Language and Dialect Atlas of Kenya*, 9 vols. Berlin: Reimer. Vol. 1, *Geographical and Historical Introduction.*

Heine, Bernd, and Mechthild Reh. 1984. *Grammaticalization and Reanalysis in African Languages.* Hamburg: Buske.

Hemphill, R. J. 1974. "Language Use and Language Teaching in the Primary Schools of Kenya." In Whiteley, ed., 1974c, 455–79.

Henderson, Lawrence. 1979. *Angola: Five Centuries of Conflict.* Ithaca, N.Y.: Cornell University Press.

Herms, I., and V. J. Porchomovskij. 1982. "On the Development of the Language Situation of the Federal Republic of Nigeria." In Brauner and Ochotina, eds., 1982, 165–200.

Hesseling, Gerti. 1981. *Etat et langue en Afrique: Esquisse d'une étude juridique comparative.* African Studies Centre, Working Paper no. 3. Leiden: University of Leiden.

Hill, C. P. 1980. "Some Developments in Language and Education in Tanzania since 1969." In Polomé and Hill, eds., 1980, 362–409.

Hirschman, Albert. 1963. *Journeys toward Progress*. New York: Twentieth Century Fund.

Hirson, Baruch. 1981. "Language in Control and Resistance in South Africa." *African Affairs* 80:219–37.

Hobsbawm, Eric, and Terence Ranger, eds. 1983. *The Invention of Tradition*. Cambridge: Cambridge University Press.

Hoffmann, Stanley. 1960. *Contemporary Theory in International Relations*. Englewood Cliffs, N.J.: Prentice-Hall.

Höftmann, H. 1982. "Le développement des langues nationales et la politique linguistique en République Populaire du Bénin." In Brauner and Ochotina, eds., 1982, 201–12.

Holm, John. 1989. *Pidgins and Creoles*. Cambridge: Cambridge University Press.

Hopkins, Tometro. 1977. "The Development and Implementation of the National Language Policy in Kenya." In Kotey and Der-Houssikian, eds., 1977, 84–96.

Houbert, Jean. 1980. "Mauritius: The Socio-political Determinant of the National Language Question in a Colonial Formation." *Argument-Sonderband (Berlin)* 8:37–52.

Hvalkof, S., and Peter Asby. 1981. *Is God an American? An Anthropological Perspective on the Missionary Work of the Summer Institute of Linguistics*. Copenhagen: International Work Group for Indigenous Affairs.

Hymans, Jacques. 1971. *Léopold Sédar Senghor: An Intellectual Biography*. Edinburgh: Edinburgh University Press.

Hymes, Dell. 1962. "The Ethnography of Speaking." In T. Gladwin and W. D. Sturtevant, eds., *Anthropology and Human Behavior*, 15–53. Washington, D.C.: Anthropological Society of Washington.

Iliffe, John. 1969. *Tankanyika under German Rule*. Cambridge: Cambridge University Press.

Itebete, P. 1970. "Language Modernization and Standardization in Eastern Africa: The Luluyia Case." Address presented to the Language Association of Eastern Africa, Conference on Language for Development, Nairobi. University of Nairobi, Africana Collection. Mimeo.

Jacquot, A. 1961. "Notes sur la situation du Sango à Bangui, résultat d'un sondage." *Africa* 31:158–66.

Johnson, Bruce Champney. 1973. "Language Use at Larteh, Ghana: A Sociolinguistic Study of a Bilingual Community." Ph.D. diss., Northwestern University.

Kariuki, Mwangi. 1986. "Determinants of Language Choice by Middle Level Managers in the Kenyan Public Service." MA thesis, Michigan State University. University Microfilms: MBP13-27678.

Kashoki, Mubanga. 1975. "Language Selection and Zoning: Some National Implications." Paper presented at the Zambia Language Group Conference on Language and Education in Zambia, Lusaka, 30–31 August.

——— 1977a. "Between-language Communication in Zambia." *Lingua* 41:145–68.

——— 1977b. "Fishing from the Same Pond: Lexical Innovation among Four Zambian Languages." Paper presented to the African Studies Association, Houston.

1977c. "Language and the Future Citizen of Zambia." Paper read at University of California, San Diego, Department of Sociology, 21 November.

1978. "The Language Situation in Zambia." In Ohannessian and Kashoki, eds., 1978, 9–46.

Kavugha, Douglas, and Donald Bobb. 1980. "The Use of Language and the Law Courts in Tanzania." In Polomé and Hill, eds., 1980, 229–58.

Kher, B. G. 1956. *Report of the Official Language Commission.* New Delhi: Government of India Press.

Kirk-Greene, A. 1971. "The Influence of West African Languages on English." In Spencer, ed., 1971, 123–44.

Kitchen, H. 1962. *The Educated African.* New York: Praeger.

Klein, M. 1968. *Islam and Imperialism in Senegal.* Stanford: Stanford University Press.

Kleinz, Norbert. 1984. *Deutsche Sprache im Kontakt in Südwestafrika.* Stuttgart: Steiner.

Kloss, Heinz. 1968. "Notes Concerning a Language–Nation Typology." In Fishman, Ferguson, and Das Gupta, eds., 1968, 69–85.

1978. *Problems of Language Policy in South Africa.* Vienna: Universitäts-Verlagsbuchhandlung.

Knappert, Jan. 1970. "Contribution from the Study of Loanwords to the Cultural History of Africa." In Dalby, ed., 1970, 78–88.

Kodjo, Edem. 1987. *Africa Tomorrow,* trans. E. B. Khan. New York: Continuum.

Kotey, Paul F. A., and Haig Der-Houssikian, eds. 1977. *Language and Linguistic Problems in Africa: Proceedings of the Seventh Conference on African Linguistics.* Columbia, S.C.: Hornbeam Press.

Kozelka, Paul. 1984. "The Development of National Languages: A Case Study of Language Planning in Togo." Ph.D. diss., Stanford University. University Microfilms: MBP84-20572.

Kropp Dakubu, M. E. 1981. *One Voice: The Linguistic Culture of an Accra Lineage.* Leiden: African Studies Centre.

Kropp Dakubu, M. E., ed. 1988. *The Languages of Ghana.* London: Kegan Paul.

Kwofie, Emmanuel N. 1979. *The Acquisition and Use of French as a Second Language in Africa.* Grossen-Linden: Hoffmann.

Labahn, Thomas. 1982. *Sprache und Staat: Sprachpolitik in Somalia.* Hamburg: Buske.

Labouret, Henri. 1931. "La situation linguistique en Afrique Occidentale Française." *Africa* 4:56.

Labov, W. 1968. "The Reflection of Social Processes in Linguistic Structures." In J. Fishman, *Readings in the Sociology of Language.* The Hague: Mouton.

Ladefoged, Peter, et al. 1971. *Language in Uganda.* Nairobi: Oxford University Press.

Laitin, David D. 1977. *Politics, Language and Thought: The Somali Experience.* Chicago: University of Chicago Press.

1979. "Language Choice and National Development: A Typology for Africa." *International Interactions* 6:291–321.

1983. "Linguistic Dissociation: A Strategy for Africa." In J. G. Ruggie, *The

Antinomies of Interdependence, 317–68. New York: Columbia University Press.

1986. *Hegemony and Culture.* Chicago: University of Chicago Press.

1988. "Language Games." *Comparative Politics.* 20:289–302.

1989a. "Language Policy and Political Strategy in India." *Policy Sciences* 22: 415–36.

1989b. "Linguistic Revival: Politics and Culture in Catalonia." *Comparative Studies in Society and History* 31:297–317.

Laitin, D., and Carol Eastman. 1989. "Language Conflict: Transactions and Games in Kenya." *Cultural Anthropology* 4:51–72.

Laitin, D., and Edward Mensah. 1991. "Language Choice among Ghanaians." *Language Policy and Language Planning* 15:139–61.

Language in Education in Africa. 1986. Centre of African Studies, Published Seminar Proceedings. Edinburgh: Edinburgh University Press.

Lanham, L. W., and K. P. Prinsloo. 1978. *Language and Communication Studies in South Africa.* Cape Town: Oxford University Press.

Laponce, J. 1984. *Langue et territoire.* Quebec: Presses de l'Université Laval.

1987. "Language and Communication: The Rise of the Monolingual State." In C. Cioffi-Revilla et al., eds., *Communication and Interaction in Global Politics.* 183–207. New York: Sage.

Lenneberg, Eric. 1967. *Biological Foundations of Language.* New York: Wiley.

Lévy, Elisabeth. 1991. "L'Algérie perd son français." *Jeune Afrique,* no. 1567 (January 9–15), 30–2.

Lewis, I. M. 1958. "The Gudabiirsi Somali Script." *Bulletin of the School of Oriental and African Studies* 21:134–56.

Leys, Colin. 1975. *Underdevelopment in Kenya.* Berkeley and Los Angeles: University of California Press.

Lieberson, Stanley. 1981. *Language Diversity and Language Contact.* Stanford: Stanford University Press.

Lijphart, Arend. 1977. *Democracy in Plural Societies.* New Haven: Yale University Press.

Linz, Juan. 1974. "Politics in a Multilingual Society with a Dominant World Language." In J. G. Savard and R. Vegneault, eds., *Les états multilingues: Problèmes et solutions,* 367–444. Quebec: Presses de l'Université Laval.

Lucy, J. 1987. "Grammatical Categories and Cognitive Processes: An Historical, Theoretical and Empirical Re-evaluation of the Linguistic Relativity Hypothesis." Ph.D. diss., University of Chicago.

Mallikarjun, D. 1986. *Language Use in Administration and National Integration.* Mysore: Central Institute of Indian Languages.

Markovitz, Irving L. 1969. *Léopold Sédar Senghor and the Politics of Négritude.* New York: Atheneum.

1977. *Power and Class in Africa.* Englewood Cliffs, N.J.: Prentice-Hall.

Marks, Shula, and Anthony Atmore. 1970. "The Problem of the Nguni: An Examination of the Ethnic and Linguistic Situation in South Africa before the Mfecane." In Dalby, ed., 1970, 120–32.

Maw, J., and David Parkin, eds., 1984. *Swahili Language and Society.* Vienna: Veröffentlichungen der Institut für Afrikanistik.

Mayer J. 1963. "L'université garant de la pureté du langage dans les pays de langue française." In Spencer, 1963, 60–3.

Mazrui, Ali A. 1966. "The English Language and Political Consciousness in British Colonial Africa." *Journal of Modern African Studies* 4:295–311.
    1968. "Some Socio-political functions of English Literature in Africa." *European Journal of Sociology* 9:295–306.
    1971. "Islam and the English Language in East and West Africa." In Whiteley, ed., 1971, 79–97.
    1975. *The Political Sociology of the English Language.* The Hague: Mouton.
    1978. *Political Values and the Educated Class in Africa.* London: Heinemann.
McRae, Kenneth. 1983. *Conflict and Compromise in Multilingual Societies.* 2 vols. to date. Vol. 1, *Switzerland.* Waterloo, Canada: Wilfred Laurier University Press.
Mehnert, Wolfgang. 1973. "The Language Question in the Colonial Policy of German Imperialism." In T. Büttner and G. Brehme, eds., *African Studies / Afrika-studien.* Berlin: Akademie.
Moiso, Bokula. 1979. *Les langues de la region du Haut-Zaire.* Kisangani: Institut de Recherche Scientifique, Bureau Régional de Kisangani, Republique du Zaire.
Morin, Francine. 1967. "The Psycho-sociological Environment of the Senegalese Student in the Primary School." Dakar: Comité Linguistique Africaine à Dakar (CLAD) document. Mimeo.
Morrison, Donald G., et al. 1989. *Black Africa: A Comparative Handbook,* 2nd ed. New York: Paragon House.
Mozambique, National Institute for Educational Development. 1982. "Bilingualism, Cognitive Development and Pre-school Experience of Mozambican Children." Project proposal, Department of Educational Research. Maputo. May.
Mwanakatwe, John M. 1968. *The Development of Education in Zambia.* London: Longmans.
Ndoma, Ungina. 1977. "Some Aspects of Planning Language Policy in Education in the Belgian Congo: 1906–1960." Ph.D. diss., Northwestern University.
    1984a. "Belgian Politics and Linguistic Policy in Congolese Schools, 1885–1914." *Transafrican Journal of History* 13:146–56.
    1984b. "National Language Policy in Education in Zaire." *Language Policy and Language Planning* 8:172–84.
Newitt, Malyn. 1987. *Portugal in Africa.* London: Hurst.
Ngalasso, N. M. 1986. "État des langues et langues de l'état au Zaïre." *Politique Africaine* 23:7–27.
Ngara, E. A. 1982. *Bilingualism, Language Contact and Language Planning: Proposals for Language Use and Language Teaching in Zimbabwe.* Gwelo, Zimbabwe: Mambo Press.
Ngugi, James. 1965. *The River Between.* London: Heinemann.
Ngugi wa Thiong'o. 1986. *Decolonising the Mind: The Politics of Language in African Literature.* London: Heinemann.
Nicolaï, Robert. 1981. *Les dialectes du Songhay: Contribution à l'étude des changements linguistiques.* Paris: SELAF.
Nikiema, N. 1980. "La situation linguistique en Haute-Volta." UNESCO doc. ED-80/WS/22. Paris: UNESCO.
Nodolo, Ike S. 1989. "The Case for Promoting the Nigerian Pidgin Language." *Journal of Modern African Studies* 27:679–84.

North, Douglass. 1981. *Structure and Change in Economic History*. New York: Norton.

Nsibambi, Apolo. 1971. "Language Policy in Uganda." *African Affairs* 70:62–71.

Nthawakuderwa, Bisima. 1986. "Authenticity and Problems of Language Planning in Zaire." In *Language in Education in Africa*, 1986, 101–39.

Nurse, Derek, and Gerard Philippson. 1980. "The Bantu Languages of East Africa: A Lexicostatistical Survey." In Polomé and Hill, eds., 1980, 26–67.

Nurse, Derek, and Thomas Spear. 1985. *The Swahili: Reconstructing the History and Language of an African Society, 800–1500*. Philadelphia: University of Pennsylvania Press.

Nwoye, Onuigbo. 1978. "Language Planning in Nigeria." Ph.D. diss., Georgetown University. University microfilms: 7913988.

Nyerere, Julius. 1968. "Education for Self Reliance." In *Freedom and Socialism*, 267–90. London: Oxford University Press.

O'Barr, J. F. 1976. "Language and Politics in Tanzanian Governmental Institutions." In O'Barr and O'Barr, eds., 1976, 69–84.

O'Barr, W. 1971. "Multilingualism in a Rural Tanzanian Village." *Anthropological Linguistics* 13:289–300.

——— 1978. Review of Laitin, 1977. *American Ethnologist* 5:797–99.

O'Barr, W. M., and J. F. O'Barr, eds. 1976. *Language and Politics*. The Hague: Mouton.

Ohannessian, Sirarpi. 1978. "Historical Background." In Ohannessian and Kashoki, eds., 1978, 271–91.

Ohannessian, Sirarpi, and Mubanga Kashoki, eds., 1978. *Language in Zambia*. London: International African Institute.

Ohly, Rajmund. 1976. "Lexicography and National Language." *Tanzania Notes and Records*, 79–80:23–30.

Oyelaran, O. O. 1990. "Language, Marginalization and National Development in Nigeria." In Emenanjo, ed., 1990, 20–30.

Parkin, D. J. 1974a. "Language Shift and Ethnicity in Nairobi: The Speech Community of Kaloleni." In Whiteley, ed., 1974c, 167–87.

——— 1974b. "Language Switching in Nairobi." In Whiteley, 1974c, 189–216.

——— 1974c. "Nairobi: Problems and Methods." In Whiteley, ed., 1974c, 131–46.

——— 1974d. "Status Factors in Language Adding: Bahati Housing Estate in Nairobi." In Whiteley, ed., 1974c, 147–65.

Peal, Elizabeth, and Wallace E. Lambert. 1962. "The Relation of Bilingualism to Intelligence." *Psychological Monographs* 76(27):1–23.

Phillipson, D. W. 1977. "The Spread of the Bantu Language." *Scientific American*, April, 106–14.

Polomé, E. C. 1980a. "The Languages of Tanzania." In Polomé and Hill, eds., 1980, 3–25.

——— 1980b. "Tanzania: A Socio-linguistic Perspective." In Polomé and Hill, eds., 1980, 103–38.

——— 1982. *Language, Society, and Paleoculture*. Stanford: Stanford University Press.

Polomé, Edgar C., and C. P. Hill, eds. 1980. *Language in Tanzania*. Oxford: Oxford University Press.

Pool, Jonathan. 1972. "National Development and Language Diversity." In J. A.

Fishman, ed., *Advances in the Sociology of Language,* 2 vols., 2:213–30. The Hague: Mouton.

——— 1991. "The Official Language Problem." *American Political Science Review* 85:495–514.

Pool, Jonathan, ed. 1987. *Linguistic Inequality.* Special issue of *Language Problems and Language Planning.* 11.

Potter, D. 1986. *India's Political Administrators, 1919–1983.* Oxford: Clarendon Press.

Pratt, R. Cranford. 1971. "The Cabinet and Presidential Leadership in Tanzania, 1960–1966." In M. Lofchie, *The State of Nations,* 93–118. Berkeley and Los Angeles: University of California Press.

Price, Robert. 1975. *Society and Bureaucracy in Contemporary Ghana.* Berkeley and Los Angeles: University of California Press.

Rabushka, Alvin, and Kenneth Shepsle. 1972. *Politics in Plural Societies: A Theory of Democratic Instability.* Columbus: Merrill.

Rajyashree, K. S. 1986. *An Ethnolinguistic Survey of Dharavi: A Slum in Bombay.* Mysore: Central Institute of Indian Languages.

Rasmusen, Eric. 1990. *Games and Information.* Oxford: Blackwell.

Reh, Mechthild. 1981. *Problems of Linguistic Communication in Africa.* Hamburg: Buske.

Reh, Mechthild, and Bernd Heine. 1982. *Sprachpolitik in Afrika.* Hamburg: Buske.

Rhoades, John. 1977. *Linguistic Diversity and Language Belief in Kenya: The Special Position of Swahili.* Maxwell School African Series, no. 26. Syracuse: Maxwell School of Communications.

Richmond, Edmun B. 1983. *New Directions in Language Teaching in Sub-Saharan Africa.* Washington, D.C.: University Press of America.

Richter, R. 1982. "On Language Problems in Ethiopia." In Brauner and Ochotina, eds., 1982, 241–60.

Ring, James A. 1981. *Ewe as a Second Language: A Sociolinguistic Survey of Ghana's Central Volta Region.* Dallas: Summer Institute of Linguistics.

Robinson, R., and John Gallagher. 1961. *Africa and the Victorians.* London: Macmillan.

Rosse, M. R. N.d. "Le Français des élèves du lycée de Thiès." Dakar: Comité Linguistique Africaine à Dakar (CLAD) document.

Rouchdy, Aleya. 1989. " 'Persistence' or 'Tip' in Egyptian Nubian." In Dorian, ed., 1989, 91–102.

Rubin, J., and Björn H. Jernudd. 1971. *Can Language Be Planned?* Hawaii: University of Hawaii Press.

Rufai, Abba. 1977. "The Question of a National Language in Nigeria: Problems and Prospects." In Kotey and Der-Houssikian, eds., 1977, 68–83.

Rustow, D. 1967. *A World of Nations.* Washington, D.C.: Brookings Institute.

Sahlins, Peter. 1989. *Boundaries.* Berkeley and Los Angeles: University of California Press.

Samarin, W. J. 1955. "Sango: An African Lingua Franca." *Word* 11:254–67.

——— 1982a. "Colonization and Pidginization on the Ubangi River." *Journal of African Languages and Linguistics* 4:1–42.

——— 1982b. "Goals, Roles, and Language Skills in Colonizing Central Equatorial Africa." *Anthropological Linguistics* 24:410–22.

Schmidt, P. W. 1930. "The Use of the Vernacular in Education in Africa." *Africa* 3:137–49.

Schwartzberg, J. E. 1985. "Factors in the Linguistic Reorganization of Indian States." In P. Wallace, *Region and Nation in India*, New Delhi: Oxford University Press.

Scotton, Carol Myers. N.d. "Language in East Africa: Linguistic Patterns and Political Ideologies." Mimeo.

1965. "Some Swahili Political Words." *Journal of Modern African Studies* 3:527–41.

1972. *Choosing a Lingua Franca in an African Capital.* Edmonton: Linguistic Research.

1983. "The Negotiation of Identities in Conversation: A Theory of Markedness and Code Choice." *International Journal of Sociology of Language* 44:115–36.

1986. "Diglossia and Code Switching." In Joshua Fishman et al., eds., *The Fergusonian Impact*, 2 vols., 2:403–15. Berlin: Mouton.

1988. "Code Switching and Types of Multilingual Communities." In Peter Lowenberg, ed., *Language Spread and Language Policy*. Washington, D.C.: Georgetown University Press, 61–82.

1990. "Elite Closure as Boundary Maintenance." In Brian Weinstein, ed., *Language Policy and Political Development*, 25–42. Norwood, N.J.: Ablex.

Scotton, C. M., and John Okeju. 1973. "Neighbors and Lexical Borrowings." *Language* 49:871–89.

Sebeok, Thomas, ed. 1971. *Linguistics in Sub-Saharan Africa. Current Trends in Linguistics*, vol. 7. The Hague: Mouton.

Serpell, R. 1978. "Some Developments in Zambia since 1971." In Ohannessian and Kashoki, eds., 1978, 424–47.

Serpell, Robert, and Muyunda Mwanalushi. 1976. "The Impact of Education and the Information Media on Racism in Zambia since Independence." UNESCO Report (February). Department of Psychology, University of Zambia, Lusaka. Mimeo.

Sesep, N'Sial Bal-a-Nsien. 1978. *La querelle linguistique au Zaire.* Lubumbashi: Centre de Linguistique Théorique et Appliquée.

Seyoum, Mulugeta. 1985. "The Development of the National Language in Ethiopia." Ph.D. diss., Georgetown University. University Microfilms: MBP86-06910.

Shibatani, Masayoshi. 1990. *The Languages of Japan.* Cambridge: Cambridge University Press.

Sirles, Craig Alan. 1985. "An Evaluative Procedure for Language Planning: The Case of Morocco." Ph.D. diss., Northwestern University.

Slobin, D. 1971. *Psycholinguistics.* Glenview, Ill.: Scott Foresman.

Sofunke, B. 1990. "National Language Policy for Democratic Nigeria." In Emenanjo, ed., 1990, 31–49.

Soyinka, Wole. 1981. *Aké: The Years of Childhood.* New York: Random House.

Spencer, John, ed. 1963. *Language in Africa.* Cambridge: Cambridge University Press.

1971. *The English Language in West Africa.* London: Longmans.

Sumaili, N'Gayé-Lussa. 1974. *Lexique parlementaire et legislatif en usage sous la deuxième législature*. Lubumbashi: Centre de Linguistique Théorique et Appliquée.

Sutton, Francis X. 1971. "Research, Scholarship and Cultural Development." Paper presented to the International Division Conference of the Ford Foundation, New Delhi. Mimeo.

Tadadjeu, M. 1987. "Le facteur linguistique du projet social camerounaise." *Journal of West African Languages* 17:23–34.

Taddese, A. T. 1970. "Amharic as a Medium of Instruction in Primary Schools." Paper presented to the Language Association of Eastern Africa, Conference on Language for Development, Nairobi. Mimeo.

Tieber, Silvia. 1990. "Political Linguistics in Namibia." M.A. thesis, University of Chicago.

Tiendrebeogo, G., and Z. Yago. 1983. *Situation des langues parlées en Haute-Volta*. Abidjan: Institut de Linguistique Appliquée.

Tilly, Charles. 1985. "War Making and State Making as Organized Crime." In P. Evans et al., *Bringing the State Back In*, 169–91. Cambridge: Cambridge University Press.

Treffgarne, Carew. 1986. "Language Policy in Francophone Africa: Scapegoat or Panacea?." In *Language in Education, in Africa*, 1986, 141–70.

Trimingham, J. S. 1952. *Islam in East Africa*. Oxford: Oxford University Press.

1962. *History of Islam in West Africa*. Oxford: Oxford University Press.

1964. *Islam in Ethiopia*. Oxford: Clarendon Press.

Tucker, A. N., and M. A. Bryan. 1956. *The Non-Bantu Languages of North-Eastern Africa*. London: Oxford University Press.

Turcotte, Denis. 1981. *La politique linguistique en Afrique francophone; une étude comparative de la Cote d'Ivoire et de Madagascar*. Travaux du Centre International de Recherche sur le Bilinguisme, no. 17. Quebec: Presses de l'Université Laval.

1983. *Lois, reglements et textes administratifs sur l'usage des langues en Afrique Occidentale Française (1826–1959)*. Travaux du Centre International de Recherche sur le Bilinguisme, no. 18. Quebec, Presses de l'Université Laval.

Tuska, Betty. 1968. "English Teaching in Rwanda and the Problems of Training Teachers of English in a Francophone African Country." Paper presented to the East African Regional Conference on Language and Linguistics. Africana Collection, University of Nairobi Library, Kenya. Mimeo.

UNESCO. 1953. *The Use of Vernacular Language in Education*. Monographs on Fundamental Education, no. 8. Paris: UNESCO.

Vallverdú, Francesc. 1981. *El conflicto lingüistico en Cataluña*. Barcelona: Peninsula.

Verdoodt, M. Albert. 1968. "Le bilinguisme au Burundi." East African Regional Conference on Language and Linguistics. Africana Collection, University of Nairobi Library, Kenya. Mimeo.

Von Neumann, John, and Oskar Morgenstern. 1944. *The Theory of Games and Economic Behavior*. New York: Wiley.

Wallerstein, Immanuel. 1974. "The Rise and Future Demise of the World Capitalist System." *Comparative Studies in Society and History* 16:387–415.

Wauthier, Claude. 1964. *The Literature and Thought of Modern Africa*. New York: Praeger.

Weber, Eugen. 1976. *Peasants into Frenchmen*. Stanford: Stanford University Press.

Weber, Max. 1968. *Economy and Society,* 2 vols. Berkeley and Los Angeles: University of California Press.

Weinreich, Uriel. 1953. *Languages in Contact*. The Hague: Mouton.

Weinreich, Uriel, William Labov, and Marvin Herzon. 1968. "Empirical Foundations for a Theory of Language Change." In W. P. Lehmann and Yakov Malkiel, eds., *Directions for Historical Linguistics,* 95–188. Austin: University of Texas Press.

Weinstein, Brian. 1976. "Francophonie: a Language-based Movement in World Politics." *International Organization* 30:485–507.

1979. "Language Strategists." *World Politics* 31:345–64.

1983. *The Civic Tongue*. New York: Longmans.

Welmers, W. 1971. "Christian Missions and Language Policies." In Sebeok, 1971, 559–69.

Westermann, D., and M. A. Bryan. 1952. *Handbook of African Languages: Languages of West Africa*. London: Oxford University Press.

White, John. 1980. "The Historical Background to National Education in Tanzania." In Polomé and Hill, eds., 1980, 261–82.

Whiteley, Wilfred H. 1969. *Swahili*. London: Methuen.

1974a. "The Classification and Distribution of Kenya's African Languages." In Whiteley, ed., 1974c, 13–61.

1974b. "Some Patterns of Language Use in the Rural Areas of Kenya." In Whiteley, ed., 1974c, 319–50.

Whiteley, Wilfred, H., ed. 1971. *Language Use and Social Change*. Oxford: Oxford University Press.

1974c. *Language in Kenya*. Nairobi: Oxford University Press.

Whorf, B. L. 1956. *Language, Thought and Reality,* ed. J. Carroll. Cambridge, Mass.: MIT Press.

Wolff, Hans. 1959. "Intelligibility and Inter-ethnic Attitudes." *Anthropological Linguistics* 1:34–41.

1967. "Language, Ethnic Identity and Social Change in Southern Nigeria." *Anthropological Linguistics* 9:18–25.

Wright, Marcia. 1965. "Swahili Language Policy, 1890–1940." *Swahili* 35:40–8.

Yanga, Tshimpaka. 1980. "A Sociolinguistic Identification of Lingala." Ph.D. diss., University of Texas, Austin.

Yates, Barbara A. 1978. "Shifting Goals of Industrial Education in the Congo, 1878–1908." *African Studies Review* 21:33–48.

1980. "The Origins of Language Policy in Zaire." *Journal of Modern African Studies* 18:257–79.

Zuengler, Jane E. 1982. "Kenyan English." In Braj B. Kachru, ed., *The Other Tongue: English across Cultures,* 112–24. Oxford: Pergamon Press.

Index

Abassi, Abdelaziz, 137
Abdulaziz, M. H., 63, 112, 140, 165n9, 170n10
Abernethy, David, 122
Abidjan, 80, 144, 152
Achebe, C., 56, 122
Acholi, 83
Adams, Charles, 78
administration, 6
 in France, 12–13
 language of, 95, 117, 119, 163
 and language policy, 83–6
 in Nigeria, 121–2
Africa
 case studies from, 120–45
 civil servants in, 94–5
 class structure in, based on language, 57–8
 distinctiveness of, 103, 104
 language future in, 103–19
 language issue in, 50–2
 nationalist leaders in, 91–4
 precolonial rulers of, 82–3
 relation between language diversity and economic growth in, 54–7
 3 ± 1 outcome for, 112–18
African history, as part of world history, 103, 119
African National Congress, 137
African states
 European languages' official status in, 104–7
 tensions in, 25, 26
Afrikaans (language), 4, 6, 56, 78, 133, 136–7
Afrikaners, 135, 136–7
Afro-Asiatic (language family), 19
age of country
 and economic development, 54
 and language outcomes, 38–41

Agency for Cultural and Technical Co-operation, 98
Ahidjo, Ahmadou, 93
Ahmadu Bello University, 99, 126
Ahmed, Ocin Ait, 143
Ahwoi, Kwamena, 170n3
Akan (language), 7, 73–4, 131–2, 143
Akan-English code switching, 115, 155
Aké (Soyinka), 77, 78–9
Akinnaso, Festus Niyi, 21
Akwa Ibom (state, Nigeria), 123
Alexander, Neville, 136
Alexandre, Pierre, 57, 129, 166n4, n11, n14, 168n4
Algeria, 18, 138
 emergent language rationalization in, 139, 142–3
Allan, Keith, 54, 96
All-Union government (India), 38, 40, 41, 44
Alsace, 13, 21
Alsatian (language), 17
Ambrose, Stanley, 83
Amharic (language), xi, 4, 58
Amin, Idi, 154
Amonoo, Reginald F., 116, 131–2, 155
Anderson, Benedict, 11, 39
Angola, 19, 133, 134, 136
 language policy of, 59, 85
Ansre, G., 169n2
anthropological linguistics, 61, 63
Apronti, E. O., 71
Arab Gulf States, 90–1
Arabic (language), 18, 76, 77, 84, 108
 dialects of, 89
 in Maghreb, 138-9
 Muslim missionaries and, 89–91
 rationalization of, 142–3
 in Somalia, 151–2
arabization, 138, 143

For EU product safety concerns, contact us at Calle de José Abascal, 56–1°,
28003 Madrid, Spain or eugpsr@cambridge.org.

www.ingramcontent.com/pod-product-compliance
Ingram Content Group UK Ltd.
Pitfield, Milton Keynes, MK11 3LW, UK
UKHW010044140625
459647UK00012BA/1607